# TENSE
# Commandments
## Federal Prescriptions and City Problems

### PIETRO S. NIVOLA

BROOKINGS INSTITUTION PRESS
*Washington, D.C.*

*Library of Congress Cataloging-in-Publication data*

Nivola, Pietro S.
  Tense commandments: federal prescriptions and city problems / Pietro
S. Nivola.
    p.  cm.
Includes bibliographical references and index.
  ISBN 0-8157-6093-0 (cloth) — ISBN 0-8157-6094-9 (paper)
  1. Urban policy—United States—Evaluation.  2.  Urban policy—United
States—Case studies.  3. Federal-city relations—United States.  I.
Title.
  HT123 .N58 2002
  307.76'0973—dc21

                                                      2002008412


Typeset in Sabon

Composition by Cynthia Stock
Silver Spring, Maryland

Printed by R. R. Donnelley and Sons
Harrisonburg, Virginia

In tribute to
New York, New York,
the city where I was born

# Foreword

U rbanists have long bewailed the relative decline of America's central cities in relation to their sprawling suburbs. Whatever the merits of this lament, market forces do not wholly explain why many big cities—such as Baltimore, Philadelphia, and Washington, D.C., to name a few—continued to shed inhabitants and net only mild increases in employment in their metropolitan regions during the past decade. Comparatively high tax rates and some unsatisfactory municipal services (most notably, the public schools) often put cities at a competitive disadvantage.

Although the sources of these, and other, city problems are numerous and complex, Pietro S. Nivola posits that cumbersome federal prescriptions have exacerbated some of the difficulties facing the nation's urban centers—that is, particular rulings and regulations that may create unwarranted fiscal and administrative complications for local authorities. The study readily acknowledges that many of the national government's interventions are necessary and beneficial. But it also sheds light on how and why "federalization" of municipal affairs in this country increased in the second half of the twentieth century and finds that some of this expansion has been counterproductive.

As the nation and its cities brace for a long and probably arduous war against terrorism, the need to reconfigure the roles of the national and municipal governments in today's intricate federal system is becoming evident. As this book suggests, an unencumbered capacity of governments at all levels to concentrate on their core functions and responsibilities seems urgent.

The author thanks many scholars and colleagues at Brookings and elsewhere for criticism, advice, and assistance with this book. He is especially grateful to Martha Derthick, Alan Ehrenhalt, Chris Foreman, Ed Glaeser, Michael Greve, Bob Katzmann, Don Kettl, Paul Light, Tom Mann, Carol O'Cleireacain, and Bob Stein.

John Bennett, Bill Fanaras, Anna Galland, Seth Green, Andrea McDaniel, and Jon Shields provided research assistance. Cyrus Afshar verified the manuscript, and Sarah Chilton of the Brookings library offered valuable help with the citations. Elizabeth McAlpine contributed her administrative skills to the project. Theresa Walker edited the manuscript, Carlotta Ribar proofread it, and Robert Swanson prepared the index.

The views expressed here are solely those of the author and should not be ascribed to the persons whose assistance is acknowledged above or to the trustees, officers, or other staff members of the Brookings Institution.

MICHAEL H. ARMACOST
*President*

*June 2002*
*Washington, D.C.*

# Contents

*Boxes*

# TENSE
# Commandments

# 1 Introduction

Each year the U.S. government publishes a report called *The State of the Cities*. The final year of the twentieth century was a very good one. Thanks to "the Clinton-Gore economic policies and effective empowerment agenda," the end-of-the-millennium edition proclaimed, "most cities are showing clear signs of revitalization and renewal."[1] Yet, the authors conceded, even in that time of great prosperity the nation's central cities still faced "challenges."

Challenges? During the 1990s dozens of large cities—including such major centers as Baltimore, Cincinnati, Cleveland, Milwaukee, Philadelphia, Pittsburgh, St. Louis, and Washington, D.C.—continued to shed inhabitants. Sprawling suburban subdivisions still accounted for more than three-quarters of all new metropolitan growth.[2] Although many other cities finally managed to regain population, few kept pace with the growth of their suburbs.[3]

Disparities in growth between the metropolitan core and its outlying counties remained wide by other measures as well. Despite thousands of acres of abandoned land at the cores of the thirty-nine largest metropolitan regions, permits issued for construction of new housing units in 1998 were still down from their level in 1986. The volume of permits outside the core areas was about four-and-a-half times larger.[4]

Suburbs captured the bulk of employment growth. One study of ninety-two metropolitan areas found that, although 52 percent of their central cities began netting some increase in private sector jobs between 1993 and 1996, 23 percent did not, and fully 82 percent of the cities recorded a declining share of private employment in relation to the rest of their respective regions.[5] The nation's capital, for example, started the 1990s holding at least a third of its metropolitan area's jobs. Seven years later the city held less than a quarter. Although Atlanta by comparison was a thriving city, its share of jobs also dropped dramatically, from 40 percent in 1980 to 24 percent by 1996. From 1994 to 1997 the central business districts in Ohio's seven major cities had a net increase of only 636 jobs. The suburbs of these cities added 186,410 new jobs.[6]

In absolute terms the enclaves of poverty left behind in the inner cities by the unending dispersal of people and jobs to distant peripheries shrank in the 1990s.[7] This was no small accomplishment, but it scarcely changed the fact that poor people remained a substantial percentage of the resident populations of many cities. At long last the strain of sustaining these dependents had diminished almost everywhere, including urban counties where dependency declined by more than 40 percent between 1994 and 1999.[8] But it remained no less true that cities were still the locus of disproportionate caseloads in comparison with surrounding communities. Orleans Parish in which the city of New Orleans is located was home to just 11 percent of Louisiana's population but 29 percent of its welfare recipients. Philadelphia County had 12 percent of Pennsylvania's people but 47 percent of all Pennsylvanians on welfare. Baltimore accounted for 56 percent of Maryland's welfare cases. Nearly two-thirds of all welfare recipients in the Washington metropolitan area were clustered inside the District of Columbia.[9]

The depopulation, impoverishment, and decay of much of urban America, however, had abated. Whether the decline would be durably halted, let alone lastingly reversed, is another matter. For the calamity of September 11, 2001, dealt a severe setback not only to New York and Washington, D.C., but to cities across the land. The terrorist assaults, arriving as the national economy had already started to falter, wiped out almost 80,000 jobs in New York and sent the unemployment rate in the

District of Columbia toward double digits.[10] The economic shock waves rippling out from "ground zero" would also shatter hopes of robust growth through 2002 for places as far away as Miami or San Francisco.[11] Even if none of this had happened, the central fact of the urban scene in the United States remains as unmistakable today as ever: far more Americans, when choosing where to live and work, still locate outside old cities rather than inside them. If anything, save for anomalies like New York in recent years, the margin of difference continues to widen, not narrow.

Most of the underlying causes of this country's urban predicament are familiar. Among them are disproportionate poverty—hence crime and blight—in the inner cities, some lingering barriers to racial or class assimilation in the suburbs, a cultural preference for the suburban way of life, stiff city tax rates heightened by the costs of supporting large unionized bureaucracies and the unsatisfactory public services some of them deliver. Less recognized is the distinct possibility that sometimes the regulatory policies of the federal government—the rules and rulings that its judges and bureaucrats, as well as its lawmakers, impose—further disadvantage the cities, hobbling their ability to attract residents and businesses. These complications are the focus of this book.

Arguably the burden of what a former mayor of New York had called the federal "mandate millstone" may have diminished a little by the end of the 1990s thanks to attempts at self-restraint by policymakers in Washington but also because municipal economies were mostly faring better.[12] How much weight was really lifted, and whether alleviating more of it would have left the cities in an even stronger position today, remains an open question.

## "Shift and Shaft"

City governments in the United States, unlike municipal administrations in most of Europe, must largely support themselves; they collect approximately two-thirds of their revenues from local sources.[13] German localities derive less than one-third of their income from local revenues.[14] Britain's local councils are now responsible for as little as a fifth of their budgets for basic functions.[15] The locally sourced share is even less in the Netherlands and, until recently, Italy.

In principle the relative self-sufficiency of local government in America is a virtue; municipal taxpayers ought to pay for the essential services they use. But in practice these taxpayers are also asked to purchase plenty of other costly projects, many of which federal law prescribes. A handful of national rules bore down on local governments before 1965. By the 1990s hundreds were weighing down on them.[16] Meanwhile federal aid to large cities was shrinking. Mayors became alarmed by the confluence of these trends and so was the U.S. Advisory Commission on Intergovernmental Relations: "The financial burdens imposed by federal laws and regulations," the commission stressed in a 1993 report, "have been increasing faster than the growth of federal aid since 1986."[17] While affluent jurisdictions absorbed this cost shifting with minimal disruption, communities of lesser means—notably many old central cities in the Northeast and parts of the Midwest—experienced difficulties.

Cities with large concentrations of low-income households and shaky sources of taxable wealth, of course, are squeezed the worst.[18] A few of these desperate places (Bridgeport, Connecticut, for instance) became insolvent.[19] The extreme exceptions aside, however, bankruptcy has not been the first problem that the profusion of federal prescriptions typically posed. Rather, their cumulative, lower-profile effects have complicated basic municipal management decisions, including those pertaining to taxing and borrowing. According to a study by the National League of Cities, nearly 40 percent of the hundreds of cities it surveyed reported that their financial needs had become harder, not easier, to satisfy at the end of the 1990s.[20] Evidently the era's economic boom had not generated sufficient growth of local revenues in about one out of five of these cities, so property tax rates rose yet again in 1998.[21] That year a group of prominent mayors repeated their long-standing complaint about how Washington's unfunded mandates tended to "destabilize" municipal budgets.[22]

The following figures tell a good deal of the fiscal side of the story. Federal aid to large cities declined in constant dollars between 1980 and 1998, the last year for which reliable data are currently available (figure 1-1). To be sure, support from state governments and increases in locally collected revenues helped offset the federal reductions, but at least in large Frost Belt cities through 1998 the local increases were not large— and in some cases, not large enough (figure 1-2). Meanwhile, externally imposed claims on municipal resources often outpaced the latter's modest increases in these cities. Glance at one example: municipal wastewater treatment. Adjusting for inflation, local expenditures to build and run

Figure 1-1. *Federal Aid to Large Cities, 1980–98*

Billions of 1998 dollars

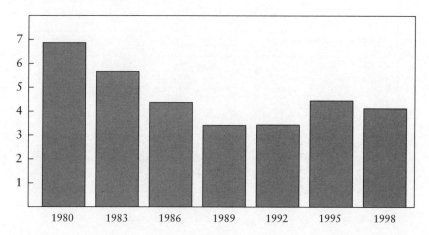

Sources: U.S. Department of Commerce, Bureau of the Census, *Statistical Abstract of the United States, 1982–83,* p. 300; *1986,* p. 290; *1989,* p. 288; *1991,* p. 302; *1994,* p. 317; *1998,* p. 328; and *2001,* p. 290 (various years).

Note: Cities include Austin, Baltimore, Chicago, Cleveland, Columbus, Dallas, Detroit, El Paso, Houston, Indianapolis, Jacksonville, Los Angeles, Memphis, Milwaukee, Nashville, Philadelphia, Phoenix, San Antonio, San Franciso, San Jose, Seattle, and Washington, D.C.

treatment plants up to federal standards ballooned from about $7.5 billion a year in 1978 to more than $23 billion a year in 1998.[23] Federal funding to offset this kind of huge annual invoice dwindled (figure 1-3).

The strain in certain cities was much greater than the aggregated figures suggest. Revenues in constant dollars available to Detroit, for example, had contracted until 1998, even as this troubled city faced new multimillion dollar expenses piled on by federal and state authorities (figure 1-4). And as revenues sagged, so did bond ratings. Thus cities such as Detroit remained hard pressed not only to defray their new obligations directly but also to meet them by borrowing.

Increases in federally mandated expenses exacted a toll in more prosperous places too. Before New York City's financial health was battered

Figure 1-2.  *General Revenue in Large Frost Belt Cities, 1980–98*

Billions of 1998 dollars

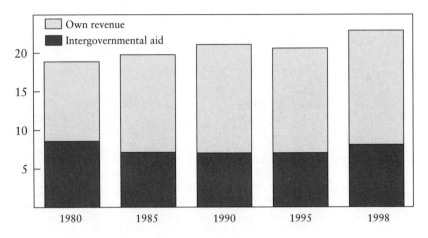

Sources: U. S. Department of Commerce, Bureau of the Census, *Statistical Abstract of the United States, 1997,* p. 302; *1982–83,* p. 300; *1988,* p. 278; *1992,* p. 302; *1998,* p. 328; *1999,* p. 326; and *2001,* p. 290.

Note: Cities include Chicago, Philadelphia, Baltimore, Indianapolis, Washington, D.C., Milwaukee, Cleveland, Boston, Columbus, and Detroit.

in the fall of 2001 the city estimated it would have to finance at least $8 billion in mandatory capital expenditures for water-quality projects alone in the next ten years.[24] New York will have to pull off investments of this magnitude amid already mountainous debts and with a tax system that probably has reached the limits of its capacity.[25] At a minimum the added financial commitments facing cities like New York seem likely to force municipal officials to forgo further rounds of badly needed tax reductions.

Finances aside, some mandates impinge directly on local administration of routine services, tying the hands of managers and at times thwarting improvements that the beleaguered taxpayers in cities consider past due. For middle-class households and businesses contemplating where to locate in metropolitan areas, these circumstances do not enhance the allure of the central cities.

Figure 1-3. *Local versus Federal Wastewater Expenditures, 1972–98*

Billions of 1996 dollars

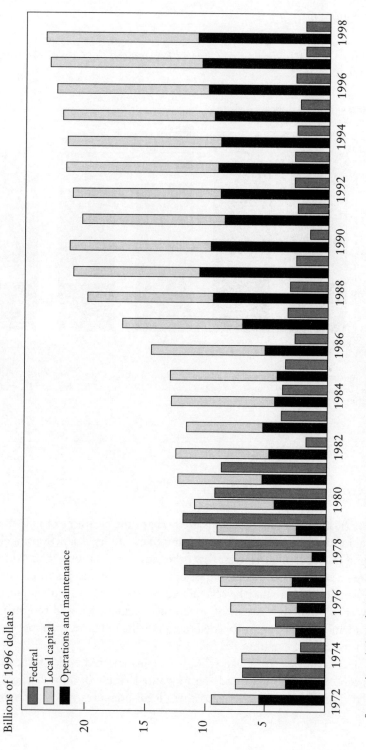

Source: Association of Municipal Sewage Agencies, *The Cost of Clean* (Washington, 1990).

Figure 1-4. *Distribution of General Revenue in the City of Detroit, 1980–98*

Billions of 1998 dollars

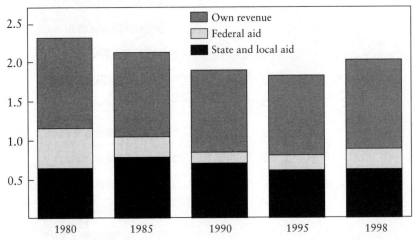

Sources: U.S. Department of Commerce, Bureau of the Census, *Statistical Abstract of the United States, 1997*, p. 302; *1982–83*, p. 300; *1988*, p. 278; *1999*, p. 326; and *2001*, p. 290.

## Exemplifying the Problem

America's urban public schools are perhaps the clearest example of a crucial local service beset by bureaucratic rules and legal sanctions, including numerous federal directives. Few other advanced nations, if any, devote as large a share of their total public education expenditures to nonteaching personnel.[26] There may be several excuses for this lopsided administrative overhead, but the growth of government regulation, and the throngs of academic administrators needed to handle the red tape, is almost certainly at least one explanation.

For decades, U.S. urban schools systems labored under forced busing orders. Many of them had the unwanted result of stimulating "white flight" to the suburbs. Even as these legal pressures gradually subsided, newer ones mounted. Increasingly the schools would need to supply various specialized services. Local authorities, for example, must set aside tens of billions of dollars a year to meet the needs of students with learning disabilities.[27] Congress, which fashioned this expensive program known as special education, has never reimbursed even a quarter of its yearly bill. Meanwhile, the number of clients swells as definitions of disability take in behaviors that in an earlier time were not considered clinical abnormalities—and as teachers, parents, and administrators dump their faltering students into the program.

Compliance costs are especially onerous for city schools, where the concentrations of learning-disabled pupils are high and the means to support them low. The District of Columbia is forced to spend roughly a third of its entire education budget on students eligible for special education, a clientele that constitutes 15 percent of the school system's overall enrollment.[28] In 1997 just over 17 percent of Baltimore's school children qualified for the program, reportedly costing the Baltimore school district as much as $221 million—again, one-third of the city's school budget.[29] Chicago's public schools enroll more than half of all the special education students in the state of Illinois.[30] Federal and state aid has fallen far short of what is needed to support this overload. And when a school system has to hire legions of counselors, therapists, administrators, and lawyers, how can it also afford to recruit what it needs most: competent teachers? The Chicago school district had to dig deep into the pockets of its taxpayers for many hundreds of millions of dollars in property tax increases between 1988 and 1993.

Wretched schools have been among the main reasons why American families have fled, or avoided, old cities. It is hard enough for distressed city school systems, which struggle to impart even rudimentary reading and arithmetic skills, to compete with their wealthier suburban counterparts. The hardship is surely compounded by federal entitlements that without adequate recompense increasingly divert the scarce resources of cities from better serving the majority of their citizens. Amid the centrally directed priorities and their fiscal impacts, it often becomes harder for local school boards to undertake essential innovations. Not long ago an in-depth study of six large urban school districts—Boston, Memphis, New York, San Antonio, San Francisco, and Seattle—found that reform-minded city officials were stymied first and foremost by inadequate financial capacity and flexibility.[31]

## Plan of the Book

Although this book is not long, it could have been shorter if the national government's voluminous commands and controls indisputably brought too few benefits to city dwellers. But the bottom line is a matter of much dispute. There are many good reasons for federal policymakers to be telling city governments what they must or must not do, even if city officials deem many of these strictures unaffordable or overbearing. Although the local objections frequently are to be taken seriously, sometimes they turn out to be decidedly unconvincing—and an overall assessment cannot help but be fraught with debatable judgments as to how competing values ought be traded off, empirical evidence weighed, and urban impacts quantified.[32] I attempt no such rigorous appraisal. Instead, I divide a frankly impressionistic critique into two parts, taking a general sweep in chapter 2, and then getting down to cases by examining in chapter 3 some experiences of particular cities.

Underlying such stories are the political pressures that, in varying degrees, thrust federal regulators into local governance. The incentives to intervene from the top are complex and somewhat different from those in other democracies and have gained momentum that has been at best only mildly suspended in recent years. This phenomenon—what I call the politics of paternalism—is the subject of chapter 4. Some readers may wonder why that chapter pulls back from a narrow concentration on the urban setting and tours instead the broader contours of American federalism that, for the most part, show the ascent of national power not only over city governments but local politics generally. But I regard this broad-brush treatment as a helpful supplement. An understanding of why any city mayor might begrudge Washington's infringements on the ability of his or her city to govern itself is ultimately inseparable from an appreciation of the centralizing forces at work in the federal system as a whole.

Chapter 5 offers some brief, basic comparisons with political systems abroad. An aim of this book is to encourage renewed reflection on an old topic—the suitable balance between national and local domains—and one way to assist such an exploration is to view municipal administration from an international perspective: how closely do the central governments of various European countries supervise the affairs of their large cities, and why have the forms of fiscal burden sharing evolved differently? Chapters 5 tries to shed light on these questions.

In conclusion chapter 6 offers a few suggestions for reformers, based in part on lessons that might be drawn from international contrasts.

## Some Preliminaries

Before going further, however, three clarifications are in order. First, the thesis of this study is *not* that federal regulations are a dominant source of urban managerial and budgetary woes. Other fundamentals, such as the implications of outsized concentrations of low-income residents and of maintaining a high-priced municipal work force, come first.[33]

Personnel salaries and benefits, for instance, have long been the chief consideration in municipal finance, especially in cities with powerful public employee unions. The ability of these unionized workers to extract from their employers unsustainable concessions played a big part in the urban fiscal crisis of the early 1970s, and though the unions have less leverage today, in many cities they remain a significant force.[34] When New York's transit workers threatened to strike late in 1999, even the comparatively frugal administration of Mayor Rudolph W. Giuliani acquiesced to a new labor contract that effectively increased pay by more than 18 percent over three years.[35] (That precedent no doubt was not lost on other unions when the time came to renegotiate their contracts.) Compared with endogenously generated costs like these, those foisted on the cities from the statehouses or from Washington have often seemed modest. Modest or not, they can still worsen an unstable situation.

Second, state governors, legislators, administrators, and judges compel more compulsory spending by local government than do decisionmakers at the federal level. Despite the large role of the states the emphasis of this book is on what the federal government has been doing.

In America the authority of the states over their local entities is essentially without limits. In contrast to the ancient charters of European cities, some of which have retained independent privileges that predated the formation of their respective nation states, the legal position of municipalities in the United States is simple: they are mere creatures of the states, which can delineate the scope of local jurisdiction at will. Cities have no separate constitutional status. On this the U.S. Supreme Court has long been unambiguous:

The city is a political subdivision of the state, created as a convenient Agency for the exercise of such of the government powers of the state as may be trusted to it. . . . The state may withhold, grant, or withdraw powers and privileges as it sees fit. . . . In the absence of state constitutional provisions safeguarding it to them, *munici-palities have no inherent right of self-government which is beyond the legislative control of the state.*[36]

But whereas state officials have *carte blanche* to meddle in practically any municipal decision (technically, a city may not be able to operate a peanut stand at the city zoo without state permission), the same cannot be said of the federal government. Its reach, the founders certainly intended, was to be anything but unlimited. Madison's language in *Federalist No. 45* was explicit: "The powers delegated by the proposed Constitution to the federal government are few and defined. Those which are to remain in the State governments are numerous and indefinite." After all, he wrote, it would have been "preposterous" for the American Revolution to have been fought and "the precious blood of thousands spilt," only to have a federal leviathan "derogate" the sovereignty of the states or even the "dignities" of "particular municipal establishments."[37]

Thus mandates emanating from Washington differ fundamentally from those imposed by the states. For better or worse, state governments have an acknowledged license to commandeer their municipal corpora-tions. Debating that prerogative is at a minimum futile. The same resig-nation scarcely befits a proliferation of *national* regulations that increas-ingly dictate local choices. Abridging local self-rule may affront principles or customs of American federalism—and therefore stands at least some chance of being readjusted.

Although the innumerable means by which state governments subor-dinate their local communities are outside the scope of this volume, it recognizes that expenses associated with various federal exactions *on the states* may be bucked to municipalities.[38] Special education certainly fits this description. So do several environmental programs. This book does not delve into the specific ways in which state governments pass their costs through to localities. Nor does it examine some of the costli-est pass-throughs. Critics might find that omitting an analysis of Medicaid administration from these pages, for instance, is a major shortcoming. States are required by law to match federal contributions by as much as 50 percent. In New York and some other states approxi-mately half of the matching funds are collected from local governments.

Thus Medicaid has ballooned into a multibillion dollar item on New York City's budget.[39]

Nonetheless, this book is broadly gauged. It looks at an array of directive or supervisory methods by which federal policymakers narrow local autonomy and complicate the work urban governments are supposed to do.[40] It is helpful not to get hung up on the technical labels that have been applied to those methods. For decades mayors and other local managers lamented that federal grants-in-aid came with too many strings attached, often tying the hands of local governments as congressional appropriations were pared. During the first half of the 1990s these and other federal rules that set an agenda but then underfunded it became the object of a concerted local protest. Congress responded in 1995 by legislating some mild relief (the so-called Unfunded Mandates Reform Act, which chapter 6 discusses). No sooner was the ink dry on this correction, however, than state and local office holders voiced another concern: too many federal regulations were said to "preempt"—that is, arrogate—local responsibilities.

As a practical matter the line between a so-called preemption and an unfunded mandate, or even an increasingly stringent condition of aid, is not necessarily bright.[41] Who should be allowed to consume alcoholic beverages, whether a local school needs to remove asbestos, what height and strength qualifications a local fire department elects for its recruits, or how a community purifies drinking water are now matters of national law. Some of the stipulations are proscriptive: the fire department cannot discriminate against persons on the basis of their muscle mass. Others are prescriptive: hazardous asbestos has to be removed and water purified. Still others (for instance, the suitable drinking age) are standards that communities have to meet to qualify for funding they cannot do without. Each of these policies is coercive. All should be put to the same test: are they socially beneficial, or do they mostly deprive localities of discretion, distort legitimate local priorities, and perhaps misallocate resources?

The query applies, moreover, regardless of whether the policies are administered directly or obliquely, by means such as individual lawsuits. Americans like to think of their practice of taking anyone, including government agencies, to court as a "private" activity. Suing an agency is said to be, in the legal vernacular, exercising a private right of action. But the nomenclature leaves the wrong impression. National legislation in this country, unlike most other democracies, commonly deputizes individuals or groups to file suits to secure from local governments certain services or standards. The outcomes of these cases often do much more than redress someone's personal grievance; they often elicit rulings with community-wide implications.

Many of the most arduous impositions on city governments in the United States derive from these sweeping federal court orders. A study of urban America's regulatory regime cannot ignore them.

# 2 *Problems*

It would be nice if America's local governments had a consistent history of good conduct. In reality much has gone wrong—at times so wrong any fair observer would have welcomed or at least understood an extensive federal usurpation of local powers. Think about the following episodes from various cities.

On the evening of May 31, 1921, a lynch mob in Tulsa, Oklahoma, descended on the municipal courthouse in search of a black man who had been charged with (and later acquitted of) raping a white woman.[1] After an altercation at the courthouse the mob invaded the city's black neighborhood, destroying thirty-five square blocks and murdering hundreds of residents. At one downtown location 123 blacks were found clubbed to death. How did city and state authorities respond as the bloodbath unfolded? The Tulsa police department deputized large numbers of the white vigilantes and, according to an account citing court records from the time, instructed them to "go out and kill." The state of Oklahoma appointed a Tulsa Race Riot Commission to launch an investigation—more than three-quarters of a century later.

In 1975 a strange thing happened: New York, the biggest city in the world's richest nation, neared bankruptcy. The sources of this fiscal crisis were complex, but at least one root cause was unmistakable: New York had spent beyond its means on redistributive social services.[2] This municipal welfare state could no longer be sustained by its vulnerable local tax base.

More recently the Atlanta metropolitan area has been experiencing a buildup of air pollution.[3] Along the eastern seaboard of the United States no metropolis belches more smog than Atlanta. It has one of the dirtiest coal-fired power plants in the country, and emission levels of nitrous oxides from motor vehicles have regularly exceeded the Environmental Protection Agency's (EPA) caps and projections. The local political establishment, however, has been slow to act. While Draconian steps such as ordering a four-day work week were rightly rejected, so were more modest proposals—like charging for parking spaces and converting to cleaner fuels. The idea of cleaner fuel, which implied a slight increase in energy prices, caused consternation in the Georgia legislature.

In 1989 a well-known journalist, staunchly committed to public education, described a problem his son experienced in a classroom of the public school system of the city in which they resided. "One of my children," the journalist wrote, "spent a year with an elementary school science teacher who had been shifted from teaching English. She was fully 'qualified' to teach, since she had her credentials, but she knew less about science than most of the children did."[4] One of the things this qualified science teacher did not know was how the moon revolved around the earth.

## The Trouble with Localism

The derelictions of local government range from the barbaric to the regrettable, the irresponsible, and the merely ridiculous. What they imply, though, is that in the absence of enforced national standards some self-governed communities have proved capable of sinking below the most elementary regard for public competency, environmental safeguards, financial prudence, or even basic human rights.

The account about the public school teacher who did not understand the orbit of the moon was hardly unique. Reports of this sort or worse are sufficiently common to stir calls for national education standards. Nor was the Tulsa race riot of 1921 an isolated incident. In a wave of hyste-

ria about rumored rapes of whites by blacks during the 1920s racial violence erupted in cities across the country.[5] The federal government may
not have had at its disposal sufficient statutory powers to quell these
atrocities or even to prosecute their perpetrators. Would that it had.

In the case of Atlanta's polluted atmosphere the argument for national
"hammers" to compel an end to the local policy paralysis went beyond a
need to protect the region's residents from possible health risks. Air pollution crosses boundaries. Concentrations of ozone can drift across hundreds of square miles. One place's foul air pollutes another region's
water.[6] Why should people living in other jurisdictions have to inhale or
swallow the poisons spewing from a neighboring urban area whose citizens year after year are not curtailing their wide-ranging effluents?

As Madison warned in *Federalist No. 10*, the inertia of local government has to do, at least in part, with the ability of entrenched interests to
capture small polities: how can municipal school systems reinvent themselves when their administrations remain in the grip of obstructive teachers' unions? Will a one-company town, whose factory is the local economy's mainstay but also its worst polluter, put in a fix? Localism begets
freeloading. When some jurisdictions become welfare magnets, others are
tempted to lower their benefits below an acceptable minimum. A city or
state whose contaminated air or water flows downstream to neighboring
cities or states has little incentive to control the spillover for their sake.
Indeed localities competing for business investment and taxable income
might reciprocally "dumb down" standards.[7]

Clearly if interjurisdictional competition and externalities arbitrarily
enrich certain communities at the expense of others or else draw too
many into a "race to the bottom," or if local mismanagement is so
endemic it corrupts the commonweal, or mischievous local factions egregiously violate the fundamental freedoms of citizens, the solution seems
plain: "extend the sphere" of governance, as Madison recommended,
shifting control from the "smaller" jurisdictions to "the Union."[8]

## Mandating without Spending

In the past half-century most of this remedial enlargement of the national
ambit has been purchased with federal dollars. As of 1990 nearly $120
billion in grants to state and local governments was being disbursed to
patch alleged shortcomings of local policies in transportation, environmental protection, economic development, job training, education, public

safety, and much more.[9] Because the purpose of this funding has not been to distribute unrestricted handouts but largely to make up for local deficiencies, receipt of the funds has been conditioned on compliance with a plethora of federal requirements. In theory those requirements could be ignored if the grantees simply turned down the money. In practice this became almost impossible. He who pays the piper calls the tune. New federal instructions are often affixed after the grant programs have been institutionalized. By then their constituencies are so well organized the programs have all but ceased to be voluntary. And typically the federal rules remain firmly in place even if congressional appropriations fall far short of authorizations. The local provision of special education for students with disabilities, for instance, is essentially governed by federal law, even though Congress has never even come close to appropriating its authorized share of this $43 billion-a-year mandate.

Federal grants feature these bait-and-switch dynamics because, despite considerable weaning during the past couple of decades, local governments remain dependent on whatever aid they can get. There are far fewer federal aid junkies today than twenty years ago (when more than three-quarters of the revenues in cities such as Detroit came from Washington), but federal aid remains a substantial source of state and local revenue, still exceeding in many places the proceeds from sales taxes or property taxes.

### Going Off Budget

Paying the piper, however, is but one way of gaining influence. In recent decades the manner in which Washington exerts control changed. As the national government's deficits grew, and Congress's propensity to throw money at domestic programs bumped against budget caps, a tendency developed for the federal government to regulate local governments more stringently while aiding them less generously.[10] At the end of 1974 some forty federal mandates reflected this pattern. Twenty years later the number had grown by almost 160 percent (figure 2-1).[11] Presidents Ronald Reagan and George Bush put up faint resistance to what the Advisory Commission on Intergovernmental Relations had come to call regulatory federalism, even in the realm of administrative rulemakings. Between 1981 and 1986 Reagan presided over the promulgation of some 140 agency rules that placed nearly six thousand new obligations on states and localities.[12]

Figure 2-1. *Federal Mandates on State and Local Governments,*
*1955–94*

Number of mandates

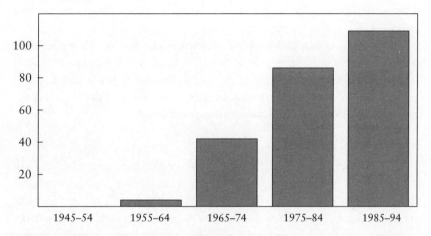

Source: National Conference of State Legislatures, as cited in Clyde Wayne Crews Jr.,
*Ten Thousand Commandments: A Policymaker's Snapshot of the Federal Regulatory
State* (Washington: Competitive Enterprise Institute, September 1996), p. 17.

To local entities, of course, many of these actions seemed unfair and
irrational. To policymakers at the national level, however, there was
method in the madness. Before a retrenchment commenced in the 1980s
federal grant giving had gotten out of control. Between 1960 and 1980
expenditures increased one and a half times as fast as the growth of the
economy. Funds were tossed hither and yon, sponsoring countless questionable "community development" needs—like the construction of a
tennis complex in an affluent section of Little Rock, Arkansas, and the
expansion of a municipal golf course in Alhambra, California.[13] Gradual
curtailment of such waste after 1980 was a positive change regardless of
whether a less profligate government might try to extend its influence by
means of off-budget regulations.

Indeed, as the federal government applied the brakes to discretionary
spending and eventually managed to bring a bloated budget into balance

in the 1990s, inflation and interest rates fell, and the national economy surged. Federal austerity yielded by way of economic growth a large net gain for the nation and for the treasuries of most states and municipalities. With plenty of states and many cities now running surpluses there was something to be said for devolving to them more chores and expenses.[14]

Passing responsibilities to local authorities can be fiscally prudent not only for the federal fisc but for society.[15] If local public works are mostly funded by Washington, their costs are harder to contain. States, cities, and counties do not print money; to spend they have to tax. Local resistance to taxation encourages cost consciousness.[16]

### Stingy or Just Thriftier?

Local politicians wish Congress would simply shovel them cash and ask no questions. What the same politicians do not always acknowledge is that when Congress declines to write blank checks, and instead subjects state and local governments to uncompensated demands, some of the demands actually conform to local preferences.[17] A federal law that, say, asks states to administer particular licensing procedures for truck drivers using interstate highways is not an oppressive request if almost every state already has adopted, or willingly intends to adopt, essentially those same procedures. Hence, while the locals are often quick to say that, at a minimum, they should be paid back for the cost of meeting federal requirements, an indiscriminate policy of reimbursements would pose a moral hazard. States and municipalities that had been poised to take the desired actions anyhow would acquire an excuse to stop, sit back, and wait for federal payments.

Nor should taxpayers from afar be expected to indulge local governments that get themselves into trouble. In the early 1990s the governor of California, Pete Wilson, repeatedly complained that Washington was leaving his state too many of the burdens of servicing immigrants. In the next breath he insisted that his state had a rightful claim to hundreds of millions of dollars in federal disaster relief for property damage from earthquakes, floods, and mudslides, even in areas in which permissive California building regulations were substantially responsible for the losses.[18] The rotting rubbish at New York City's primary municipal dump discharges into the tri-state region not only one million gallons of polluted water each day but also large quantities of methane, a major contributor to global warming. People residing in Oregon or Oklahoma—or, for that matter, New Jersey and Connecticut—should not be taxed to detoxify the garbage New Yorkers generate. Efficiency and equity requires that the polluters pay. Most federal environmental regulations operate on that logical principle.

Besides, though federal grants for mandatory pollution abatement have shrunk, other parts of the federal welfare state continued to support the nation's cities. Even during the Reagan years, the social safety net frayed less completely than many observers feared. Measured in constant dollars, federal welfare payments, Food Stamps, Medicaid, child nutrition, and supplemental feeding for women and children—all programs essential to cities—held up reasonably well between 1980 and 1990.[19]

Some would argue that the ability to deduct local property taxes and to exclude interest income earned by state and local debt instruments from the federal income tax represents a $70 billion concession to local control.[20] In 1988 the Supreme Court decided that Congress was free, if it wished, to tax the interest on municipal bonds.[21] Their tax-free status nonetheless has remained intact and continues to favor the beneficiaries with preferential rates of interest. The deductibility of local income and property taxes enables localities to raise more revenue than they otherwise could. Along with these constants at least one other remains in the equation: about half of the billions of dollars in revenues received annually from the sale of minerals, timber, and other commodities on public lands is shared with states and localities.

In sum in the United States as in any other country exactly what the central government "owes" subnational jurisdictions is a debatable matter. And certainly there are times when the Union, in Madisonian terms, has reason to take charge of local affairs—and can legitimately do so even without further indemnifying local governments.

## The Yellow Line

But there also can be too much of a good thing.

Consider a small sample of the municipal functions now touched by national regulations. Federal law draws a line, commonly bright yellow, behind which passengers are forbidden to stand when they ride city buses. In many states, federal law may have a say in how firefighters should be deployed when fighting a fire. Federal law has influenced decisions about how long some unruly students in public schools can be suspended. Federal law has a bearing on how much a city pays for everything from snow removal services to contracts for sidewalk ramps. Federal law can affect whether the recruits for a police department are physically fit. Whether your child can walk to school or must commute by bus may depend on federal law. The degree to which a city's vacant industrial land parcels have to be cleared of toxic waste is dictated by federal law. The salary your child's teacher is paid may be affected by federal law that reaches well beyond the national minimum wage. Federal law addresses what protective measures must be taken to secure municipal landfills, school buildings that contain asbestos, and housing units with lead paint. Federal law determines how a city has to purify its drinking water.

None of these examples are flights of fancy.

When charges for basic municipal services rise, personnel costs are typically the reason. In the wake of the Supreme Court's opinion in the 1985 case of *Garcia* v. *San Antonio Metropolitan Transit Authority* the entire local public sector became liable for retroactive pay to employees filing claims for overtime compensation.[22] Before that time, Congress had moved in 1974 to include state and local governments under the minimum wage and overtime pay provisions of the Fair Labor Standards Act, but two years later this exercise of the commerce clause power had been overturned.[23] *Garcia,* and the subsequent statutory reinstatement of FLSA coverage in the local public sector, can help explain the high cost of operating a fleet of city snowplows during a Sunday night snowstorm.

The Americans with Disabilities Act of 1990 (ADA) tells every municipality to install ramps so that streets and sidewalks can be wheelchair accessible. But when any federal funds help construct these special accommodations (or any other local public works projects) the Davis-Bacon Act, a vestige of the New Deal, requires that the municipal contracts go not to the lowest bidders but to those who pay the "prevailing" (that is, union negotiated) wage of laborers working comparable projects in the geographic vicinity.[24]

Antibias suits brought under the auspices of federal statutes are now so pervasive they shape the employment practices of every municipal agency. Sometimes this litigation appears to have discouraged police departments from testing rigorously for the physical qualifications of the men and women that apply for jobs. For example, after it interrupted such testing in 1986 because of legal challenges, the New York Police Department found itself with some hires who were unfit.[25]

The federally ordained special education program, frequently enforced in painstaking detail by judicial consent decrees, now takes so large a bite out of the budgets of urban school districts that many are unable to raise their regular classroom teachers' salaries, which lag behind those of wealthier suburban districts.

Beginning in the 1960s a number of federal court decisions greatly expanded the rights of students to appeal school suspensions.[26] Despite more modulated opinions by the Supreme Court in later years few teachers or principals can ignore the legal minefield they enter when they contemplate disciplinary actions, especially against students said to be suffering from learning disabilities.[27]

Whether children in a city attend neighborhood schools or are bused sometimes over great distances often hinges on whether and with what methods a federal court order is regulating the racial composition of the city's school system.

As for the instructions to firefighters and the federal pettifogging about where to stand on local public buses, the first fall under standard operating procedures formulated by the Occupational Safety and Health Administration (OSHA).[28] The second is a Department of Transportation (DOT) regulation, which reads as follows:

> Every bus which is designed and constructed so as to allow standees, shall be plainly marked with a line of contrasting color at least 2 inches wide or equipped with some other means so as to indicate to any person that he/she is prohibited from occupying a space forward of a perpendicular plane drawn through the rear of the driver's seat and perpendicular to the longitudinal axis of the bus. Every bus shall have clearly posted at or near the front, a sign with letters at least one half inch high stating that it is a violation of the Federal Highway Administration's regulations for a bus to be operated with persons occupying the prohibited area.[29]

### Crossing the Line

The immersion of the central government in most of these matters seems hard to understand. Why should a national cabinet department or regulatory bureaucracy concern itself with how "standees" ride city buses or with the deployment of firefighters? If local transit authorities or fire departments cannot be left to decide such minutiae, what, if anything, are local governments for? Surely few of the activities in question—putting out fires, riding buses, disciplining troublemakers in schools, hiring police officers, remunerating city workers or contractors—blow fallout across jurisdictions the way some forms of environmental pollution do.

Indeed even some of the national strictures intended to protect the environment seem overly preoccupied with localized problems, not with perils that spill across jurisdictions. Leaking landfills are undesirable, but they seldom contaminate the watersheds in adjacent states or regions.[30] Asbestos or lead paint in buildings is dangerous if absorbed in large quantities, but whatever the risks, neither substance wafts from one community to another. The same holds for the toxic waste sites regulated by the Comprehensive Environmental Response, Compensation and Liability Act, otherwise known as Superfund. Federal tutelage in environmental protection is easy to justify for forms of pollution that traverse boundaries. But Superfund sites do not migrate; they are located in certain places and stay there. And for all but a few pathogens in drinking water, the risks associated with high concentrations of contaminants are borne almost entirely by people in the immediate vicinity who might consume the impure water for a lifetime. Why, then, should the standards of national regulators trump those of localities on how stringently to filter the local drinking water?

Nor can a plausible case be made that the federal involvement in *all* these particulars is meant to restrain potentially destructive competition among communities and thus prevent a downward spiral of standards and services. How many cities, if left to their own devices, would practice fire prevention techniques so ineptly that they require federally approved manuals specifying thumb rules like the number of personnel that must remain outside a burning structure to back up those who go inside? Before Congress acted to rid the Republic of asbestos at least thirty-one states already had programs to inspect and abate the potentially hazardous substance.[31] Long before the EPA promulgated expensive new rules to curb lead poisoning, few state and municipal code enforcement agencies were oblivious to this public health issue.[32] Granted local regulators also were aware that the cost of de-leading buildings could be high and so would compete with other urban needs such as the desire to supply "affordable" housing. But recognizing that trade-off is not "dumb," it is appropriate. Unfortunately, certain local services may suffer *because* of federal legalities that have unintended consequences. The physical condition of as much as a fifth of New York's "finest" was said to have deteriorated for a while after the department grew fearful that its pre-employment fitness test, if kept up, might be deemed discriminatory.[33]

Federal supervision is emphatically warranted on the grounds of upholding basic civil liberties or rights. Yet the legal doctrines that started out establishing fundamental protections—like defending due process for persons who were being wrongfully or arbitrarily punished—later began to wander far afield. Today some assertions of constitutional rights bear scant resemblance to the noble national cause of combating appalling injustice—the likes of Tulsa, for instance.

How these departures came about is a question this book revisits later on. For now, we might keep in mind that while state and local governments have not always been good guarantors of rights and freedoms, neither has the national government. August presidents, congressional leaders, and Supreme Court justices presided over such brutalities as the Cherokee expulsion, the Dred Scott decision, Attorney General A. Mitchell Palmer's raids, and the wholesale internment of American citizens who happened to be of Japanese ancestry. Blind trust in the sagacity or moral superiority of politics at the federal level is naive.

Finally, if James Madison were alive today, he would be startled by how often federal regulation seems to empower local oligarchies more than it liberates citizens from them. Take the supposedly minimal requirements of the Fair Labor Standards Act (FLSA). In the context of the local public sector even this seemingly unassailable law is less innocuous than it appears. Local public employees have, as the chief of New York City's sanitation workers' union once boasted, a natural advantage that no private sector union has: "We have the ability to elect our own boss" (that is, the employer).[34] He could have added that the threat of a strike in most cities is unlike that posed by work stoppages in private industry. When the Supreme Court's *Garcia* verdict opened the floodgates for overtime claims under the FLSA, the taxpayers in some cities became hostages. They had little choice but to acquiesce to the demands of their service providers, for unlike consumers in a free market, the city dwellers (unless they leave town) could not readily switch to alternative suppliers. Far from countervailing the power of municipal monopolies, *Garcia's* interpretation of the FLSA played into their hands.

## A Rising Toll?

Of course some of the federal prohibitions that seem to play a perverse role may not truly matter much. The DOT's rule for city bus riders may seem abstruse and pedantic, but it is not expensive. Guidance supplied by

OSHA for firefighting sounds officious, but it touches a limited number of jurisdictions indirectly, and even there, hardly seems too taxing. Contemporary legal constraints on the recruitment practices of critical municipal service organizations such as police departments are more telling but, again, exactly what they amount to is unsettled.[35] Local law enforcement agencies and correctional systems, toiling under a variety of federal injunctions, still managed to help drive down urban crime rates in the past decade.

But surely a number of federal prescriptions have had uneven impacts on local governments and have piled impressive costs on some cities.

## One Size Does Not Fit All

The point of federalizing standards is to set norms for society as a whole and hence ensure uniformity. However, uniform rules of little significance for some jurisdictions can be onerous for others. The reach of the amended Fair Labor Standards Act is illustrative. It extends to public employers the mandatory minimum wage and other provisions that the FLSA originally reserved only for private firms. Not only does this generic regulation of workplaces carry different implications for municipalities than markets, its effects vary from one location to the next. The law would not have for most suburban towns, with no unionized employees, comparatively small payrolls, and bountiful tax bases, the same costly consequences it has had for some major cities.

A federal lawsuit that contests traditional fitness tests can pose difficulties for a big city's police force like New York's, which has to cope with crime-ridden slums. The same suit would be of little consequence for, say, Beverly Hills, a place so affluent and sheltered that, as the joke goes, the police department has an unlisted phone number.[36]

### Green Mandates

The unequal impacts of federal environmental regulations are sometimes notorious.[37] In 1987 Congress concluded that every municipality in the United States would have to treat storm water much the same as discharge of polluted water from industrial plants. This requirement, appropriate for humid climates, was ill-suited to arid regions such as much of the Southwest. Never mind that Phoenix averages only seven inches of rainfall a year. This city nonetheless was required to spend large sums each year monitoring the runoff from extremely infrequent rain storms.

Between 1974 and 1994 American taxpayers poured $213 billion into upgrading their municipal water-treatment plants. Now the EPA predicts that $200 billion more will be needed through the year 2014 to bring local wastewater systems up to newly specified design criteria. To that estimate must be added another $132 billion for the replacement of aging plants. The projected total, therefore, rises to $332 billion—a figure that does not include the soaring increases in operating and maintenance expenses associated with more advanced technologies. If the recent past is prologue, local governments will be expected to come up with more than 90 percent of the funding for these capital improvements, plus 100 percent of annual operating expenses.

And for at least some cities the bill will be needlessly steep. Under the Clean Water Act cities have to install secondary wastewater treatment facilities that remove the remaining organic matter not treated in primary facilities. While secondary treatment is usually necessary for landlocked communities, according to a 1993 study by the National Academy of Sciences, the same precaution may not be essential for many seaport cities. Tides at coastal cities help flush organic residue from water bodies. Although the EPA has granted a number of waivers, arguably more oceanside cities ought to receive dispensations.[38]

So stringent are the federal criteria for cleaning up local land containing toxic wastes, and so unsparing have been the liability provisions, that developers and lending institutions have resisted investing in many abandoned industrial and commercial sites. A recent survey of more than two hundred cities by the U.S. Conference of Mayors reported no fewer than 81,000 acres of brownfields, including some undoubtedly entangled in Superfund suits. These sites continue to languish in the inner cities, costing them possibly as much as $2.4 billion in lost property tax revenue each year and foreclosing opportunities to create as many as 550,000 jobs. Meanwhile policymakers bewail the "sprawl" wrought by businesses that, steering clear of the legal liabilities, opt to locate on virgin acreage in the suburbs.

Under the rules of the Safe Drinking Water Act localities everywhere have been busy examining their water supplies for pesticides and other toxic residues that pose substantial risks only in particular areas. Before it was finally relieved from some of this duty in the mid-1990s Columbus, Ohio, found itself guarding against approximately forty pesticides. Many of them had long since been discontinued in the vicinity, including one product used chiefly on pineapple plantations in Hawaii.[39]

At times the nationalized regulations appear to have created new problems at the regional level. New York, for instance, ran afoul of a national prohibition on ocean dumping of sewage sludge. Banned since 1988 from disposing of any sludge at sea, the city resorted to dewatering and composting its waste. But this practice emits nitrogen-rich effluents that endanger marine life in nearby estuaries. In March 1998 the state of Connecticut filed suit against the city for contaminating Long Island Sound.[40]

## Rights and Wrongs

If environmental standards often do not admit enough diversification, latitude, and cognizance of costs at the local level, the federal regulations that fall under the capacious category of civil rights permit even less. For the most part this is as it should be. "Rights tends to be viewed as absolutes," explains Robert A. Katzmann, "overriding considerations of cost effectiveness."[41] But no society can afford to extend "total justice" to an ever-increasing variety of petitioners.[42] What began in the 1960s as a long-awaited effort to secure equality of opportunity for African Americans has expanded into a vast apparatus of federally mandated protections and preferences for many additional groups. Whether every class of claimants has needed maximal compulsory remedies is a good question. So is whether each remedy should be determined from the top down.

Consider the rights of persons with disabilities. The ideal of accommodating the physically impaired is just and desirable, but should every municipality be told how to improve handicapped access in its public facilities? To modernize public buses and retrofit subways, as demanded by the Rehabilitation Act of 1973, New York concluded in 1980 that the requisite capital improvements and annual operating bills would amount to a budget-busting expense. Mayor Edward I. Koch figured, "It would be cheaper for us to provide every severely disabled person with taxi service than make 255 of our subway stations accessible."[43]

Mercifully, after pitched legal battles, the federal planners relented and lowered the costs. New York, with an old and extensive transit system, should never have been sidetracked from opting for alternatives to the federal retrofit policy. For this city it should have been obvious from the outset that investing in advanced paratransit or even subsidizing taxi rides would secure a greater net gain for the seriously disabled and for beleaguered local taxpayers.

In 1973 during the congressional debate on the Rehabilitation Act, the bill's authors seemed to have had no clue that in venues like New York the legislation's burdens might well exceed its blessings. One of the chief sponsors admitted afterward that neither he nor any of his colleagues "had any concept that it would involve such tremendous costs."[44] The deliberations were not altogether different sixteen years later when Congress took up the Americans with Disabilities Act of 1990, an even bolder piece of legislation mandating "fair and just access."[45] Local authorities pleaded for greater leeway or else for federal aid to cushion compliance costs, but Congress seemed untroubled. It wrote into the ADA a raft of requirements and almost no financial assistance.[46]

At congressional hearings on the ADA a representative of the Memphis Area Transit Authority guessed that the measure, if adopted, would force that city to eliminate hundreds of thousands of transit trips annually.[47] Dire warnings like this one about the fiscal havoc the bill portended proved mostly exaggerated. Nevertheless the law's seeming insouciance about local dissimilarities hit some communities hard. Faced with an ultimatum to construct some 65,000 wheelchair ramps by the mid-1990s the city of Phoenix reported that "it would be physically impossible to find enough skilled labor in the Valley to conduct such a massive construction program, even if the deadline were several years away."[48] Ordered to incorporate curb cuts and sidewalk ramps in its plans for downtown street repaving, officials in Philadelphia guessed that more than a third of its planned repavements would be unaffordable.[49] The Washington Metro in the nation's capital is America's most modern and beautifully designed subway system. Nonetheless it was directed to tear up parts of forty-five station platforms and install bumpy tiles along edges to accommodate the sight impaired. Interestingly the two leading organizations representing the blind—the American Council of the Blind and the National Federation of the Blind—disagreed about whether this multimillion dollar effort would protect sight-impaired transit users or perhaps endanger them.

## Zero Tolerance

How to handle municipal overtime pay, regulate the town water supply, or resurface city streets and sidewalks used to be judgments that local authorities dispatched. Now, more and more of these daily administrative duties are subject to federal guidance. Whatever the rationale for guiding so many quotidian decisions, however, the government's agenda would be less troublesome for many cities if its specifications sought to set only modest baselines. Alas the specifications are sometimes utopian.

## Environmental Perfection

A number of U.S. environmental mandates certainly seem to qualify for that description. Their targets, timetables, and technologies seem specified without regard to whether the perils the rules are meant to diminish are great or small. Indeed policy in important instances proceeds as if risk should be banished at any price. This feverish pursuit of environmental purification, sometimes tolerating virtually no margin of health risk, is unreasonable for many municipalities and thousands of businesses.

When the EPA revised its goals for curbing effluents from municipal incinerators in 1995, for instance, it ordered the virtual elimination of emissions of mercury and lead as well as dioxin.[50] Most of these toxic substances had already dropped dramatically; overall lead emissions, for example, were down 98 percent between 1970 and 1995. The city of Tampa, which had finished building a state-of-the-art incinerator only ten years earlier, now had to refit that modern installation with another round of pollution control equipment costing scores of millions of dollars.[51]

How much the latest incineration standards would improve public health was uncertain. In a review of epidemiological research on the health of persons living near city incinerators in the United Kingdom one study discerned no consistent pattern of ill health.[52] The findings were interesting because the studies surveyed relied primarily on data from the 1970s and 1980s when pollution controls on incinerators were underdeveloped. After at least a decade of stringent regulation it was likely that the remaining health hazards from these facilities would be small— especially in the United States where a person's average exposure to poisons such as mercury is now less than half the average in Europe.[53]

In 1994 the Congressional Budget Office estimated that under the Comprehensive Environmental Response, Compensation and Liability Act the expense of cleaning up the nation's toxic waste dumps would run between $106 billion and a staggering $463 billion.[54] How could this environmental project cost more than twice the entire gross domestic product of Sweden? The excesses of Superfund bear some responsibility. Costs escalate when sites have to be decontaminated so pristinely that a child playing on them could safely eat their dirt for seventy days a year.[55]

Thus the program had completed merely 52 of 1,320 designated sites as of 1993. City governments have incurred directly only a fraction of the multibillion dollar Superfund bill. But the persistence of old brownfields, at least partly shadowed by Superfund liabilities, continues to be for inner cities a financial sinkhole.

Radon in drinking water became another preoccupation of federal regulators in the 1990s. Radon in water, however, is a negligible part of a larger problem: radon leaking into homes and offices from surrounding soil—a health hazard that the EPA ironically does not regulate at all.[56] The health threat from radon in water comes chiefly from inhaling the gas as it evaporates, particularly during showering; the amount that escapes in this fashion is not greater than 2 percent of what already is naturally in the air.[57] No matter; regulations were proposed that would require water to be far more radon free than the air. What prophylactic effect such regulations would have was unclear. The sign of their effect on municipal utilities, however, was predictable: their costs would rise.

For local governments a final significant example of an environmental program driven by strong aversion to risk, hence beset by escalating costs, was the Asbestos Hazard Emergency Response Act of 1986. Asbestos in school buildings was a concern of state and local officials well before Congress took up the issue. But the goal of federal enactment was to minimize health risks in all school districts. Whether the presence of asbestos was, always and everywhere, a hazard worth regulating has never been self-evident. A symposium at Harvard University concluded in 1989 that the risk of dying from low-level exposure to asbestos was approximately 400 times lower than from, say, exposure to passive cigarette smoke.[58] The risk in schools is extremely low.[59] Hence, the cost of banning asbestos has been estimated to exceed $100 million per life saved.[60] And the process of ripping the feared substance from old structures, like those in many cities, sometimes risked increasing the volume of airborne fibers to harmful levels that could persist for years.

Yet among the demands on the stretched resources of America's embattled urban school systems has been the pressure to pour tens of millions of dollars into precautionary inspections and renovations to eliminate what has been, as health risks go, mostly a lesser one. New York City delayed opening its public schools in the fall of 1993 so that classrooms could be inspected for asbestos. The city spent $100 million on the task— money that could have been put toward a more pressing problem at the time: the insufficient number of security guards.[61]

*Hypersensitivity*

In bygone days almost anyone joining a big city police force, fire department, sanitation crew, or inner city school system understood that he or she would be entering an often unpleasant, indeed perilous, occupation. The clients of these tough "street-level bureaucracies" were not always polite company, and neither would be some of the supervisors and coworkers. Nasty or boorish encounters would occur; they went with the territory.

Expectations are rather different nowadays. U.S. legal theories have added new meanings to the pursuit of admissible and equitable employment conditions. "Hostile" work environments, unintentional discriminations ("disparate impacts"), even precautions misconstrued as insults or slights—all these imperfections and more are actionable.

Taxpayers, not philanthropists, pay the salaries of municipal employees. One would think that city officials accountable to voters might be permitted to set, say, basic health eligibility criteria and then unceremoniously ask prospective employees for their medical histories, especially if the jobs in question were physically demanding, stressful, or dangerous. Not so fast. To attain a bias-free environment for applicants with disabilities, such queries now have to be conducted with extreme delicacy, if indeed, they can be conducted at all. In one of many revealing vignettes in his 1997 book *The Excuse Factory,* Walter K. Olson relates what happened to a policeman in Boston who was disciplined after his superiors discovered that he had lied under oath about having received inpatient psychiatric care on five occasions. The policeman had to be reinstated, with back pay and damages.[62] What about the subway cleaner in New York who was refused a promotion to train operator because his corpulence prevented him from passing a basic stress test? He had standing to sue for alleged discrimination, did, and got the job.[63]

Sometimes the kinds of pains taken to ensure benign work environments are not without ironies. "A Los Angeles Police Department official," Olson recounts, "said the department was moving against a range of 'inappropriate' male doings even though 'very, very few' of them 'would rise to the level of true sex harassment.'"[64] But some years later misconduct of a different sort was disclosed in the LAPD: some members of the force had trafficked in narcotics and were accused of planting evidence, framing suspects, and shooting some unarmed ones.[65] What had been done to prevent *these* doings? Apparently too little according to newspaper accounts. Some of the officers implicated in the scandal seem to have been hired without adequately checking their backgrounds, which included histories of arrests and alcoholism.[66]

At all levels of government in the United States efforts to protect the civil rights of workers have moved beyond the original mission—to attain basic equality of opportunity for an oppressed minority in the labor force. State and local jurists often have been just as uncompromising as many federal ones in their efforts to sanitize employment procedures. (The Boston policeman took his grievance to a state court, though his could as easily have been a federal case.) The evolution of employment law at the federal level, however, has provided the legal foundation, and the main inspiration, for all concerned. Without it some local authorities might still choose to regard as discriminatory such practices as the screening of psychiatric records of job applicants, but other jurisdictions could decide that inquiring straightaway about the mental health of the applicants—not least those applying to become gun-toting police—is prudent, efficient, and fair to the taxpaying public.

The law also has been evenhanded, purging prejudice or insensitivity in private employment relations as well as public ones. This does not mean, however, that what goes for the goose is necessarily the same as what happens to the gander. When a corporation shells out hundreds of thousands of dollars to settle a bias suit, its stockholders and customers, if they get nicked at all, can always take their business elsewhere. But when a local government has to settle, in the name of upholding civil rights, what turns out to be a phony accusation contrived by a few querulous employees the checks it has to write (to conduct long investigations, retain lawyers, pay consultants, award compensatory claims, and so on) are drawn from tax revenues, collected from citizens by coercion.[67] The trouble with such extortions is not just that they rankle local residents; if the defendant is a community that is already in financial straits, the debit on the public purse can do palpable damage.

## Adversarial Legalism

Which brings up a third feature of the ubiquitous federal presence: it has helped stoke a firestorm of litigation. Between 1991 and 1995 the cost of routine liability claims in New York City increased 57 percent in constant dollars.[68] By 1992 these legal bills were totaling more than the city's entire budget for its parks and libraries.[69] The trend in some other cities was worse. During the same period Minneapolis experienced a 187 percent increase in liability expenditures.[70]

And that was only one portion of the jagged legal landscape. Alongside the mounting malpractice complaints, traffic accident claims, zoning appeals, slip-and-falls, and countless other petty municipal torts came new causes to sue city governments, now increasingly in the federal courts. Several Supreme Court opinions had widened the general exposure of cities to civil actions.[71] These and other stimulants made themselves felt.

### The Long Arm of the Lawsuit

Litigation in the federal courts exploded after 1960. That year there was a total of only 2,483 civil filings under the categories of civil rights-related cases, for example, whereas the number of such cases reached 98,153 by 1995.[72] Of these lawsuits, the ones that targeted the local public sector left virtually no facet of municipal administration undisputed. Major cities found themselves awash in court orders determining everything from the racial balancing of schools to the placement of foster children and the schooling of learning-disabled students, to the provision of shelters for the homeless, the use of city jails, buses, and even public fire alarm boxes.

Fire alarm boxes? In 1996 a federal judge halted the New York City Fire Department's plan to replace 16,300 antiquated alarm boxes with public telephones wired to an emergency system. The rationale: hearing-impaired persons might be unable to use the phones; the new system violated a federal guarantee of "equal access" to public facilities.[73]

For years a federal court had told New York how to run its jails. Conditions in the jails needed reform. But under the terms of its decree, active since 1978, the court-appointed "special masters" became fastidious. No particular was spared—down to the ratio of cups of borax per gallon of water required to mop the bathrooms.[74]

In 1996, at the other end of the country, the Los Angeles Metropolitan Transit Authority (MTA) settled a federal suit in which the MTA was accused of discriminating against minorities because city buses on certain routes were very crowded. One of the plaintiffs characterized the conditions on the MTA's buses as "a brutal violation" of civil rights. The terms of the consent decree got into specifics: there could be no more than an average of fifteen people standing during bus rides for any twenty-minute peak period by the end of 1997; then no more than an average of eleven people by June 2000; then no more than eight by June 2002.[75]

While court orders like those in Los Angeles and New York had delved into details those in some other cities were detailed—and drastic. To relieve overcrowding in Philadelphia's prisons, for instance, a federal judge barred pretrial detention of any suspect not charged with a violent crime. The long-range purpose of this shock treatment was to ameliorate the city's jails, but in the meantime, according to the court's critics, the result was that the number of fugitive drug dealers soared.[76] By one count more than three-quarters of Philadelphia's drug dealers became fugitives within ninety days of their arrests.

To be sure, most legal threats to city authorities would fizzle well short of producing judicial injunctions, usually because the underlying grievances simply could not stand up even by the standards of the world's most accommodating civil justice system. That did not mean, however, that cities could ignore the threats. To limit liabilities millions of dollars have been spent each year paying lawyers, keeping legally bullet-proof records, purchasing insurance, commissioning consultants, administering sensitivity training to personnel, and so forth.[77] Among the strange federal suits against which the city of San Diego had to defend itself a few years ago was one from a man seeking $5.4 million in damages to redress his discomfort at having had to share a rest room with members of the opposite sex during a rock concert at Jack Murphy Stadium.[78] The Court of Appeals for the Ninth Circuit recently sat to hear a complaint filed by AlliedSignal, Inc., against the city of Phoenix.[79] What was the company's grievance? The city's water disinfection policy, though supplying water indisputably safe enough for humans to imbibe, did not wipe out some bacteria that allegedly damaged the firm's sprinkler systems.

In part the basis for the increase in federal cases against cities and states had existed for about a hundred years. A federal law passed in 1871 stripped state and local officials of immunity from suits by citizens who had been deprived of any "rights, privileges, or immunities secured by the Constitution and laws of the United States."[80] A century later this dormant power—the origin of which had been an inadequate attempt to protect newly freed slaves from the Ku Klux Klan—began to stir in unforeseen ways. By 1980, it seemed, local officials could find themselves in federal court if they deprived a citizen of just about *anything* to which he or she could plausibly claim to be entitled under federal law (and not

just those federal laws protecting civil rights). For example, persons con-
tending that a local public assistance office had denied them welfare benefits could sue in federal court, even though the original federal welfare
law, enacted in 1935, said virtually nothing about which level of government had the last word on eligibility. Cities such as New York, where
public assistance was substantially a local function, were suddenly
swamped with such claims. New York's welfare rolls shot up from 49,000
in 1974 to 90,000 in 1979.[81] The upsurge almost certainly was related, at
least in part, to changes in the legal environment.

### Private Attorneys General

Meanwhile Congress expanded the avenues for citizen suits of another
kind: to enforce state and local compliance with the Clean Air Act of
1970, the Clean Water Act of 1972, and then almost every other environmental law.[82] Not only were these statutes enforceable by private advocates, their ability to litigate was enhanced by asymmetric fee-shifting
provisions. Plaintiffs who prevailed would have their attorneys' fees paid,
sometimes by direct legal aid, more often by taking compensation from
defendants, whereas plaintiffs who lost were off the hook.

The citizen suit provisions proved a powerful, and often prudential, way
of putting teeth into environmental protection programs. But for cities the
ensuing bulge of environmental litigation could also become wearisome.
The process of cleaning up toxic waste sites, for instance, soon became an
invitation to long legal altercations that dragged even the most minor
transgressors into the fray. Under the Superfund scheme primary polluters
have a powerful incentive to spread responsibility by suing third parties,
many of whom may account for only infinitesimally small shares of the
environmental injury. So in a California landfill case the city of Monterey
and twenty-eight other municipalities were hauled into a cleanup settlement and confronted with multimillion dollar charges on the grounds that
they, too, had polluted the waste site.[83] How much hazardous refuse had
they contributed? A fair estimate was less than 1 percent.

And the pollution abatement remedies devised in courtrooms have
sometimes reflected the passions of litigants more than considered opinions based on scientific assessments. In *City of Chicago* v. *Environmental
Defense Fund*, for instance, Chicago was instructed to retool at great
expense its incinerators to treat *all* incineration ash as a hazardous substance. Until then the EPA had wisely excluded harmless kinds of household refuse from its definition of hazardous waste.[84]

*Litigious Workplaces*

Employment cases, which already accounted for about a quarter of all civil suits against city governments by the mid-1980s, multiplied as well.[85] A growing number were brought by people expecting to be made whole by one or another of the federal civil rights statutes. Energized by various bold enactments, such as the Age Discrimination in Employment Acts of 1975 and 1986, the Americans with Disabilities Act of 1990, and the Civil Rights Act amendments of 1991, federal antibias suits fanned out to service a lengthening queue of clients. As in environmental advocacy cases plaintiffs acquired new incentives to sue. After 1991, for example, the burden of proof in cases of alleged racial or ethnic discrimination was tilted against defendants. The mere composition by race of an employer's payroll could be used as *prima facie* evidence of racism, leaving the truth to the accused, not the accusers, to establish. The accusers, moreover, could have the fees of their attorneys and expert witnesses recovered in multiples when prejudice was proved. And compensatory and punitive damages became available, with the odds of collecting large sums significantly improved by the use of jury trials.

Novel legal assaults on municipal employment practices also came from federal authorities acting directly. Closely scrutinized by the Equal Employment Opportunity Commission and the Department of Justice's Civil Rights Division have been the testing procedures for city job candidates. In city after city the physical fitness tests conducted by police and fire departments as well as other municipal agencies came under suspicion of victimizing some protected classes (women, for instance), while the pencil-and-paper examinations administered under typical civil service systems risked charges of excluding others (for example, blacks and Hispanics). Statistical discrimination was found even when respectable quotients of minorities ultimately made their way into hiring pools. Minority candidates were 30 percent of those who took a special civil service exam designed to increase minority representation in New York City's police department in the early 1980s. Nearly two thousand blacks and Hispanics reached the final pool. But that was not enough, according to a federal judge, who proceeded to set a standard for the department whereby half of all new hires had to be black or Hispanic until they reached at least 30 percent of the total force.[86]

Federal surveillance of municipal personnel selection continued well into the 1990s. Among the many actions reportedly brought by the

Justice Department (DOJ) in 1998, for example, were complaints against municipalities in Texas, Louisiana, and Massachusetts for not attaining the correct percentages of designated minorities in police and fire departments, school faculties, and even poll workers.[87]

### Suing the Schools

While the municipal workplace became increasingly litigious other sources of legal strife engulfed the delivery of city services, most notably the schools. For decades numerous cities had grappled with court-ordered desegregation plans, many of which had the unwanted consequence of aggravating racial imbalances by accelerating the exodus of white families from urban school systems.[88] These ordeals had finally run their course by the late 1990s, although not everywhere. As of 1995 several major city school districts, including those of Nashville, Buffalo, Indianapolis, and Memphis, were still operating under their original court orders or were still being supervised by a federal court though their original desegregation plans had been revised.[89] And as late as 1998 the DOJ was filing additional briefs requesting continued judicial supervision of the decades-old desegregation case in St. Louis.[90] But even as most of the forced busing experiments receded legal activists pressured school systems to secure other entitlements—such as a right to asbestos-free classrooms and the right of all children with disabilities to receive special educational services.

In 1975 Congress passed the Education of All Handicapped Children Act.[91] The aim of the law was to nationalize standards and procedures by which schools educated the handicapped. Teachers, administrators, and parents were to design jointly "individualized educational programs" for these children. The extensive tests and evaluations needed to prepare the programs could not be "racially or culturally discriminatory." Parents dissatisfied with a program were entitled to appeal up the line, ultimately to the federal courts. Schools would have to mainstream students "to the maximum extent appropriate" and provide for them "related services" such as physical therapy, psychological counseling, and recreational facilities. No school could change the placement of a special education student without parental approval. School districts would be required to identify all possible candidates for special education. This so-called child-find process involved discovering not only the eligible children, but also figuring out which ones were already enrolled but inadequately served.

Enforcing so elaborate a national code stirred legal conflicts as inevitable local infractions pertaining to one provision or another were revealed or perceived. "Every decision you make in special education you ask, 'Am I going to get sued for this?'"[92] That fear, voiced by the principal of an elementary school in Dade Country, Florida, could have been expressed by any number of other school officials around the country in the mid-1980s, at least in districts with sizable special education enrollments. One survey of state and local education boards published in 1987 indicated that more than a quarter of them had been sued.[93]

As the level of disputation rose the Supreme Court tried repeatedly to set boundaries. A decision in 1984 denied parents the ability to recoup attorneys' fees and one in 1989 went so far as to invoke Eleventh Amendment immunity of states from certain federal suits.[94] However, Congress promptly reversed these setbacks. Reauthorizations of the handicapped education act in 1986 and 1990 further enfranchised its citizen litigants, covered their legal expenses (now for administrative hearings as well as trials), and extended the whole program to preschool children.[95]

Predictably the law, presently titled the Individuals with Disabilities Education Act (IDEA), ratcheted the volume of litigation another notch (figure 2-2). As in other spheres of adversarial excess (certain environmental programs, for instance) IDEA raised some bizarre expectations, not just legitimate requests, in the nation's courts of law. The superintendent of one California school district reportedly described confronting plaintiffs' lawyers who demanded such "related services" as karate lessons for a kindergarten child with an immune system disorder, horseback riding lessons as rehabilitation therapy for a child who had had seizures, and school trips to Disneyland for a child who was depressed.[96]

And predictably the distribution of the legal troubles has been uneven: besieged disproportionately have been the districts with large special-ed constituencies—the school systems of cities like New York, Baltimore, and Washington, D.C., that would have to cope for years with laborious consent decrees.[97]

## Curing or Abetting the Mischiefs of Faction?

The Individuals with Disabilities Education Act is a monument to best intentions gone astray. Back in 1975, when Congress voted almost unanimously to plant this federal foothold in local public education, the lawmakers hardly anticipated what lay ahead. As its original title indicated

Figure 2-2.  *Special Education Litigation in Federal Courts, 1950–99*[a]

Number of cases

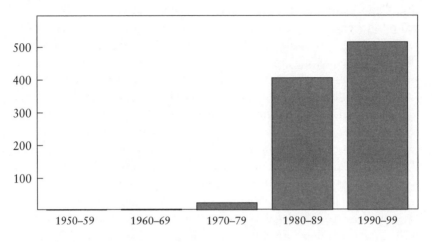

Source: Perry A. Zirkel, "The 'Explosion' in Education Litigation: An Update," *West's Education Law Reporter,* no. 114 (1997), p. 348.

a. Data for 1990–99 are a projection that is based on the actual number of cases through December of 1995.

the legislation was intended to assist the comparatively small number of children who were *handicapped*—that is, blind, deaf, paralyzed, or otherwise gravely impaired. In the ensuing quarter-century, however, definitions of disability widened to include categories of emotional, mental, or behavioral characteristics that had scarcely denoted a "handicap" in years past. Twenty-five years ago, for instance, there was no clinical classification for inattentive pupils. Now, diagnosed as suffering from "attention deficit disorder," they could be eligible for special services.[98] Twenty-five years ago underachieving students were simply called slow learners. Now, they, too, could qualify for special treatment; according to the U.S. Department of Education, "a severe discrepancy between achievement and intellectual ability" could signify that such students were learning disabled.[99] Partly in this fashion, IDEA eventually amassed about 6.1 million clients—and with them, colossal costs.[100]

The lawmakers of 1975 envisioned an expense that might rise to $8 billion nationwide, 40 percent of which would be defrayed by federal grants.[101] By the late 1990s the initiative's annual total was more than five times larger.[102] In the meantime, the federal contribution settled between 8 and 15 percent as congressional appropriators fled the oncoming budgetary behemoth.[103] State and local governments were left to confront it. New York City found itself allocating a quarter of its school budget to special-ed, an obligation so massive it crowded out more than $1 billion of other local priorities, from programs boosting gifted and talented kids to improved street lighting.[104]

Oversubscribed with students in special education, all of whom were entitled to customized "appropriate education" plans and some of whom required extraordinary facilities, many cities resorted to placing substantial percentages in private institutions. The premium for these schools, on top of the rest of the program's lopsided overhead, drove its average per pupil expenditures to twice the average for regular instruction, and in some cities (New York, for instance) to nearly three times the cost of instructing regular students.[105]

## Malfunctions

No affluent, civilized society can neglect the educational needs of disabled children. In 1975 the decision to assist them with what was supposed to be a large infusion of federal funds was decent and humane. But a responsible government also cannot, in effect, bring forth a blizzard of demands and then renege on its promise, shift the expense to communities that can least afford it, and run the risk of lowering the welfare of the remaining citizens in those communities. It is not too much to say that federal policy for special education has erred in just about all these ways. Its constraints on claims and eligibility are unclear; its appropriated funds have consistently fallen far below authorizations; and it has weighed most heavily on overtaxed cities with weak school systems.

Washington, D.C., is certainly a case in point. Few urban schools are more decrepit than the ones in the nation's capital. Repairing the overall system ought to be this city's first priority. Yet special education devoured almost half of all the money the city was able to budget for improvements in 1999.[106] Admittedly Washington's status is unique. Where state governments take charge of financing special education, it preempts a smaller share of municipal school budgets. But where the states have passed the burden through to municipalities, considerable local turmoil has resulted. In New York, as in Washington and various other major cities, the underfunded federal mandate has forced significant, disproportionate reductions in the resources available to regular classes.[107]

The compulsory and largely uncompensated dedication of vast sums to the exigencies of a minority at the expense of other urbanites, who need to educate their children, too, would seem to be the most questionable aspect of the federal special education scheme as presently constituted. But it is not the only one. How much of a net benefit some parts of the expanding program have yielded, even to beneficiaries, has not always been evident. When Congress was debating an extension to preschool children in 1986, for instance, the Congressional Research Service reviewed available studies and found them inconclusive about the cost effectiveness of such early intervention.[108] A 1999 study found no significant differences in achievement scores between learning-disabled children placed in special education and those in regular classrooms.[109]

Further, IDEA, as interpreted in the courts, sometimes has frustrated the ability of schools to protect classrooms from disruptive, even violent, students. Emotionally disturbed children are more likely than the average child to exhibit behavior punishable by suspension or even expulsion from school. Under the law, however, expelling or suspending these students raises the question of whether they are being denied an "appropriate education" and whether the punishments conform with the requirement that "the child shall remain in the current educational placement until the local education agency and the parent agree on a new placement."[110] For the most part the lower courts adjudicating such cases have barred expulsions and sharply limited suspensions. Thus a student diagnosed as having a weakness in "written language skills" was not expelled from a school into which he had helped bring a .357 Magnum handgun.[111] A different school re-enrolled a student who frequently kicked and pushed his teacher, eventually sending her to a hospital emergency room.[112] Another school kept an eight-year-old who repeatedly set fires, exposed himself, and destroyed a classroom. Another was not allowed to remove a student who had caused "a schoolwide disturbance." Yet another school was prevented from ousting a student who had been dealing drugs, and so on. In 1997 Congress amended IDEA, giving schools more flexibility to discipline violent special education students. Nonetheless the procedural hurdles have remained high.

In 1996–97 public schools in the United States were the sites of many thousands of violent assaults.[113] The frequency of these incidents was on average approximately four times worse in inner city schools than in predominately white suburban ones. How closely this differential has been associated with the corresponding ratios of special education enrollments is not known. But surely heavy concentrations of youngsters that manifest disorders such as "serious emotional disturbance" are inauspicious for urban schools struggling to stop the flight of middle-class families to safer districts.

## Clientism

One reason to have lingered over the tribulations caused by IDEA is that the regeneration of the nation's urban centers may be slowed by national policies that debilitate more than strengthen perhaps the single most important service cities must provide: viable schools for the majority of residents. But another good reason is that special education exemplifies a final inefficacy of many federal regulatory programs: they acquire stakeholders that retard reform. The national commitment to special education is in need of federal resources but also of restructuring.[114] Few policymakers at any level of government, however, are eager to rethink the federal role in ways that might disturb the program's organized armies of administrators, psychologists, social workers, lawyers, and other ensconced guardians and clients.[115]

This silo of professional advocates and client groups, embedded in states and school districts but aligned more closely to power brokers in Washington, is far from unique.[116] In fact nearly every intergovernmental program the federal government hatches eventually spawns a protective constituency. Gaze again at the public contracting provisions of the Davis-Bacon Act that can add a costly premium to municipal construction projects. Somehow the interests (chiefly organized labor) bonded to this Depression-era law remain potent enough to keep it unshaken. Or marvel at the disparate-impact test that has laid siege to municipal employment practices. At the behest of the civil rights bar and bureaucracy, and a retinue of other organized proponents, this policy, too, has become a federally enforced legal fixture, even though it is hard to adduce from the original Civil Rights Act of 1964.[117] These custodians have operated much like other successful iron triangles in American politics: "They have entrenched themselves deeply in networks of clientele groups, legislative committees, and program agencies."[118]

No faction has wielded more clout in modern city politics than the millions of organized municipal employees. Unlike the private sector where the percentage of unionized workers has declined sharply since the 1950s, the local public sector's has increased.[119] The membership of the National Education Association, for example, climbed from around 766,000 during the 1950s to more than two and half million now.[120] In the face of organizations so strong and determined to tenure their members, managing municipal personnel is a challenge. Basic tools of efficient management—including a clear capacity to fire, suspend, demote, or reassign incompetent employees—are lacking or limited. Frequently the unions stand in the way, and even if they do not, civil service systems often provide so many avenues of appeal they compound the difficulty.[121] Separating a Chicago park worker for incompetence requires some eighty-four steps. Removal of an inept employee in Boston can be contested before four different panels, none of which has authority over the others and any of which might overturn the dismissal, award back pay, or at least reinstate pension benefits.

As if this maze did not contain enough traps, federal legislation inadvertently has set additional ones. By banning automatic retirements, for instance, and protecting job holders with disabilities federal laws shield older employees and handicapped ones from capricious discrimination but can also frustrate fair efforts to unseat some whose ill health may pose a genuine liability, or even some who are manifestly unfit. When the city of Toledo disqualified an insulin-dependent diabetic as a candidate for its police force, a federal district court reinstated him.[122] When a Connecticut municipality tried to terminate the employment of a school superintendent who had "walked off the job," he invoked (among other excuses) alcoholism as a disability and obtained a settlement of $240,000.[123]

In principle a prime justification for elevating governance from the local to the national level is to overrule factions that may arrogate power and exploit or even tyrannize other citizens in a local polity. The first aim of federal civil rights protection, for instance, was (or should have been) to halt all local lynchings, indeed to avenge the 4,742 African Americans who were tortured, hanged, and burned to death by racist bands between the 1880s and the 1960s.[124] But in practice a good deal of national oversight no longer serves this type of core purpose. On the contrary, federal programs often install or solidify cartels, so to speak, that ought to have their local influence shorn, not enhanced, especially when they hinder local innovation or stymie sound public administration.[125]

This is not to say that the client lobbies always pose insurmountable obstacles to locally inspired reforms. Albeit after many decades, the malfunctioning federal welfare program, for example, was successfully overhauled and devolved.[126] Nor does it mean that the lobbies are necessarily so dominant as to be able to extract from congressional appropriation committees the funds needed to honor Congress's ambitious goals. The clients are commonly powerful enough, however, to make state and local governments cough up the difference, and to keep them playing by the federal rules even when those rules are flawed.

In this sense a final paradox of the politics of federalization is that it sometimes seems to ensure, not curb, the mischief of factions.

## Summary

If each of these federal interventions decidedly improved the quality of urban life, the misgivings expressed in these pages could be shrugged off. But there is a point at which routinely subjecting municipal decisions to national supervision and regimentation risks doing more damage than good.

Federal regulation today reaches into so many details of municipal administration that picayune concerns are nationalized alongside weightier ones. Much of this spectacle is merely a nuisance. A federal court that interferes with the ability of a city to test, say, municipal clerk-typists for grammar, spelling, and punctuation (as the Fifth Circuit ruled a number of years ago) might trifle with the local community's own valued standards but probably does not put it in jeopardy.[127] At times, however, the stakes have been higher. The safety of community residents can be compromised, for example, by rulings that limit the testing of would-be firefighters and police recruits for endurance, strength, or agility (as some of the opinions handed down by the federal courts have done), or by rulings that turn loose hundreds of arrested suspects, including some charged with robbery, stalking, carjacking, drug dealing, and manslaughter (as a federal injunction against pretrial detention did for several years in Philadelphia).

Some federal mandates sock cities with unnecessarily large costs. Costs can soar, for example, amid the national campaigns for risk-free environments—such as perfectly bias-free workplaces, toxin-free tap water, asbestos-free schools, lead-free housing, hazard-free redevelopment sites, and more. The persistence of some 21,000 brownfields languishing in cities is a stark example of the debacle that a zero-risk mentality can create.[128]

Federal law has also enmeshed municipalities in new litigation, some of which manacles their managers, demoralizes their personnel, and ties their budgets in knots. Due in no small part to federal policy, the terms and conditions of municipal employment are cited as the realm most roiled by legal disputes or the threat of them.[129] City schools used to be relatively simple and trusted neighborhood institutions. Since the 1960s, however, they have been buffeted by federal regulatory and judicial directives, leaving many preoccupied with legal bills and compliance issues more than with the quality of instruction for most students.[130]

By the early 1990s New York City's costs of complying with the ten largest court orders and mandates, specifying protocols for various municipal functions, were said to corner 26 percent of the city's tax revenue.[131] Even if every dollar earmarked in this litigious fashion were a dollar well spent (a dubious proposition), local taxpayers could fairly ask whether less adversarial means would have allocated the desired resources better, or at least without as much costly friction. By the early 1990s the cumulative cost of settling New York's liability claims had reached bewildering proportions.[132]

Alongside these considerable vexations lies the fact that some federal regulations are relatively rigid templates, superimposed on cities and towns regardless of their diverse circumstances. In certain locations, therefore, the mandated expenditures are simply a waste of money. (Should Phoenix really be made to spend significant sums to monitor the runoff from practically nonexistent rain storms?) In other instances the costs of meeting a given standard, though not pointless, will vary wildly among localities. For example, all municipalities will have to bring their groundwater treatment up to the nationwide standards of the Safe Drinking Water Act. The charges for households could vary by several thousand percent between small and large cities.[133]

U.S. environmental strictures are hardly the only ones that beget interjurisdictional inequities. Many central cities in the United States continue to contain disproportionate percentages of the low-income residents of metropolitan areas. Hence these cities bear a disproportionate share of poverty-related public expenditures. National regulations can contribute to the imbalance when their costs are not adequately reimbursed and are a function of local poverty rates. The federal special education mandate, as we have seen, falls into this category, but so do quite a few others.[134]

At the end of 1996 the District of Columbia was home to 45 percent of the Washington region's poor.[135] A consequence, as in other cities that have to shoulder comparable concentrations of poverty, is that the expense of administering almost any city service is inherently higher in the District than in the surrounding suburbs.[136] Whatever the other reasons for the District's extraordinary administrative cost structure, the heavy lifting is scarcely alleviated by some thirty-nine federal court decrees, some of which have compelled steep increases in the costliest of municipal items—like overtime compensation for city workers.[137]

## Race to the Bottom—or the Top?

It is generally assumed that Washington intervenes in local decisions primarily to prevent intergovernmental rifts and rivalries from degrading basic norms for public health, safety, or welfare. Federal authorities, the theory goes, chiefly step in to set suitable baselines—for Atlanta's air quality, or New York's fiscal practices, or the competence of school teachers in a bunch of cities. But in reality much federal preemption of local policies works the other way around. It subjects state and local governments to national directives even when those governments are emulating, indeed outdoing, one another to run standards up, not down.

In 1986 Congress moved to extend to preschoolers the universal right to special education for handicapped children. But forty-two states already had begun programs of this sort.[138] Similarly, by the time Congress proclaimed that no schoolchild should be exposed to asbestos risks most school districts already had programs to repair dangerous buildings. In 2001 a new administration in Washington proposed to coax the states to start rating the performance of all their local elementary and secondary schools. But less noticed during the national education reform debate was that seventeen states already assigned such ratings, four more were poised to initiate them in 2002, and at least two more planned to do so soon thereafter.[139] The concept of school accountability, in other words, was percolating and spreading at the local level well in advance of any coercive federal measures.

Proponents of central direction, however, frequently seem unimpressed. By their logic, if so many state and local initiatives have already blazed a trail, national standards only complete what the locals have started. The latter, it would appear, are as likely to have their independence shorn when they are proactive and progressive as when they are laggards.

Principled arguments are hard to advance for at least some of the specialized, coerced expenditures that have been pressed upon cities. But worthy or not, federally mandated programs, once established, are not easy to redesign. Program preservationists prevail.[140] The cementing of policies by vested interests was not what the framers of the Constitution had in mind when they sought to enlarge the orbit of national authority. What the founders intended was to check and counterbalance the power of calcified local elites.

## Final Considerations

Although plenty of the federal government's urban mandates are presumed to confer more benefits than costs to cities, the net benefits are hard to determine when the estimated costs of particular federal regulations turn out to be moving targets. Example: the Environmental Protection

Agency originally predicted that the burden of its rules for managing overflows from municipal sanitary sewers would total $10.3 billion. By March 1999 the estimate was raised to almost $82 billion.[141]

Further, while cities have had to contend with new requirements imposed by the federal government, its copayments have diminished during the past couple of decades—this, even though federal revenues grew at almost twice the rate of municipal revenues after 1992.[142] A good deal of what the nation's cities are asked to do should not be propped up with federal tax dollars. But in certain spheres of policy a better balance has to be struck between making a habit of bailing out local governments and the habit of passing the buck.

State treasuries cannot be counted on to fill the breach. During the 1990s almost thirty states adopted tax and expenditure limits.[143] Meanwhile major federal expansions of Medicaid added new multibillion dollar liabilities to state budgets. By the second half of 2001 the national economy was sputtering, and terrorism hijacked substantial revenues from all levels of governments, further limiting the ability of many states to aid their cities.

A number of cities have been incurring expenses so enormous their outlays have exceeded those of many state governments.[144] By 1992 Chicago was spending more than any one of a dozen states. Los Angeles spent more than any one of thirty-two states. New York City spent more than did forty-eight states. Local taxation in some of these places has risen to the highest levels in the country.[145]

What has such taxing and spending meant for urban households? Federally mandated expenditures were estimated to claim at least one-fourth of the city budget of Columbus, Ohio, as of 1996.[146] The environmental items alone were expected to add around $850 to the annual tax bill of an average family.[147] And that surcharge was likely to be only a first installment. Facing an array of expensive new rules—governing everything from solid waste disposal, to the disinfection of drinking water, surface water treatment, and the percentage of "zero emission" vehicles in municipally owned vehicle fleets—the citizens of Columbus and of many other large cities are likely to see ongoing increases in municipal taxes and fees.[148]

# 3 Tales from Six Cities

To see how federal rules encumber some cities it is helpful to examine them at closer range. A handful of sites was selected for this purpose: Baltimore, Philadelphia, New York, Chicago, San Francisco, and Los Angeles. This selection does not pretend to be representative, let alone scientific. (This is not a fatal flaw. Is anyone really sure what a suitable cross-section of American cities should comprise?) Nevertheless the half-dozen cities meet several salient criteria. They are all big, with half-a-million or more inhabitants, and include the nation's three largest urban centers. They are also reasonably diverse, situated in at least three distinctive geographic regions of the country, and subject to varying jurisdictional settings, such as differing arrangements with state and county governments.

Further, although these cities have shared some similar experiences coping with particular federal regulations, the most noteworthy war stories are not everywhere the same, nor of equal import. But the ones sampled help illustrate a variety of conflicts, even if the sample hardly does justice to the full range of regulatory issues and expenses that huge cities like New York, Chicago, or Los Angeles have had to confront.

Finally, although certain cities flourished in recent years while others continued to struggle (San Francisco's resurgence in the 1990s, for instance, dwarfed Baltimore's and Philadelphia's), none is a fiscal basket case; that is, the assortment does not include the likes of Bridgeport, Connecticut, East St. Louis, Illinois, or Camden, New Jersey—cities that became literally wards of their state governments, having failed to satisfy the most minimal state and federal standards, never mind the arduous ones.[1] By contrast, at the close of the twentieth century every city chosen for this chapter was fairly capable of discharging the essential functions of municipal government—though sometimes less satisfactorily than might have been possible. For each has had to haul additional administrative baggage, some of it sent down problematically by the federal government.

## Baltimore

A century and a half ago Baltimore ranked among the country's three largest cities. From its bustling port the world's fastest clipper ships plied the seas, and looking west the nation's first railroad (the Baltimore & Ohio) moved materials and merchandise in and out of the city's teeming factories. Today Baltimore is fourteenth in size among major U.S. cities, and its population continues to slip away—6.5 percent in the 1980s followed by another 6 percent in the 1990s. Despite the billions of dollars that have been poured into rebuilding the downtown, including a redeveloped Inner Harbor, a national aquarium, a cavernous convention center, and two state-of-the-art sports stadiums, the city has been unable to reverse a net loss of jobs. By contrast the city's suburban counties have chalked up impressive employment growth: some 326,800 jobs, nearly a 50 percent increase, since 1980.[2] Between 1993 and 1995 the suburbs of Baltimore gained 9.5 jobs for every job *lost* in the city.

Within its urban region Baltimore remains the main repository of metropolitan poverty. Average family income in the city was 59 percent of the average in the suburbs in 1990. Of the region's 137,000 poor blacks, 86 percent lived in the city.[3] Although some of the weight of this maldistribution has since lifted, poverty-related pathologies remain acute.[4] Baltimore had the second highest rate of violent crime among the thirty most populous American cities in the late 1990s (although for the first time in a decade the city's homicide rate finally fell below 300 victims in the year 2000).[5] The 2,420 incidents per 100,000 residents reported in 1997 were barely better than the number in 1990, when 2,438 incidents per 100,000 were recorded.[6] Overall crime (including nonviolent incidents) rose throughout the 1990s.

With the preponderance of the region's economic base now situated in the suburbs, and the high-maintenance tasks of coping with poverty and dependency still falling primarily on the city government, Baltimore levies a lot of taxes. City imposts take approximately 11 percent of the income of the average middle-income family, a burden that has placed this municipality among the top six cities with the steepest levels of taxation (a whisker below New York's 11.4 percent).[7]

In part reductions in intergovernmental aid have foreclosed the possibility of much local tax relief ( figure 3-1). Federal aid dropped by 77 percent between 1980 and 1995, from $385 million to $90 million a year. The state of Maryland picked up some of the slack, raising its annual contribution from $803 million to $965 million during those years, but that was not enough to offset the overall 11 percent decline of intergovernmental funds since 1980, to say nothing of the far greater decline dating back to 1975.

Figure 3-1. *Distribution of General Revenue in the City of Baltimore, 1980–98*

Billions of 1998 dollars

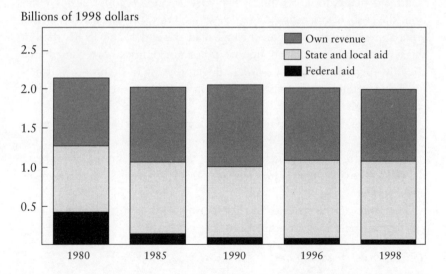

Sources: U.S. Department of Commerce, Bureau of the Census, *Statistical Abstract of the United States, 1982–83*, p. 300; *1988*, p. 278; *1992*, p. 300; and *1999*, p. 326 (various years).

*Paying for the Clean Water Act*

Amid these fiscal constraints the city has been on the receiving end of some expensive instructions from policymakers in Washington. A case in point is the Environmental Protection Agency's (EPA's) requirements for wastewater management, which have loomed as the costliest environmental regulations for almost all major cities.

Through the 1980s Baltimore's expenditures on wastewater treatment plants remained modest compared with the obligations faced by other large cities, thanks to generous federal and state assistance and extensive sharing of the expense with neighboring county governments.[8] (Baltimore's plants serve residents of some surrounding counties and have been jointly financed.) Thus only one-fifth of the $458 million (in 1998 dollars) spent on plant construction during that decade fell to the city.

Things changed in the 1990s. Of the $529 million that went into new construction in this period, the federal government covered a little over a fifth, while Baltimore's share climbed above a third. Since 1998, as federal and state money virtually dried up, the city seems to have borne the brunt (more than 60 percent) of the $163-plus million in new capital spending.

At the same time operation and maintenance expenses of the city's two treatment plants took off during the past decade. Accounting for inflation, the costs of operating one of these facilities (the Black River plant) were approximately 200 percent higher at the end of the 1990s than at the start of the 1980s. Although neighboring counties have contributed roughly 40 percent to its operating budget, the city of Baltimore still supplied $23 million to run this installation in 1999, nearly twice what it spent in 1981.

These vicissitudes in financing the Clean Water Act's big-ticket items do not seem to bode well for a city whose level of disposable revenue has remained more or less static for the past twenty years. But to date at least, the bill for environmental projects has not blown a big hole through the city's budget.

The same cannot be said for the federal role in a much larger municipal responsibility: public education.

*The Schools: Teaching and Taxing Uncle Sam's Way*

Since 1988 Baltimore's public school system has been operating under a U.S. court decree that watches over the federal special education program.[9] The original consent decree has undergone several revisions,

Figure 3-2. *City of Baltimore's Total Expenditures on Special Education, 1988–98*[a]

Millions of constant 1998 dollars

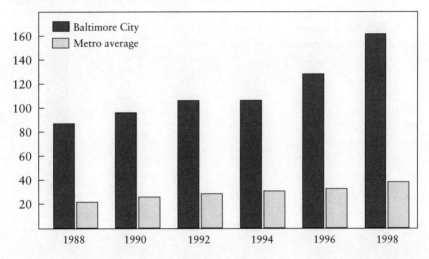

Sources: State of Maryland, Department of Education, *Selected Financial Data—Part 4 (Ten-Year Summary), 1997–98* (Annapolis, 1999), tables 7, 9, 10.
a. Includes nonpublic placements.

adding in 1992 such pricey items as a computer tracking system to monitor compliance and in 1998 an agreement to hire additional administrative staff and train 1,000 specialized elementary school teachers. Estimates vary as to exactly how much the city's school district has had to spend on the imperatives of special education. The low end, according to the state's Department of Education, was around $160 million in 1998 (figure 3-2). But other calculations, counting more inputs, have put the figure as high as $221 million in 1997—fully one-third of the city's entire education budget—before the latest amendments to the court consent decree took effect.[10]

Root causes of this budget buster are well known. The city's extensive impoverished neighborhoods are hothouses for family disintegration, drug abuse, violence, and trauma, all closely associated with high percentages of emotional disturbance, mental retardation, and other grave

Figure 3-3.  *Cost of Special Education for Nonpublic Placements in Baltimore and Surrounding Metropolitan Counties, 1975–98*

Millions of constant 1998 dollars

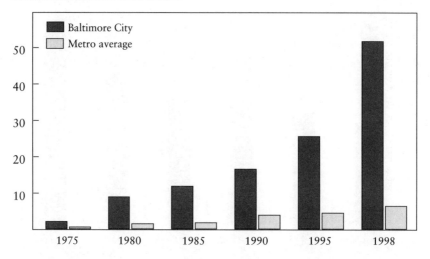

Sources: State of Maryland, Department of Education, *Selected Financial Data—Part 2, 1974-75*, table 1;  *Part 2, 1979–80*, table 1; *Part 2, 1984–85*, table 1; and *Part 4, 1997–98*, table 10 (Annapolis, various years).

learning disorders. Special education students are classified by the severity of their disabilities. In Baltimore more than 60 percent are said to suffer severe disorders, falling into categories that describe only a third of the special education enrollees in the surrounding suburban districts.[11] With so many hardcore cases Baltimore's program has to place in expensive private institutions more than twice as many students as any other school system in the metropolitan area.[12] The cost of these nonpublic placements reached almost $52 million in 1998 (figure 3-3).[13]

That year, however, the city spent more than four times that much on special education overall, so the quotient of severe disabilities amid the city's caseload and the resulting volume of nonpublic placements hardly explains all of the program's budget. In part, under the watchful eye of court-appointed monitors, the city has classified more students as eligible for special instruction. The consent decree also contains enforcement provisions that claim millions of dollars annually. One such provision—a so-called compensatory awards program—seemed to offer to families of students deemed ill served by the city the option of receiving either additional services such as extra tutoring or summer camps or goods like computers and cell phones.

Baltimore's school system as a whole gets a great deal of help from the state and federal governments. Although the feds pitched in just 5 percent of the city's cost for special education in 1998, the state picked up another 31 percent. Moreover other programs, such as Title I and school lunches, raised overall federal aid to $100 million, or roughly 12 percent of the 1998 school budget.[14] On a per pupil basis federal grants contributed $940 for each student in the Baltimore schools, several times the assistance received by any other jurisdiction in the metropolitan area. Maryland, in turn, makes a strenuous effort to equalize school resources among districts throughout the state. In 1998 state aid averaged $4,692 per student in Baltimore, which was $1,708 more per pupil than went to the region's next most-aided district, Carroll County. Intergovernmental aid thus approached almost three-quarters of the city's whole education budget and enabled the city's *overall* per pupil expenditures to surpass those of surrounding districts.

But the overall level of per pupil spending is a misleading statistic. Baltimore's average is engorged by the city's extraordinary special education expense, most of which external aid does not reach. The bulk of special education spending is billed to the city's taxpayers. In fact, out of the local tax dollars that are raised to run the city's public schools, *half* winds up in special education.[15] No suburban county in the vicinity has to allocate its hard-earned educational resources in this fashion (figure 3-4). So significant is the budgetary impact of the federally imposed special education requirements in Baltimore that the inflow of intergovernmental aid, though substantial, does not level the playing field.

As table 3-1 plainly suggests, exceptional outlays for special education students crowd out per pupil spending for the instruction of regular students in the city, whereas the much more modest costs of the program in the suburbs enable at least four of the region's five suburban districts to shortchange their regular students less egregiously.[16] Measured in such key indicators as teachers' salaries, the schools in the city are not holding their own in relation to the superior ones outside.[17]

Figure 3-4.  *Baltimore Metro Area's Distribution of Local Dollars to Special Education and Regular Expenditures, 1998*

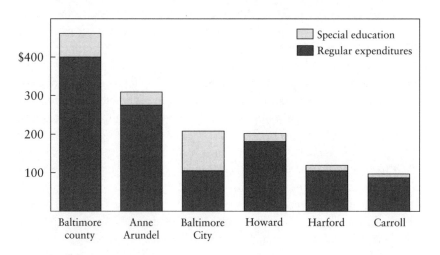

Sources: State of Maryland, Department of Education, *Selected Financial Data, Part 4,* 1997–98, table 10.

## Philadelphia

Among the nation's historic urban places none experienced a starker reversal of fortune than did Philadelphia in the second half of the twentieth century. America's largest city in the late nineteenth century had continued to grow, from 1,293,679 residents in 1900 to 2,071,605 by 1950. In the subsequent forty years, however, Philadelphia lost a quarter of its population. The decline scarcely abated in the 1990s, when another 168,000 people decamped.[18] The aggregate numbers, moreover, masked the extreme degree to which particular parts of town were depopulated. Between 1950 and 1990 one neighborhood in North Philadelphia lost nearly half its inhabitants, down from 210,000 to 109,000. Another collapsed from 111,000 to 39,000.[19]

Once the seat of the nation's mightiest banks and of industries that produced everything from Stetson hats and Breyer's ice cream to oil, ships, and locomotives, the city's economy now is a shell of its former

Table 3-1. Distribution of per Pupil Expenditures in Baltimore Metro Area Public School Districts, 1998

| Total cost per pupil[a] | | Share spent on special education[b] | | Share spent on instruction for regular students[c] | | Other (includes administration, health, transportation, fixed, and maintenance costs) | |
|---|---|---|---|---|---|---|---|
| 1. Baltimore City | $6,826 | 1. Baltimore City | $1,567 | 1. Howard | $3,133 | 1. Howard | $2,788 |
| 2. Howard | 6,672 | 2. Baltimore Co. | 794 | 2. Baltimore Co. | 3,019 | 2. Baltimore Co. | 2,657 |
| 3. Baltimore Co. | 6,470 | 3. Howard | 75 | 3. Anne Arundel | 2,901 | 3. Anne Arundel | 2,587 |
| 4. Anne Arundel | 6,176 | 4. Anne Arundel | 688 | 4. Harford | 2,858 | 4. Baltimore City | 2,583 |
| 5. Harford | 5,681 | 5. Harford | 557 | 5. Baltimore City | 2,676 | 5. Carroll | 2,455 |
| 6. Carroll | 5,624 | 6. Carroll | 504 | 6. Carroll | 2,665 | 6. Harford | 2,267 |

Sources: State of Maryland, Department of Education, *Selected Financial Data—Part 3 (Analysis of Costs), 1997–98* (Annapolis, 1999), table 3; data for special education transfers from State of Maryland, Department of Education, *Selected Financial Data—Part 2 (Expenditures), 1997–98* (Annapolis, 1999), table 6; and State of Maryland, Department of Education, *Fact Book, 1997–98* (Annapolis, 1999), p. 3.

a. Excludes expenditures for adult education, equipment, and state share of teachers' retirement.

b. Includes nonpublic transfers.

c. Includes instructional salaries, textbooks and supplies, and other instructional costs.

self. Even during the prosperous 1990s, around 100,000 jobs vanished.[20] In 2000 the U.S. Conference of Mayors reported more abandoned industrial sites in Philadelphia than in any other U.S. city, save New York and Chicago.[21] About 50,000 properties of one kind or another stand vacant, and brownfields tie up at least 2,000 acres of prime urban land.[22] Although Philadelphia's unemployment rate had come down from its level in 1990, at 6.2 percent in 1998 it was still almost twice as high as the level in the city's suburban counties.[23] The city of Philadelphia is clearly the poorhouse of its metropolitan area. In 1993 more than 26 percent of the city's inhabitants fell below the poverty line.[24] Although the percentage is lower now, the median household income of Philadelphians in 1998 was still nearly a third below the median of the metropolis as a whole.[25]

## Fiscal Strain

A city in these straits has fiscal worries. Early in the past decade Philadelphia was broke. The city had run out of cash to pay its bills, including interest payments on loans. Its credit rating had plunged to junk bond status as City Hall faced a cumulative deficit of almost $1.25 billion over the next five years. At the root of the fiscal crisis were the unrelenting costs of coping with the city's large underclass and with outsized payments made to municipal employees.[26] Aided by the rebound of the U.S. economy after 1992, an uptick in state and federal aid, and better financial management under new mayor Edward G. Rendell, the financial picture brightened. Reforms of the city's disability pensions, employee health plan, wage structure, and overtime compensation rules yielded significant savings.[27]

Yet, referring to the city's recovery, the mayor cautioned, "We look a lot better than we really are."[28] Among the liabilities that created uncertainties were tense labor relations and, perhaps more important, high taxes.[29] Between 1981 and 1992, Philadelphia hiked taxes on households and firms nineteen times. When Rendell took office Philadelphians were the most heavily taxed residents of any major city in the country. Although he subsequently was able to shave down some of the fees on businesses, in 1997 (the last year for which comprehensive comparative data are available) Philadelphia still recorded the third worst overall tax burden among the fifty largest cities—trailing only such extreme outliers as Newark and Bridgeport.[30] In 1997 the city taxed 12.2 percent of the income of a typical middle-income family. A similar family living in New

York or Chicago would have paid roughly 15 percent less in local taxes, and half as much in Los Angeles.[31]

Differences in tax rates may help explain why in 1997 Philadelphia succeeded in attracting only one new business for every 275 residents, compared with one in 97 in San Francisco and one in 66 in Houston. (Between 1990 and 1995, 2,127 business establishments evacuated or disappeared in Philadelphia, contributing to a 3 percent net loss of jobs. It was only after 1997 that the city finally began to reverse this trend.)[32] Not only was Philadelphia overtaxed relative to other cities; its overall tax rate exceeded that of the region's suburbs. Between 1972 and 1992 the disparity between the total per capita tax burden in the central city and in adjacent Montgomery County (another high-tax jurisdiction), for instance, had widened threefold (figure 3-5). Unless this type of gap closes completely many firms and families contemplating a future in Philadelphia will wonder what, if anything, their extra tax dollars are buying.

Figure 3-5. *Comparison of per Capita Total Taxes in Philadelphia and Surrounding Counties, 1971–92*

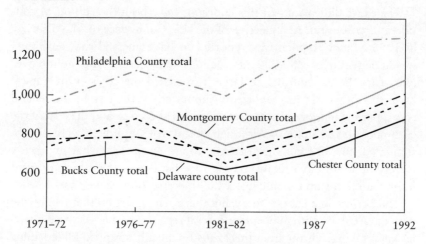

1992 dollars

Sources: *1977 County and City Extra: Annual Metro, City and County Data Book,* p. 407; *1983 County and City Extra: Annual Metro, City, and County Data Book,* p. 475; *1988 County and City Extra: Annual Metro, City, and County Data Book,* p. 443; and *1993 County and City Extra: Annual Metro, City, and County Data Book,* p. 562 (Bernan Press, various years).

*Roadblocks*

Mismanagement and an infirm economic base were the main sources of Philadelphia's financial troubles. In this context of fiscal instability, however, ambitious federal tutelage that placed the city's limited capacities under added strain seemed especially inopportune.

Title II of the Americans with Disabilities Act, for example, dictated that communities build curb ramps on streets and sidewalks to achieve "program accessibility" by a certain date: January 26, 1992. Congress offered no financial assistance to perform this feat, and many municipalities concluded that the 1992 deadline was hopelessly unrealistic. In Philadelphia, however, disability rights activists wasted no time dragging the city into federal court to force compliance. Confronted with a judge's ruling that curb ramps be constructed on all resurfaced streets, city officials first tried to fight back, appealing all the way to the U.S. Supreme Court. When the high court declined to review the case, the city submitted a plan that it said would take ten years and $100 million to complete.[33] Rejecting the delay, attorneys for a second group of plaintiffs were back in court, and by early 1996 had extracted a settlement in which the city agreed to have ramps installed at all intersections no later than the end of the year 2001.

The exact dimensions of this endeavor have been the subject of considerable confusion. At a meeting of the U.S. Conference of Mayors early in 1996 Mayor Rendell was reported to have guessed that curb cuts would be required at 80,000 intersections, at a cost of $180 million over two years, an expenditure so large it exceeded the city's entire capital budget.[34] Other figures, reportedly submitted by the city to the federal court, put the number of street intersections at 20,525 and the cost of the curb cuts at $20 million. Although the mayor's numbers were unsubstantiated, the $20 million price tag, too, seemed somewhat imprecise. According to the city's financial report for fiscal year 1999, the city spent more than that sum redoing just 12,000 intersections since fiscal 1990.[35]

The bottom line may be fuzzy, but there is no question that complying with the ADA, as with many other federal regulations, has not been a trivial undertaking. Throughout the 1990s financially strapped Philadelphia had to come up with tens of millions of dollars to fulfill an ideal that Congress conceived but never funded.[36] Granted, the disconnect between ends and means would have been more conspicuous if the rest of the city's federal and state-supported programs also had been starved for cash. The

Figure 3-6. *Distribution of General Revenue in the City of Philadelphia, 1980–98*

Billions of 1998 dollars

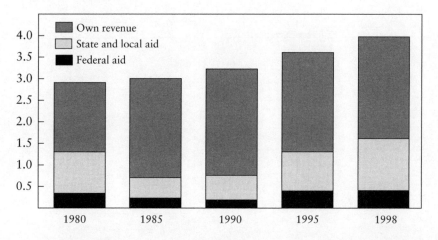

Sources: U.S. Department of Commerce, Bureau of the Census, *Statistical Abstract of the United States, 1972*, p. 427; *1977*, p. 304; *1982–83*, p. 300; *1988*, p. 278; *1992*, p. 300; *1999*, p. 326; and *2001*, p. 290.

external funding for various other programs during the 1990s did not remain constant, as it had between 1985 and 1990 (figure 3-6). Other designated needs—airport improvements and welfare payments, for example—saw an increase in federal and state aid to Philadelphia in the mid-1990s. Earmarked grants, however, are not fungible; Philadelphia could not fashion ADA curb ramps out of airport funds.

## Undiminished Crime

That urban decay breeds crime is axiomatic. Philadelphia, however, followed a perplexing track: the city of late was decaying less; yet, even more than Baltmore, and unlike other large American cities in the 1990s, its crime rate continued to climb (figure 3-7). By conservative estimates, 7,319 crimes were committed per 100,000 persons in 1999, compared to 5,233 in 1986.[37] Certain categories of nonviolent crime, larceny and theft, for instance, were up 40 percent between 1992 and 1999.[38]

Figure 3-7. *Total Percentage Change of Crime Index in Selected Cities,
1986–98*

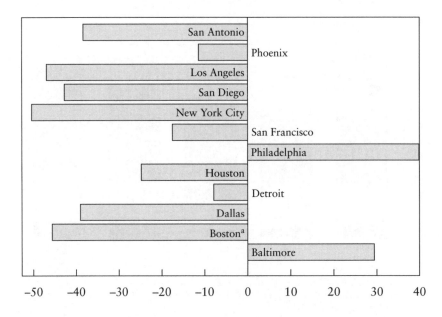

Sources: U.S. Department of Commerce, Bureau of the Census, *Statistical Abstract of
the United States, 1984–86; 1998; 1990–99;* and Federal Bureau of Investigation, *Crime
Reports 1997, 1998* (Washington).
    a. Boston figure is for 1988–98.

Whatever else may have accounted for this anomaly, there is reason to
suspect that, particularly through the first half of the 1990s, federal legal
actions directed at Philadelphia's jails unwittingly contributed. In the
spring of 1982 inmates in one of the city's prisons filed a class action in
federal court alleging that confinement in an overcrowded jail violated
their civil rights. Following consent decrees issued in 1986 and 1991 the
city agreed to limit the classes of crimes for which defendants could be
jailed, provide for the early release of pretrial detainees, and grant a
court-appointed special master extensive administrative jurisdiction over
matters ranging from construction of a new downtown detention center
to the handling of inmates' mail and other day-to-day operations.[39]

What impact did these developments seem to have on public safety? In
1992 it was reported that 67 percent of released defendants failed to

show up for trial.[40] The percentages that failed to appear were especially high among persons arrested for drug dealing (76 percent), burglary (74 percent), and theft (69 percent). All told, the failure-to-appear rate was said to be "roughly four times the rate found in earlier studies of Philadelphia defendants." Seventy-six percent of all drug dealers became fugitives within ninety days of their arrest—a percentage almost three times the national average.[41]

Not surprisingly, the increase in the number of fugitives was correlated with additional crimes; when these individuals were back on the street they represented a riskier pool of defendants than those normally freed on bail. In congressional testimony in 1995 Philadelphia's district attorney reported that, throughout 1993 and the first six months of 1994, defendants released because of the prison cap committed 9,732 new crimes, including 79 murders, 959 robberies, 2,215 drug deals, 701 burglaries, 2,748 thefts, 90 rapes, and 1,113 assaults.[42]

To attribute, as some critics did, Philadelphia's rising crime rate primarily to the early-release and nonadmission provisions of the consent decrees is probably an oversimplification. However, it appears implausible that the timing of their implementation and some of the city's crime wave (waxing, as it did, while crime in other cities waned) was a mere coincidence.

Whether the federal decrees were equally implicated in the difficulties Philadelphia continued to have controlling crime after 1995 is another matter. In October of that year the federal court granted a request to return responsibility for admissions and releases to the state courts that serve the city. Also, by then a new national law, the Prison Litigation Reform Act of 1996, had begun to take effect. It entitled cities to seek relief from judicially administered prison plans, Philadelphia's being the nation's most fabled example.

Still, Philadelphia stayed in the shadow of pending federal contempt citations through the remainder of the decade. Eighteen years after the initial lawsuit had been filed the city was formally allowed to retake control of its jails. "Eighteen years," concluded the district judge in September 2000, "is generally the age at which a child is declared emancipated."[43]

Inasmuch as the workings of *Harris* v. *City of Philadelphia* may have had a hand in making an unsafe city even less safe, the cost of the case to local taxpayers was probably substantial. No one has added it up, but at a minimum a proper calculus would have to consider revenues drawn down by an expanded bureaucracy of lawyers, consultants, and other professional staff whose sole function for nearly two decades was to carry out some 250 judicially prescribed policies and procedures; millions expended arresting and rearresting offenders, only to have them pass through a revolving door to the street; and the dislocation of businesses and households plundered by burglars and thieves that had been prematurely set free. To be sure, the judicial remedy was not without benefits: it pushed the enlargement of facilities and eased crowding, thereby bettering the lot of inmates. Whether this end could have been attained by less controversial means remains an issue much debated.

## New York

Residents in three Brooklyn neighborhoods file a federal complaint against city officials on the grounds that the stench from a nearby garbage transfer station violates their civil rights.[44] A federal judge, also in Brooklyn, rules that a city agency has failed to provide "adequate services" for people with acquired immune deficiency syndrome (AIDS).[45] Another city agency, the parks department whose work force is almost 50 percent minority, is charged with employment bias.[46] Federal prosecutors accuse the police department of engaging in racial profiling.[47] The city's Metropolitan Transit Authority is sued for the disparate impact of raising subway fares from $1.25 to $1.50.[48] Plaintiffs for a group of handicapped children sue the city for alleged failure to provide them an appropriate education.[49] A federal court orders the city's fire department to redesign a physical exam to make it less discriminatory toward women applicants.[50]

An out-of-towner glancing episodically at the *New York Times* over the years might conclude that scarcely a week goes by when New York City's government is not being raked over the coals by a federal lawsuit or investigation. Even if New Yorkers are accustomed to the incessant confrontations—most of which are mere metro-section curiosities—some dragged on for years and became more than a sideshow.

For example, under a long-standing consent decree the New York City Board of Education found itself increasing expenditures on special education services at twice the rate of its spending on regular teaching.[51] By 1994 the special education program was costing nearly $2 billion a year and tying up much of the school system's budget.[52] For a city in which 60 percent of all elementary-level students still do not read at an acceptable level of proficiency, and 70 percent do not perform adequately in math either, a different mix of local spending priorities might seem in order.[53]

Still, New York is no ordinary town. Judgments and claims in the hail-storm of legal actions that come down on the city every year neared $350 million for 1998, up from about $160 million ten years earlier.[54] For any other municipality numbers like these would be disquieting, but for New York, where the expense budget in 1997 neared $33 billion, they were taken in stride.[55] Even sinking a couple of billion dollars a year into fed-erally favored services, like the sixty-three schools that administer the Individuals with Disabilities Education Act (IDEA), did not appear to make much of a dent in this city's enormous assets.

And before the devastation of September 11 those assets seemed to be getting more and more impressive. New York's economy had rebounded later than the economies of many other big cities in the 1990s. The city's jobless rate remained above 9 percent, twice the national average, as late as 1997.[56] But by 2000 unemployment had dropped to 5.5 percent as the local private sector created jobs at a faster pace than the national econ-omy.[57] Fully 88,000 jobs were added that year alone. In the heart of the city, Manhattan, the vacancy rate for office space fell below 4 percent (it had hit 20 percent during the recession nine years earlier).[58] Economic vibrancy yielded fiscal dividends that would have been unthinkable a quarter century ago when the "Big Apple" seemed to be dangling at the brink of bankruptcy. With tax revenues reaching $38.7 billion in 2000 the city government luxuriated in a $3.1 billion budget surplus. New York City's Independent Budget Office confidently projected $41.6 bil-lion in revenues for 2004.[59]

## Debits

Alas, the good times did not keep rolling. September 11 tore an estimated $90 billion out of the city's economy.[60] Expecting to lose some 87,000 jobs, the city stared at a rising rate of unemployment that seemed likely to hit 8 percent by the end of 2002.[61] From a budgetary standpoint a $4 billion gap was the prospect for the subsequent fiscal year.[62]

Even before the autumn of 2001, however, structural liabilities had continued to complicate New York's finances. Because New York com-bines the services of municipal and county governments, the city dis-charges more functions that lay a claim on its resources. In its 1998 bud-get, for example, New York spent almost $5 billion on health and human services.[63] Unlike most other large cities, New York has to shoulder directly a substantial share of local welfare and Medicaid expenditures. One cannot simply compare New York's spending on hospitals, say, with that of Chicago or Los Angeles. Cook County and Los Angeles County, not the city treasuries, pay for this item. That New York spends more than ten times as much per capita on social services, hospitals, and health as the average big eastern or midwestern city may be startling, but part of the divergence is because New York handles activities that are not the usual province of city governments.[64]

To pay for most of its colossal all-purpose government New York has had to tax its citizens aggressively. (State aid in 1997 supplied barely 27 percent of the city's revenues, federal aid less than 5 percent.)[65] Only three other cities—Washington, D.C., Philadelphia, and Cleveland—levy as full a range of taxes as New York. For every $8 earned by a New Yorker in 1994 almost $1 went to City Hall.[66] By contrast residents of San Francisco (the city with the next highest tax burden that year) paid barely one-half the New York level. Subsequently the administration of Mayor Rudolph W. Giuliani managed some tax reductions, but at least through the mid-1990s, the level of taxation in New York had hovered near the point of diminishing returns: further marginal increases risked repelling new jobs or even precipitating net employment losses.[67]

Another reason why New York has exacted almost every type of tax, and mined many to their limits, has had to do with the magnitude of the city's debt service. Between 1990 and 2000 New York's net general debt per capita increased 95 percent, from $2,490 to $4,854.[68] As figure 3-8 shows, per capita debt in 1999 was the highest in the nation, and more than double the average carried by residents in fourteen other big cities around the country. As of mid-2000 the city's gross debt outstanding surpassed $40 billion, a sum bigger than the budget of Switzerland. The cost of repaying the borrowed money plus interest has had to be met by transfers from the city's general fund—that is, by city tax revenue.[69]

Whatever the many other ingredients of New York's extraordinary indebtedness over the years, from here on the looming obligations associated with federal mandates—most notably the public works required by environmental programs—will be a prominent part of the picture. Compliance with U.S. environmental policies has weighed upon the capital accounts of local governments throughout the country. The projects in store for New York, however, carry potential price tags so breathtaking that their financial reverberations could be unusual.

## Troubled Waters: Getting from Potable to Pure

To provide water to its 8 million residents New York City draws on two watersheds that cover nearly two thousand square miles and feed into a

Figure 3-8. *Debt per Capita for Selected Cities, 1999*

Dollars

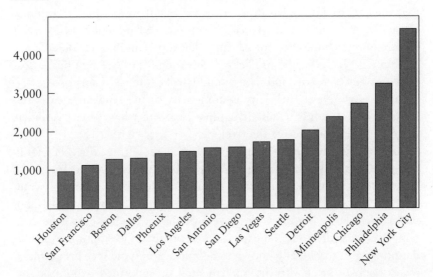

Source: *Fiscal Year 2001 Annual Report of the Comptroller on Capital Debt and Obligations* (City of New York, November 2000).

system of reservoirs north of the city. The larger of the two, known as the Catskill/Delaware watershed situated west of the Hudson River, supplies about 90 percent of the city's water. The other, the Croton system on the east side of the river, provides the rest. Since the nineteenth century, when the extensive network of aqueducts and tunnels was constructed to draw from these sources, the water they have furnished has been unfiltered.

With enactment of the Safe Drinking Water Act of 1986 federal and state regulators began tightening the screws on New York to secure, then gradually upgrade, water quality. By 1992 the city had promised to build within the decade a filtration plant for the Croton area, but as site selection and other obstacles caused seemingly interminable delays city officials eventually found themselves visiting a less scenic venue: the U.S. courthouse. In the face of a federal suit pressuring the city to move ahead, a consent decree was reached in 1998 that choreographed a wide range of steps to protect the entire east-of-the-Hudson watershed.[70]

Not all of the planned measures could be characterized strictly as environmental safeguards. (For example, to make way for the new filtration apparatus the city was expected to dig up but then rebuild a golf course.) The centerpiece of the plan, however, is a state-of-the-art purification plant, projected to be one of the world's largest. Current estimates are that this facility (along with related work, like the replacement of faulty sewage systems in some areas) could approach $1 billion, but because it may require technologies not yet fully developed and its scheduled completion date is 2007, the predictions are rough guesses; significant cost overruns between now and then would hardly come as a surprise.[71]

If the work New York City is doing east of the Hudson seems substantial, however, it is trifling in comparison with what the city is undertaking on the other side of the river.

In 1991 the city's Department of Environmental Protection (NYCDEP) applied for a waiver from the EPA's so-called Surface Water Treatment Rule, which would have required filtering the enormous flow of water from the Catskill/Delaware region—an average of 1.2 billion gallons of water each day.[72] No filtration system of such scale has ever been contemplated anywhere else on earth. But to obtain an exemption from this daunting task, technically known as a "Filtration Avoidance Program," a host of substitutes had to be implemented. Among them would be, for instance, new land-use restrictions affecting several counties far away from the city limits to prevent degradation of the region's water supply from sewage discharge, pesticides, soil erosion, and other diffuse sources of pollution.

How the city of New York, which owned merely 7 percent of the land in question, could impose these controls on myriad far-away municipalities, towns, and hamlets was a perplexing question. In 1993 the city approached the EPA with a proposal to acquire thousands of acres in the vicinity of reservoirs. Fearful that the land-acquisition scheme would be carried out by eminent domain, communities in these areas filed suit to block the idea.[73] It was only after a prolonged mediation process, involving city and state officials (led by Governor George Pataki), the EPA, several conservation advocacy groups, and representatives from scores of townships, that an agreement was finally negotiated in 1997.

As part of the settlement New York City agreed not only to purchase a lot of properties and conservation easements from willing landowners at fair market value but much, much more.[74] The city would now fund, among other experiments, a complex program of land stewardship, including efforts to alter local forestry management and farming practices. City tax dollars and loans were also earmarked for such community responsibilities as the repair or replacement of residential septic tanks, local sewer extensions, wastewater treatment, bridge, and roadway modifications to reduce unwanted runoff, even payments to local municipalities to help them cover the fees of their attorneys and consultants in property tax disputes over city-bought land. As if this range of activities did not suffice, a "good neighbor" slush fund would have city taxpayers pay for things that appeared to bear little relationship to environmental protection. New firehouse equipment, road-paving assistance, and a pump for a community swimming pool have been among the city-funded donations to watershed communities.[75]

City officials have justified these concessions as comparatively cost effective: in effect, the package commits the city to transferring hundreds of millions of dollars to upstate jurisdictions, but if it succeeds in meeting the EPA's standards for drinking water—and thereby avoids construction of a Catskill/Delaware filtration plant—"Gotham" will have realized a savings in the multiple billions of dollars.

The trouble is: no one knows whether the elaborate concoction of conservation measures, community capital improvements, and subsidies courtesy of city taxpayers will be successful over the long haul. An interim progress report released by the EPA in May 2000 commended New York for significant accomplishments but also listed multiple corrective actions that were still needed "to ensure the long-term viability of filtration avoidance."[76] Conceivably the city could struggle at great expense to avoid filtering water only to fall short of a satisfactory EPA "determination" at the end of the day.[77] New York, in sum, confronts a real possibility of having to erect a gargantuan filtration facility at a staggering additional estimated cost of $8 billion.

## Drainage Debacle: From the Sewers to the Sound

New York's water management problems point in all directions: not only upstream from the Catskills but downstream into the city's harbor and out to the Long Island Sound. Whether the city will be able to protect its drinking water without sifting every glassful through the world's most expensive filter is only one of the great environmental issues hanging over policymakers, not to mention ratepayers, in New York. According to an EPA estimate prepared in 1996, New York City also would need to invest $5.6 billion in wastewater treatment equipment in the upcoming years, and a further $5.5 billion to reduce nitrogen effluents and other contaminants discharged into the Sound in part by a dozen sewage treatment plants within the city's drainage district.[78]

Only about one-third of New York's sewers separate the flow of sanitation discharge from storm water. During heavy rains the rest of the sewer pipes are frequently overwhelmed and spill millions of gallons of raw sewage into the harbor and the Long Island estuary.[79] Short of replacing several thousands miles of antiquated combined sewer lines the city has proposed a system of storage tanks designed to capture excess wastewater and hold it until it could be fed gradually into nearby treatment plants. Whether this lower-priced remedy will meet with EPA approval, however, remains unclear. Even if it does, each tank is expected to cost at least a quarter of a billion dollars—and the city might need to install ten or more of them.

Solving the sewer problem would lessen some of the pollution of Long Island Sound. To cut down the city's share of nitrogen discharges and other oxygen-consuming materials harmful to fish and wildlife in this body of water, however, additional measures, including modification of sewage treatment plants, will be necessary. In 1998 the New York City Department of Environmental Protection expected the immediate capital costs of modifying four of its plants to be in the millions, not billions, of dollars.[80] The city must hope that this forecast will hold. Through 1999 New York had received $2.8 billion for the construction of wastewater treatment improvements, sewer system rehabilitation, and combined sewer overflow control facilities.[81] Whether this level of support will extend to the next generation of refinements (for example, the retrofitting of facilities for nitrogen control) is an open question.

## Taking Stock

Uncertainties beset New York's long-range budgeting for environmental protection. Will preservation of watersheds suffice as a substitute for a filtration system? Or will new legal actions by environmental groups and ultimately the EPA force the city to follow the Croton formula: preservation *plus* a twenty-first-century plant for good measure? Can the city count on receiving in the future state and federal financing that was enjoyed in the past? Will federal and state regulators further ratchet the standards for water quality in vulnerable ecosystems like the Long Island Sound where dispersed pollutants from agriculture and development may eventually offset the abatement efforts of New York's wastewater plants? And will this mean that lawsuits will continue to target New York's plants and operations (as a federal case, filed by environmentalists and the State of Connecticut, did in 1998) simply because point sources of pollution are easier to identify and enjoin than nonpoint sources?[82]

Suppose that from the standpoint of officials mindful of New York's fiscal constraints the worst-case scenario were to unfold: that is, the city is faced with a full filtration mandate west of the Hudson; every water pollution control plant along the East River has to be repeatedly retooled; federal contributions to municipal wastewater treatment programs continue to dwindle; and so forth. The financial impact on the city government would still be only partial and indirect. The cleanup would be backed not only by some combination of state grants or low-interest loans but financed by the bond issues of a separate agency, the New York City Municipal Water Finance Authority. Even so, a binge of borrowing by the water authority would likely compete with some of the city's other lines of credit, thereby augmenting its already steep debt service. Debt issues aside, local residents would certainly encounter sharp rate hikes for metered water. New York's water rates rose in eleven of the fifteen years between 1986 and 2000, often at several times the general rate of inflation.[83] The upward trend would almost certainly accelerate.

To mention these concerns, of course, is not necessarily to infer that the U.S. environmental objectives at issue—for example, the provision of safe drinking water from regional reservoirs, and protecting marine life in the Long Island Sound—are of dubious merit. What can be debated, though, is whether these well-intended ends are being pursued by suitably equitable and efficient means.

## Chicago

After shrinking for decades Chicago finally began to regain inhabitants in the 1990s. Slightly more than 18,350 more people lived in the city in 1998 than in 1990. For the most part Chicago began to recover residents because this city, not just its metropolitan area, experienced exceptionally robust economic growth since the early 1990s. The city netted approximately a 13 percent increase in jobs between 1990 and 1998.[84] Unemployment plunged from 11.3 percent in 1990 to 5.4 percent in 1999 and then just 4 percent in the fall of 2000.[85] After 1993 Chicago's increases in white-collar jobs (158,900) surpassed those of New York (122,500) and Los Angeles (88,300).[86]

Chicago's regeneration got a lift from other favorable fiscal preconditions as well. Although the average residential property tax rate in Cook County has remained generally higher than that of the "collar counties," Chicagoans are taxed significantly less heavily than, say, New Yorkers and Philadelphians. And Chicago's residential taxes have declined since the 1980s; by 1999 the effective tax rate on a residence valued at $100,000 was merely 1.41 percent, one of the lowest residential tax rates in the state and well below the rates prevailing in Oak Park, Evanston, Palatine, and other nearby communities.[87] So even if other drawbacks—urban crime, for instance—discourage families and firms from locating in town, at least the level of local taxation has not been adding insult to injury.

As it turned out, the overall crime rate fell sharply during the past decade. Whereas there were 112.4 crimes per 1,000 residents reported in 1990, 82.4 per 1,000 took place in 1999. In 2000 there were 627 homicides in the city, the fewest in thirty-three years.[88] Chicago has remained a dangerous place, however. At the end of 2001 its homicide rate was nearing 660, possibly the worst of any major city in the country.[89] And the crime statistics of Chicago looked awful in comparison with those of its suburbs; a person is about three times more likely to become a victim of crime there than in suburban DuPage, Kane Lake, McHenry, or Will counties.[90]

Ratepayers in Chicago have enjoyed another advantage: unlike the administrative arrangements in New York, Los Angeles, or Washington, D.C., a multijurisdictional Metropolitan Water Reclamation District (MWRD) handles wastewater treatment. Amid the rising costs of complying with clean water regulations, the MWRD has had an enviable record of efficiency in building and operating its seven water reclamation plants. In a 1996 survey of large sewerage agencies (serving populations of 2 million or more) the MWRD reported the lowest average cost for collection and treatment of sewage: $450 per million gallons of wastewater, compared with $1,143 per million gallons by the agency's counterpart in Los Angeles and $1,795 by the Water and Sewer Authority of Washington, D.C.[91] The wastewater management system in the Chicago district has done an unusual thing for a major U.S. metropolitan area: the average user fee paid by city households was *lower* in 2000 than it was in 1980.[92]

For all the encouraging reports about Chicago in recent years, the not-so-good news is that various regulatory strictures have seemed out of sync with some of the city's needs. Especially in the current economic climate, inharmonious government policies can pose risks for Chicago's continued revival. The net increase in the city's population between 1990 and 1998 brought the total number of residents to 2,802,079, but this figure was still well below the 3,005,072 of twenty years ago. Despite the city's favorable water rates and residential property tax rates, countless other local levies, including the license and permit fees and other imposts on local businesses, jack up the tax bill in Chicago. Indeed, given their lower median income, Chicagoans feel they are overtaxed more than do the residents of proximate suburbs.[93] Perhaps most important many prospective city dwellers will locate elsewhere as long as there is no real end in sight to the city's worst failings—substandard schools, for instance, and notorious slums.

## Schools: Better but Still Lagging

The massive Chicago public school system (559 schools, 425,000 students) initiated notable efforts to improve the performance and accountability of students and teachers in 1988 and again in 1995. The reforms were not without beneficial results. The scores of elementary school pupils on standardized tests rose in the course of the 1990s, and after 1996, so did those of high school students (figure 3-9).

Nevertheless the system is not even close to achieving the stated goals of the 1988 Chicago School Reform Act: that every school should match the national norms in student achievement. In 1990 only 8.2 percent of the city's elementary schools were able to report that at least half of their students could read at the national norm. By the year 2000 the share of schools meeting this standard had increased to 21.3 percent. Almost four out of five schools, in other words, remained substandard.[94]

Changes at the high school level were less remarkable. Only in the past few years have reading scores begun to overtake their 1990 level; thus the overall improvement through the past decade was small. In the year 2000 only 15 percent of city high schools had more than half of their students matching national norms for reading and math—up from 9 percent in 1990 but still a low percentage.

Another important measure of whether a school system is sound is the high school dropout rate. From the graduating class of 1998 (the most recent data available) almost 42 percent had dropped out, a rate similar to that prevailing in the 1980s.

How much these statistics could be bettered by increasing or realigning educational resources is hard to say. We do know this, however: Chicago received less external aid in 1998 than in 1980 (figure 3-10). Meanwhile,

Figure 3-9.  *Percentage of Chicago Students at or above National Norms, 1990–2000*

Percentage of students

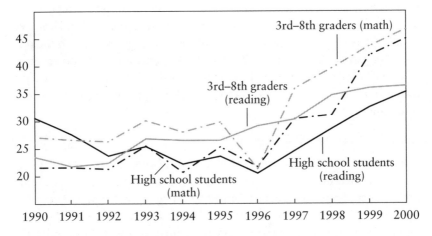

Source: G. Alfred Hess Jr., "Changes in Student Achievement in Illinois and Chicago, 1990–2000" (Center for Urban School Policy, Northwestern University, August, 2000).

as in Baltimore, New York, and many other big cities, spending for expensive programs such as special education, which totaled $445 million in 1994, or about 26 percent of the school system's budget, keep needing more revenues.[95] Since 1995 expenditures under the special education program have risen $14.4 million a year.[96] And the tab is likely to run higher. A recent class action suit ended in 1998 with a settlement that essentially dictates larger quotas for placements.[97]

## Overregulated Housing

Of the past half century's U.S. urban policy blunders perhaps none left a deeper and deadlier mark than the decision to condense a critical mass of indigent inhabitants into isolated public housing complexes. Most of these dwellings soon became the principal breeding grounds of inner-city social degradation and the command posts for violent predators. Many central neighborhoods of American cities will never be reclaimed unless

Figure 3-10. *Distribution of General Revenue in the City of Chicago, 1980–98*

Billions of 1998 dollars

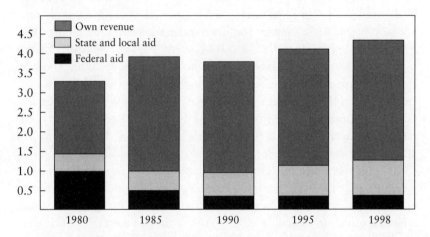

Sources: U.S. Department of Commerce, Bureau of the Census, *Statistical Abstract of the United States, 1972,* p. 427; *1977,* p. 304; *1982–83,* p. 300; *1988,* p. 278; *1992,* p. 300; *1999,* p. 326; and *2001,* p. 290.

policymakers close down the worst projects, convert salvageable ones to mixed-income residences, and replace the failed settings with a larger supply of scattered "affordable" housing.

Chicago has made progress on the first of these imperatives. In 1995 the Chicago Housing Authority settled a federal class action suit, filed in 1991, and agreed to raze several rundown high-rises.[98] Federal law, however, has not been entirely helpful to the city in meeting the second part of the bargain: supplying suitable substitutes. According to a survey of local housing developers who work on city projects, the Davis-Bacon Act's prevailing-wage stipulations inflate construction costs of new or renovated moderate-income housing by 25 to 30 percent.[99] To be sure, the carrot of federal financing can sweeten the deal for these developers, but often not enough, they say, because the added red tape includes compliance costs associated with such items as the Asbestos Hazard Emergency Response Act and the Americans with Disabilities Act.

If the housing rehabilitation contractors had been queried again a few years later, they certainly would have highlighted another federal requirement: lead-based paint removal. In September 1999 the U.S. Department of Housing and Urban Development (HUD) released its final rules for lead-based paint. The regulations, which cover all federally assisted housing built before 1978, require the city to earmark a substantial portion of federal housing funds for lead hazard control. Chicago housing officials had planned to refurbish about 4,800 housing units in 2000. The new lead treatment rules will substantially raise the bill for jobs like this one. Because no additional federal aid has been offered to offset this expense—and no exemptions are allowed, even for dwelling units of childless occupants—the upshot could well be a sizable reduction of the city's effort to alleviate a shortage of moderately priced ("affordable") housing.

Large parts of the inner city remain in desperate need not only of a serviceable housing stock but many other essentials, including places to work, shop, and recreate. In an attempt to revive one such neighborhood, covering some fifteen square miles on the south and west sides of the city, by designating it the city's first federally assisted empowerment zone, local planners in 1995 petitioned to have no fewer than seventy-two HUD regulations relaxed. Among the seemingly modest requests was one seeking permission for children currently enrolled in Head Start to remain in the program even if their family incomes changed. Another just asked for access to unused funds in a community development grant the city had received. The department allowed seven of the seventy-two requested waivers, disappointing city officials who wondered whether, thus constrained, they might ever be able to attract adequate private investment to the zone.[100]

## San Francisco

A visitor to City Hall in San Francisco in recent years would be dazzled. The building's gold dome, which looks as if it had just been replated, glistens in the sunshine. Inside, majestic corridors of fine Italian marble shine as if they were buffed daily. The spotless rest rooms are elegantly appointed and fitted with the most modern of plumbing fixtures. All this is a far cry from, say, Philadelphia, where City Hall has been crumbling from decades of neglect, and where the city has been so strapped for funds to complete basic repairs it was considering leasing most of the hundred-year-old landmark's nine floors to private enterprises.[101]

Before the onset of the dot-com bust in the spring of 2000 and the national economic downturn a year later, San Francisco was doing exceedingly well. The city's economic boom during the 1990s began earlier than the recoveries of the other large cities examined in this chapter. Although the unemployment rate in New York, for example, stood at 9.3 percent in 1994, San Francisco's was down to 3.1 percent that year—below California's statewide average.[102] Crime rates in San Francisco also dropped dramatically. Between 1981 and 1997 violent crimes were down 35 percent, property crimes 20 percent.[103] These decreases compared favorably with what was happening in surrounding suburbs, some of which showed significant increases in violent crime. Between 1994 and 1996 San Francisco's population grew four times more quickly than New York's. Although in the San Francisco region, as in virtually all U.S. metropolitan areas, growth of the suburbs far outpaced that of the central city, there were nonetheless 70,000 more people living there in 1998 than in 1980.[104]

During those good times vacancy rates in the central business district fell to negligible levels and property values soared.[105] In 1998, with municipal tax receipts up 12 percent, the city enjoyed a $100 million budget surplus.[106]

## Correcting the Fire Department

Yet prosperity and high rents were not the only signatures of San Francisco at the end of the twentieth century. There also was the reality that this city had been riven by three decades of strife occasioned by federal suits over the racial, ethnic, and gender composition of the police and fire departments. The thirty-year war in the courts had not left these crucial municipal services unscathed.

Take the fire department. It had been in and out of federal court since 1970, when the National Association for the Advancement of Colored People (NAACP) and other community organizations first sued the city for discrimination in hiring practices. During the next fourteen years, five attempts were made to devise an entrance exam that might be recognized as suitably unbiased, but to no avail. A new round of litigation confronted the department in the mid-1980s. The Black Firefighters Association, now joined by complainants representing other minorities and women, brought a class action. The Department of Justice filed a separate complaint.

While these lawsuits were raining down, the number of minority fire-fighters was going up. (As of 1987 there were eighty Latinos, seventy African Americans, and thirty-five Asian Americans.)[107] The figures, how-ever, fell well short of what the plaintiffs and a federal district judge deemed adequate. Thus a 1988 consent decree set explicit targets for the department's next 500 hires: 55 percent minority applicants; 10 percent women.[108] As was also typical in municipal antidiscrimination disputes, the department came under pressure not only to meet hiring quotas but to demonstrate affirmative action in promotions and assignments.

A decade later, with minorities constituting 40 percent of the depart-ment, and women 10 percent, all judicial supervision of the fire depart-ment's personnel practices was terminated.[109] Did the years of contesta-tion in the courts (and $30 million in legal expenses) gradually modernize the San Francisco Fire Department from an antediluvian exclusionary fra-ternity to a new age organization, more representative of, and presum-ably more responsive to, the community it serves?[110] Or did the long period of discord sow rancor and recriminations that would take years to bury? Time would tell. For all the significant rewards of the city's affir-mative action tussles, however, it would be hard to deny that they also took a toll on the fire department's *esprit de corps*.

In 1989 an official of the local firefighters union had warned members of the city's fire commission that morale was low because of what he euphemistically called "different promotion opportunities."[111] Long after they had brought a reverse-discrimination case that was summarily dis-missed in 1990 resentments lingered among white firemen who had been passed over in key appointments and promotions. A lead story in the *San Francisco Chronicle* in June 1995 reported persistent morale problems and racial tensions in the department.[112] And this disruptive situation smoldered. An anonymous newsletter, circulated monthly at several fire stations and dripping with sarcasm about the coerced departmental reforms, caused a furor in 1999.[113]

Maybe, as the city supervisor explained, this incident was simply a "sick hate crime."[114] But perhaps the implications of such troubles were also a bit broader. For a city that sits on an earthquake fault line and that had gone up in flames at other times in its history, a fire department focusing on a single task—fighting fires—might seem essential. Whatever the merits of making the organization juggle other social goals (such as federally sanctioned diversity preferences), the internal convulsions result-ing from some of them were prolonged and distracting.

## The Schools: Federally Supervised Identity Politics?

In 1970 African Americans represented more than 65 percent of the enrollment in twenty of the elementary schools in San Francisco.[115] In ten of these schools black enrollment ranged from 89 percent to 97 percent. As in dozens of other big cities at the time, patterns like these provided grounds for federal civil rights litigation. San Francisco's began in 1971 when one David Johnson charged the San Francisco United School District (SFUSD) with creating and maintaining a racially segregated school system.[116]

A federal district judge promptly ordered the SFUSD to use whatever means necessary (busing, altered attendance zones, cessation of "tracking," and so on) to obtain "substantially the same" ratios of black and white children in all public elementary schools. In the ensuing years none of these measures accomplished much desegregation. What they met with instead was an acceleration of white flight to the suburbs and some intense opposition from at least one other local group: elements of the Chinese community that proceeded to establish separate "freedom schools." Between 1967 and 1983 more than 32,000 students abandoned the city's public schools.[117] By 1978 the SFUSD was back in court, this time with the California State Department of Education as a codefendant in a wide-ranging suit that the NAACP hoped would bring new, more potent remedies.[118] Four and a half years of pretrial legal maneuvers culminated in a complicated settlement in 1983.

Much of the complexity of the 1983 consent decree stemmed from a simple fact: desegregation in San Francisco could not be, quite literally, a black and white issue. By the early 1980s the student population of the city was only one-fourth "white"—not enough to right the racial imbalances of the district's schools citywide. Several other ethnic groups would also have to be shuffled around. Thus the judicially approved "guidelines" for assigning students meant, first, identifying nine distinct racial and ethnic categories: "Spanish surname," "other white," black, Chinese, Japanese, Korean, Filipino, American Indian, and "other nonwhite." Next, no school would be permitted to contain fewer than four of these racially or ethnically designated groups in its student body. Then came this dictum: no particular group would be allowed to exceed 45 percent of the enrollment at any given school.

That enforcing these requirements would soon offend one constituency or another was hard to avoid. In theory families were to be given some choice in the assignment of students to schools. In practice the constraints of the racial-diversity scheme forced more than a third of all students to attend a school that was not their first, second, or even third choice.[119]

Asian students quickly bumped against the 45 percent ceiling on admissions to the city's best schools. To incorporate minorities deemed more disadvantaged hundreds of Chinese Americans were turned away each year from one of California's top secondary institutions, San Francisco's Lowell High School, despite entrance exam scores from these applicants equal to or better than those of other groups.[120] "It's just absurd," fumed a representative of the Asian American Legal Foundation. "The school district moves children around like racial objects."[121] It was only a matter of time before the victims of enrollment quotas at schools like Lowell would seek judicial redress. In *Ho* v. *San Francisco Unified School District* aggrieved Chinese Americans struck directly at the 1983 consent decree's use of race-based criteria in admissions.[122]

Following the U.S. Supreme Court's *Adarand* doctrine of 1995, which now subjected any state-sponsored scheme of "race-based classification" to stricter scrutiny, the federal district and appellate courts presiding over San Francisco's desegregation plans eventually began revising their standards.[123] In 1999, rather than go to trial in the *Ho* case, the SFUSD agreed to discontinue its preferential placements policy in favor of a race-neutral lottery—and to lift the rest of the 1983 decree's coercive provisions by the end of 2002.

### *"Reconstitution"*

There is little question that San Francisco's schools have been rocked for decades by often bitter race and identity politics, and that race relations were not always warmed by the federally supervised formulas for desegregation. Whether on balance the repeated legal confrontations and the rifts they deepened among ethnic communities left the school system and the city worse off, however, is a different story. For in San Francisco what began as a mandate to integrate the schools evolved into a larger experiment in educational reform.

This agenda, called "Reconstitution," included bold measures aimed at improving the quality, not just the racial mix, of about 33 percent of the city's elementary schools, 40 percent of its middle schools, and 75 percent of the high schools.[124] Over the strenuous objections of the teachers' union and its allies, administrative, faculty, and staff positions were dissolved in ten schools and replaced by new, carefully selected personnel who, pre-

sumably, would be committed to upholding "clear learning goals and rigorous performance standards."[125] A half-dozen schools in one impoverished predominantly black district, Bayview-Hunter's Point, underwent
the most drastic restructuring—as well as the most significant infusion of
resources: approximately two-thirds more dollars per student were spent
there than the systemwide average.[126] However tumultuous court-ordered
desegregation was for many American cities, for a time it also conferred
on them a sizable financial windfall. In San Francisco's case federal and
state aid underwrote the 1983 court decree, along with its assortment of
ancillary programs, to the tune of an extra $37.6 million a year.

The fruits of all these efforts were mixed. An evaluation in 1992 suggested that a core of thoroughly reconstituted schools showed "substantial gains" in academic achievement, but that the rest "had produced no
significant results for minority children."[127] Subsequent studies seemed to
confirm improvements in the prime-target schools of Bayview-Hunter's
Point, where test scores reportedly rose above those typical of inner-city
schools.

Wholly reliable measurement of progress in San Francisco's school system, however, has been elusive. Throughout the 1990s the SFUSD's policy of testing only English-proficient students enrolled in the system for at
least two successive years appeared to substantially overstate the district's
overall performance on standardized tests.[128] In any event, even the
reported results revealed widening gaps among groups. The original
intended beneficiaries of the drive for educational integration, African
Americans, for instance, dropped further behind the city's whites and
Asians in achievement scores. (Among African Americans in San
Francisco the average reading score for continuously enrolled students in
the spring of 1998 was more than 20 percent below the national norm.
On math tests the black students appeared to backslide.)[129] No less dis-
turbingly, in the subset of students tested, systemwide performance on
reading and math exams indicated, if anything, deteriorating scores year-
to-year at the high school level between 1993 and 1997.[130]

We will never know whether these outcomes might have been different
in the absence of the radical reorganization that sprang from the desegregation initiative. Possibly they could have been a lot worse. But
arguably some of the directions that education policy took partially under
federal auspices in San Francisco may have been counterproductive.

The mission of the reform program did not limit itself to the pursuit of
"clear learning goals and rigorous performance standards." Its ideals—as

enunciated in the so-called Philosophical Tenets of the Consent Decree—also embraced softer themes. Schools would teach how to "live" amid "cultural diversity," and they would have to recognize that "all individuals learn in many different ways and at varying rates," that "each individual learns best in a particular way," and that learning has "affective dimensions." As for the respective roles of teachers and pupils: "All individuals are both potential learners and potential teachers."[131]

One wonders how such a regime could be consistently reconciled with the quest for "clear learning goals and rigorous performance standards." If everyone is interchangeably a "potential" learner and teacher, for example, who is responsible for what? Facing up to the continuing crisis in academic achievement, particularly among black and Latino students, may not have been facilitated by a mission statement that seemed to draw rather vague lines of accountability: "If students fail," it felt, "all partners should accept full responsibility for this failure."

And if "each individual learns best in a particular way," how can his or her progress be evaluated by means of standardized examinations? For a while the SFUSD dispensed with such tests for thousands of students. Between 1993 and 1997 the number of students exempted because of insufficient proficiency in English climbed from 1,631 to 6,390. In 1997 six of the city's high schools obtained no test scores from at least an eighth of their students.[132] Only late in 2000 did the school district reach a settlement with the state of California and agree to administer state-mandated tests in English to all students, whether proficient in the language or not.[133]

### Fiscal Setbacks

Like other cities that had been ordered to alter the racial and ethnic composition of their public schools, San Francisco received upward of $30 million a year in state aid for that purpose. Unlike some cities that had been similarly subsidized for several decades—Kansas City, Missouri, for instance, where the entire school system nevertheless remained so substandard that state overseers suspended its accreditation in April 2000—San Francisco measurably enriched the education students received in some of its schools (the ones in Bayview-Hunter's Point, for example).[134] A steady flow of external funds almost certainly assisted this process.

But as the SFUSD's racial balancing act grew in complexity and became vulnerable to charges of reverse discrimination, the special funding on which the city had come to rely year after year was jeopardized.

When the federal courts finally closed the curtain on the 1983 consent decree, the state Department of Education (which had been named as a codefendant) was automatically released from its obligation to aid the city's integration program. Because in San Francisco most of the effort to reinvent its schools has been tethered to desegregation, the impending loss of tens of millions of dollars annually raises the question of whether the city's educational reform, with its already serious programmatic limitations, would soon face budgetary ones.

## Los Angeles

Like New York, America's other urban behemoth, Los Angeles, has its hands full dealing with federal directives. Perhaps even more than in New York, however, the variety of punitive prescriptions aimed at Los Angeles is now so extensive this city has been called "a virtual ward of Washington."[135]

As this chapter was being written Los Angeles was wrestling not only with EPA regulations but with such problems as how to manage mandatory Social Security benefits for employees without threatening the municipal pension plan; how to pay out many millions of dollars in overtime claims springing from lawsuits under the U.S. Fair Labor Standards Act; how to comply with a U.S. court decree specifying the percentages of passengers permitted to stand on city bus rides; how to meet the Americans with Disabilities Act's desiderata for sidewalks, driveway aprons, bus shelters, stairways, bridges, and countless other public facilities in an urban area that covers 470 square miles; and how to live with the functional equivalent of a federal takeover of its police department.[136]

### Environmental Woes

At the top of the heap of antipollution expenses confronting Los Angeles is the same underfunded federal mandate that figures conspicuously in almost every other big city's fiscal calculus: the annual bill for wastewater management. Los Angeles spent $77 million on this operation in 1980 but $687 million in 1998—an 800 percent increase in inflation-adjusted dollars.[137] Federal aid, which had defrayed almost all of the capital-improvements portion at the start of this period, had all but vanished by the end of it (figure 3-11).

There is nothing wrong with expecting a city's residents to pay for most of their own water pollution controls—unless key components of

Figure 3-11. *Federal Share of Los Angeles's Capital Expenditures on Wastewater Infrastructure, 1980–2000*

Percent

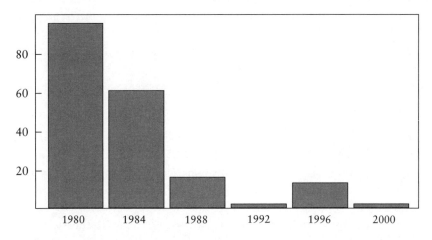

Sources: Schedule 14 in City of Los Angeles, *Budget: Fiscal Year 1979–80*, p. 134; City of Los Angeles, *Budget: Fiscal Year 1980–81*, p. 133; City of Los Angeles, *Budget: Fiscal Year 1981–82*, p. 127; City of Los Angeles, *Budget: Fiscal Year 1982–883*, p. 123; City of Los Angeles, *Budget: Fiscal Year 1983–84*, p. 126; City of Los Angeles, *Budget: Fiscal Year 1984–85*, p. 135; City of Los Angeles, *Budget: Fiscal Year 1985–86*, p. 136; City of Los Angeles, *Budget: Fiscal Year 1986–87*; City of Los Angeles, *Budget: Fiscal Year 1987–88*; City of Los Angeles, *Budget: Fiscal Year 1989–90*, pp. 137–38; City of Los Angeles, *Budget: Fiscal Year 1990–91*, pp. 137–138; City of Los Angeles, *Budget: Fiscal Year 1991–92*, pp. 154–55; City of Los Angeles, *Budget: Fiscal Year 1992–93*, pp. 161–62; City of Los Angeles, *Budget: Fiscal Year 1993–94*, pp. 159–60; City of Los Angeles, *Budget: Fiscal Year 1994–95*, pp. 171–72; City of Los Angeles, *Budget: Fiscal Year 1995–96* pp. 185–86; City of Los Angeles, *Budget: Fiscal Year 1996–97*, pp. 190–91; and City of Los Angeles, *Budget: Fiscal Year 1997–98*, pp. 191–92.

the city's system become overregulated, raising the prospect of unnecessary rate hikes and taxes. A recent dispute about L.A.'s sewers, for example, seemed headed in that direction.

Two years ago the EPA and the Los Angeles Regional Water Quality Control Board joined a lawsuit filed by Santa Monica Baykeepers, an environmental organization that had cited the city for allowing sewage to be flushed too frequently into streets, rivers, and the Pacific Ocean.[138] City public works officials were understandably puzzled by the action.[139] Six hundred million dollars were already being spent to improve L.A.'s sewer lines, and the city planned to add another $1.4 billion for renovations in the next ten years.[140] In 1999 the EPA had found Los Angeles well below the national average in number of spills per mile even though the city's collection system was the largest in the country.[141] Moreover, inasmuch as the spillage problem involved storm-water discharge, it had been compounded temporarily by the El Niño rains of 1998. After these unusual meteorological conditions passed, incidents of weather-related overflow were reportedly rare. The normally dry city of Los Angeles did not call for the same precautionary system of storm drains and pipes as cities in wetter climates. For the most part, what repairs the Los Angeles sewers did require were already under way, and arguably, no federal court case was needed to make progress.

The quandary illustrated but hardly exhausted all those posed by national pollution-abatement rules. Los Angeles, like most large cities, has had to work with regulations that, for example, curb lead and copper content in water but also discourage the use of a chemical (zinc ortho phosphate) ideal for controlling pipe corrosion. And city officials were baffled by a proposed EPA rule to limit radon in drinking water. As the Association of California Water Agencies plainly concluded, "There is no effective regulatory enforcement vehicle capable of reducing radon to an 'acceptable' level."[142] The range of environmental policy predicaments was considerable.

## *Where Angels Fear to Tread: The LAPD*

But in Los Angeles the vagaries of the Surface Water Treatment Rule or the rest of the Clean Water Act are sources of relatively minor friction compared with the head-on collisions between the federal and city governments over another issue: the behavior of the local police force.

In the spring of 1992, after a state court acquitted four police officers in the notorious Rodney King incident, the black neighborhoods of Los Angeles rioted. The policemen were then retried, this time on federal charges of violating King's civil rights. In April 1993 two of the four officers in the case were found guilty and sent to prison.

A few years later another police crisis erupted. A contingent of one of the force's antigang squads in a section called Rampart was alleged to have planted evidence, falsified reports, injured unarmed suspects, and more. After an incriminated cop, named Rafael Perez, pleaded guilty to charges of cocaine theft and began leveling accusations at some seventy other officers, the Los Angeles Police Department (LAPD) found itself in the throes of a wide-ranging corruption probe.

Local investigators, relying on the LAPD's own detectives, launched the inquest. What its results later suggested, as Peter J. Boyer in the *New Yorker* concluded in a meticulous chronicle, was that few knowledgeable observers "believe the wrongdoing was as widespread as Perez once suggested."[143] Nonetheless, what came to be called the Rampart scandal lent new impetus to a civil inquiry that the Department of Justice had opened against the LAPD in 1996 but that had produced no discernible result. Now, the Justice Department's Civil Rights Division determined that, among other misdeeds, the LAPD engaged in "excessive force, false arrests, and unreasonable searches and seizures."[144] The division proceeded to file a complaint to obtain injunctive relief from this alleged "pattern or practice of misconduct," some of which was said to include violations of constitutional protections.[145]

Rather than battle federal inquisitors in a protracted lawsuit, in November 2000 the city accepted a court consent decree with a number of laborious provisions. Henceforth the LAPD would need to monitor the law enforcement activities of all its officers through a new computerized tracking system.[146] The department would have to create new internal units to investigate future complaints of transgressions. It would have to conduct more regular and extensive audits through a specialized unit. Perhaps most notably, police officers would be prohibited from "relying" on race, ethnicity, or national origin when making traffic and pedestrian stops. At the same time the department would have to collect data on the race, ethnicity, or national origin of persons who were the subject of traffic and pedestrian stops and analyze this information for possible signs of bias or other improper conduct. In sum, what had started out as the Rampart affair—that is, the disclosures in the testimony of a single cop in one division of the police force—had ballooned into a sweeping indictment of the department's "discriminatory policing" and a federally supervised purge of profiling.

From afar it is not easy to tell whether the LAPD was exceptionally afflicted by "a deep sickness," to use the term of one longtime departmental observer and hence wholly warranted so formidable a federal foray into the organization's routine operations.[147] Los Angeles, after all, had been a crime-infested city at the start of the 1990s. By 1997 violent crime was down a third, property crime almost two-fifths—progress close to that recorded in New York.[148] If improved policing was duly credited for much of the pacification in New York, the police in Los Angeles, too, must have been doing something right.

Partly because the police in Los Angeles have been a skeletal force compared with that of New York, the LAPD had developed into a strike force more reliant on mobility and aggressive tactics.[149] No doubt the tactics sometimes crossed the line to abuse. But while the Justice Department probed rights abuses, the fact remained that various neighborhoods were under siege by brutal gangs. Whether residents in these embattled areas were as concerned as the Justice Department with the behavior of L.A.'s undermanned police department, or more worried about the emboldened gangs, was a question seldom asked amid the Rampart furor.[150]

And there was this final twist to the Los Angeles police corruption saga: in the course of the city's own detective work, indications surfaced that crimes may have been perpetrated by a handful of unlikely suspects: "gangsta cops."[151] It seems that some minority recruits with links to a notorious street gang, the Bloods, had managed to join the department. Whatever the possible explanations for how and why such individuals could have entered the ranks of the LAPD, veterans of the department reportedly contended that the department's general hiring standards had deteriorated.[152] If there was truth to this contention, an irony of the LAPD's travails was that the same federal authorities who chastised the department for the conduct of its personnel voiced no reservations about recruitment practices that may have contributed to the problem.

## So What?

For all its troubles Los Angeles has remained a resilient place. Its population, unlike that of many other major U.S. cities, did not stop growing during the past thirty years.[153] Its economy cranked out a net increase of 191,266 jobs between 1990 and 1998.[154] Contrary to early predictions, Proposition 13, the 1978 ballot initiative that capped property tax increases in California's municipalities, constrained but hardly crushed the state's biggest city. A strong economy enabled the city of Los Angeles to keep raising revenue.[155] While New York traditionally has had to share the burden of certain costly social programs, Los Angeles has fewer such fiscal responsibilities.[156] And, at least until recently, the escalating costs of key services have been substantially offset by increases in state aid.[157]

Education is a case in point. The explosive expense of special education, a bane of budget makers in many urban school districts, for example, has not stung Los Angeles as much as some other large cities. The reason: Sacramento has defrayed more than 70 percent of local program expenditures.[158] In addition the Los Angeles Unified School District spans more than 700 square miles, extending to some thirty municipalities besides Los Angeles. A district of that magnitude draws revenue from the metropolitan region, not just its central city.

Further, although no American city has been more scorned by environmentalists than Los Angeles, much of its forlorn reputation is no longer deserved. The number of smog alerts in the L.A. metropolitan area declined from 121 in the peak year 1977 to 7 in 1996.[159] By 1997 California's South Coast Air Quality Management District was able to predict that the number would fall to zero in 2000.[160] And some other environmental complexities that loom large in New York or Chicago— for example, the legal morass associated with the Comprehensive Environmental Response, Compensation, and Liability Act—are lesser issues in Los Angeles. In 1994, when the city was asked to list the most taxing environmental mandates it faced, it made no mention of brownfields and Superfund litigation.[161]

Even the California energy crisis, which brought brownouts to large parts of the state in 2001, scarcely affected Los Angeles. The city had opted out of the state's misbegotten electricity deregulation plan. While California as a whole experienced shortages, a municipally run power authority in Los Angeles generated surplus power and by 2001 was selling it lucratively to neighboring jurisdictions.

Yet, all these strengths notwithstanding, Los Angeles, like other big cities, has had to devote a large part of its limited resources to the preferences of federal regulators. In 1994 the city had conservatively estimated that federally mandated programs would cost the city government approximately $4.2 billion over the ensuing five years.[162] Annualized, this estimate implied that the equivalent of one-fifth of the city's entire budget was spoken for by Washington.[163]

## Conclusions

Although these impressions hardly measure precisely how much any of the cities viewed in this chapter have been bruised by various federal regulatory activities, their scope in places like Los Angeles invites scrutiny: is so much mandatory spending, and the comparatively stiff taxation it entails, indispensable to the city's well-being?[164] Or would some of the diverted revenues be better used for other purposes?

*Local Choices*

For instance, maybe a different order of environmental investments (like a comprehensive high-tech system of congestion pricing on local highways) would yield a larger social payback than plowing additional millions of dollars into larger sewer mains more suited to cities in wet climates where continual and abundant rainfall justifies greater drainage capacity.

And perhaps permitting city officials to spend their money on, for example, the careful recruitment of more police officers would improve public safety in Los Angeles to a greater degree than making the city invest in racial data filing and "analysis." The latter program might restrain some abusive police behavior, and at any rate is the priority of federal overseers, but how it was supposed to enhance the police's number-one responsibility of suppressing violent crime was far from clear. (Indeed residents in Rampart reported that officers, now operating under a regulatory microscope, cruise down the street in their patrol cars and make fewer arrests—"a practice known within the L.A.P.D. as drive and wave"—even as gang-related homicides in the city's poor neighborhoods have doubled.)[165]

Just as doubts linger about the net benefits of certain federally enforced imperatives for Los Angeles, questions persist about other ones elsewhere.

The water New Yorkers drink today is better, not worse, than it was in the past. But it can always be said to have deteriorated if U.S. safety standards are a moving target, ever narrowing the acceptable margins of risk. Further, a watershed protection plan that, at least in part, compels a downstream municipality (New York City) to subsidize upstream communities (where the pollution originates) is not a plan that adheres to the polluter-pays principle. That such a strategy also perennially brandishes over New York the regulatory equivalent of a sword of Damocles—in the form of a multibillion dollar filtration requirement—seems insensible, especially if the climate for financial aid to urban pollution-abatement programs stays austere and the local economy does not soon resume a robust rate of growth.

In addition, although some federal regulations apply pressure to preserve the New York region's water, arguably others have had the unintended consequence of muddying the process, thereby imposing on this city unnecessary costs. For example, a federal ban on ocean dumping of sewage sludge has forced New York to spend upward of $2 billion on installations that turn processed sewage into fertilizer.[166] But the dewatering and composting of waste emits nitrogen-rich effluents that pollute water bodies. Part of New York's contamination of Long Island Sound arises from the need to squeeze refuse dry in order to transport it to landfills. Ironically that practice was developed to comply with U.S. law.

### Blunt Instruments

In Philadelphia the long-standing federal court order that imposed limits on the inmate population in the city's jails drew scorn and outrage. (One polemicist held the district judge "responsible for as much crime in the City of Brotherly Love as any street gang.") [167] Some of this reaction was simplistic. With 2 million people incarcerated in the United States, it has been incumbent on the federal judiciary at the very least to disallow atrocious conditions, including extreme overcrowding, in some local prisons. Philadelphia had regularly exceeded acceptable caps and had dithered on enlarging its facilities.

That said, the court's decree looked like too blunt a tool. In lieu of individualized bail review, in which local judges could consider a criminal defendant's prior record, a "charge-based" formula was superimposed: suspects charged with "nonviolent" crimes (which could include stalking, carjacking, robbery, drug dealing, manslaughter, or even terrorist threats) could no longer be subject to detention pending trial. This arrangement seemed bound to increase the fugitive rate, including the rate among individuals who would prove far more likely to commit new and serious crimes. [168] A city in sound fiscal condition might have solved the problem swiftly by embarking on a crash program of prison construction projects. Philadelphia's finances, however, were anything but sound—and the criminal justice block grants the city received in the early 1990s were inadequate.[169] In sum, the uncoordinated roles of two federal institutions were at work: a court that compelled drastic remedies, but with no idea whether a second entity, namely, Congress, would assist with implementation.

### Unsettled Outcomes

San Francisco offers a rich example of the intricacies of federal plans to integrate city schools. The consent decree governing San Francisco's school district *was* backed up by substantial outside resources. But no court order can be extended ad infinitum, and when this one finally terminated, it left some confusion in its wake. For the federal legal proceeding had raised great expectations of better schools, directed the state government to underwrite them, essentially institutionalized that support over almost twenty years, and then abruptly caused it to be withdrawn. That this chain of events has given the city a more stable system than one that might have evolved without so long and turbulent a federal intervention is uncertain. The difficulties of San Francisco's schools may well have been a contributing factor in the city's ongoing decline of households with children. San Francisco ended the last decade with 4,100 fewer children under eighteen years of age than it had in 1990—turning it into the American big city with the smallest percentage of children.[170]

In Chicago, where housing issues have long been a source of contention between the city and the federal government, relations recently have improved. Two years ago the Department of Housing and Urban Development gave final approval to Mayor Richard M. Daley's $1.5 billion ten-year plan for overhauling the Chicago Housing Authority and rebuilding approximately 25,000 of its dilapidated public housing units. This large undertaking, known as "The Plan for Transformation," included a substantial number of additional waivers from federal regulations.[171] Nonetheless, time will tell just how far the new local flexibility, and "transformation," will go.

## Heavy Lifting

Last, there is the continuing story of Baltimore's special education expenditures. If the year 2000's budget cycle was an indication, the comparatively disadvantageous distribution of Baltimore's school resources seemed headed from bad to worse. The city's special education spending ran approximately $10 billion over budget in fiscal 1999. Expecting another such bulge in 2000, the Baltimore school district requested an additional $15 million for the program. But with so substantial an increment requested for special education, the school chief was only able to propose $5.5 million for purposes of reducing class sizes and $2.4 million to hire sixty new reading teachers for the district's middle schools (where 60 percent of all entering students fail to meet grade standards). The budgetary crunch special education has created for the rest of the system, explained the state's schools superintendent, is unmistakable: "When you have a finite budget, the money in this accelerated category is coming from regular education."[172]

Squeezing regular education is a ruinous course for Baltimore. In the interjurisdictional competition for jobs and residents a city in which merely 15 percent of students received satisfactory scores on the state's School Performance Assessment Program in 1998—an average result several times worse than in any of the nearby suburban districts—remains in a weak position. Yet unless Congress overhauls the national special education mandate, Baltimore's predicament, like that of many other big city school systems, is unlikely to ease.

# 4 The Politics of Paternalism

How did the U.S. government become so steeped in what had once been the separate competences of the nation's municipalities? And in what ways has the enlarged federal role in this country come to differ from the relationship between central and city governments in some other Western democracies? To put these inquiries in proper context this chapter sketches various sources of centralization in American federalism as a whole. Chapter 5 then draws comparisons with foreign experience.

## The Thirties and Sixties

Before the New Deal, federal arrogation of state and local prerogatives had been held rather firmly in check, not least by a defiant Supreme Court.[1] Indeed the defiance sometimes reached extremes—as when Congress's efforts to bar trade in goods produced by child labor drew the court's censure. "If Congress can thus regulate matters entrusted to local authority," fulminated Justice William R. Day, "all freedom of commerce will be at an end. . . , and thus our system of government be practically destroyed."[2]

The Great Depression altered this stance. In the face of the economic crisis and a president determined to alleviate it through national legislation, diehard defenders of "local authority" were forced to give ground. After the high court's tactical retreat in 1937, established norms were upended. Reinterpretations of the commerce clause, among other muscular clauses of the Constitution, gradually became so elastic they licensed formerly unthinkable forms of federal regulation. According to the court in *Wickard* v. *Filburn,* for instance, even a farmer who only grew grain to feed his own livestock now came within the ambit of federally regulated interstate commerce. For the most part the Tenth Amendment, which the court came to regard as "but a truism," was brushed aside.[3]

National mobilization during the Second World War extended the tendencies that had gained force in the 1930s, but the expanding centralism became more contentious in the immediate postwar period.[4] A coalition of governors petitioned the Truman administration to loosen some of the conditions attached to federal aid. Presidential commissions in 1949, 1955, and 1957 repeatedly recommended that proper perimeters of federal and local jurisdiction be drawn and respected. Local governments throughout the South did not jump to implement the Supreme Court's landmark school desegregation decision in 1954.[5] Nevertheless none of these momentary countercurrents turned the tide. Before long the central government would resume enlarging its local operations.

Stirred in part by the social agitation of the 1960s but also aided by a buoyant economy (hence a torrent of federal tax revenue), Washington went on a spending spree: 240 new grant programs were launched between 1964 and 1966.[6] Expenditures, which had stood at less than $8 billion in 1962, were many times larger by the early 1970s. Virtually all these funds were narrowly earmarked for particular social purposes embraced by Congress and President Lyndon B. Johnson. While some of the money surely helped states and localities pay for what they needed, not a few categorical grants moved in other directions. For example, the community action agitators and local litigants funded by the feds to squeeze new services out of City Hall may have pleased the visionaries of the Great Society but not necessarily the mayors and other local office holders whose jurisdictions were targeted.[7]

Whether a given federally aided activity proved worthwhile to local officials or not, they could not easily defect once work got under way. Programs were often locked in by crossover sanctions: failure to execute one program in every detail might mean the loss of funds for other, entirely separate projects. What began with federal inducements that communities could presumably take or leave had a way of becoming more coercive. Considerable regimentation developed, not only because local clienteles served by the programs would almost always ensure their perpetuation with local tax dollars if congressional appropriations wilted, but more often because disparities in "maintenance of effort" among communities would be cited as inequitable, thus adding pressure to stiffen national standards.[8]

If Harold Laski was to conclude as early as 1939 that "the epoch of federalism is over," one wonders what epitaph he would have reserved for federal-local relations during the Great Society, when Washington penetrated much more deeply into the affairs of cities and states.[9] The 1960s differed importantly from previous waves of federal activism. The New Deal had certainly revolutionized the use of the commerce power to regulate private enterprise but had applied fewer rules to the local public sector. Thus the old-age insurance provisions of the Social Security Act excluded state and local employees because in 1935 few thought that Congress could constitutionally impose a payroll tax on state and local governments. The Fair Labor Standards Act (FLSA) did not apply to state and municipal workers because in 1938 few people thought that regulating the employment practices of states and municipalities was a constitutional federal prerogative.[10]

In the era of the Great Society these restraints began to fall away. Congress and the Supreme Court perforated what was left of the "legitimacy barrier" that had kept the federal government from inserting its standards into the day-to-day management of local functions. In 1966, for instance, Congress extended the FLSA to cover local public employers.

## Quantum Leap

What transpired during the 1960s was but an opening wedge for wider action later on. Some of the forces at work now were unlike the kinds (wars, depressions, or urban civil disorders) that had helped expand the role of the national government in earlier decades.

While Washington's spending on grants to state and local governments grew at an inflated-adjusted rate of more than 13 percent annually between 1960 and 1970, it climbed at an even faster clip (nearing 16 percent a year) during the years 1970–78.[11] The binge of federal grant giving in the 1970s coincided with structural changes in Congress, particularly the demise of the institution's norms of strict seniority that had kept a tight circle of autocratic, mostly southern conservative, chairmen in control of key committees and their legislative agendas. After 1974 in place of the old arrangements flourished a proliferation of free-wheeling legislative actors, supported by a burgeoning congressional staff and empowered by entrepreneurial subcommittees that became the new springboards for legislative initiatives. Grant programs coaxing the states and localities to service this or that category of clients multiplied in part because they were the "quintessential products of the decentralized congressional structure," one that afforded more members opportunities to get the federal government involved.[12]

The increase in conditioned categorical grants during the 1960s and 1970s was striking, but it was not the only sign of the ascent of federal influence over time. Perhaps an even more graphic indicator, one that tracked the flow of federal dollars only in part, would be a longitudinal tally of national statutes preempting state and local laws—that is, statutes that prohibited states and localities from exercising particular powers, or replaced local rules with federal ones, or required the local authorities to satisfy certain standards.[13]

Some years ago the U.S. Advisory Commission on Intergovernmental Relations conducted a thorough count of these so-called preemptions. The commission's compilation painted an astonishing picture (figure 4-1). There were more preemptions enacted between 1960 and 1969 than in any previous decade, but what happened during the 1960s paled in comparison with the explosion that followed. A greater volume of preemptive legislation was enacted after 1970 than in the entire preceding history of the Republic.

Interestingly, Republican administrations repeatedly proved unable to halt this turn of events. President Richard Nixon's "new federalism" promised to change the system of federal grants from a means of interposing intergovernmental regulations to one that would restore local discretion through the use of unconditional revenue sharing and flexible block grants, but to no avail. Federal assistance became more, not less, entangled in restrictive red tape.[14] In 1981 President Ronald Reagan asked Congress to roll eighty-three categorical grant programs into six large block grants, intended to give local recipients much needed latitude. In the end, nine small block grants were enacted, each with complex provisions for eligibility and compliance.

For all their protestations against the Washington-knows-best mindset, Republican presidents signed a spate of laws that further indentured

Figure 4-1. *Number of Federal Preemption Statutes Enacted
per Decade, 1790–1999*

Number[a]

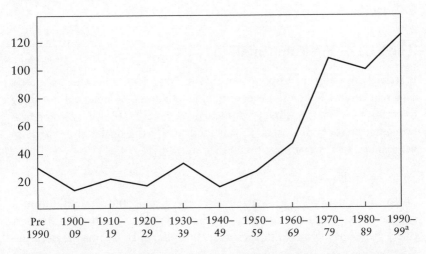

| | Pre 1990 | 1900– 09 | 1910– 19 | 1920– 29 | 1930– 39 | 1940– 49 | 1950– 59 | 1960– 69 | 1970– 79 | 1980– 89 | 1990– 99[a] |

Source: U.S. Advisory Commission on Intergovernmental *Relations, Federal Statutory
Preemption of State and Local Authority: History, Inventory, and Issues* (Washington,
1992), p. 9.

a. Estimation based on preemption data for 1990–91. Available data for subsequent
years are sketchy. See David B. Walker, "The Advent of an Ambiguous Federalism and the
Emergence of New Federalism III," *Public Administration Review,* vol. 56 (May–June
1996), p. 272.

local authorities as "field hands" of the federal government.[15] Between
1981 and 1991 federal legislation effectively obligated them to enforce,
among many other new rules, a nationwide minimum drinking age,
national standards for the licensing of bus and truck drivers, nationally
approved special services and facilities for the disabled, national intentions to monitor spillage from thousands of city storm sewers, a national
directive to inspect school buildings for asbestos, national provisions to
test seventy-seven additional chemicals in municipal water supplies, a
national ban on mandatory retirements and on numerous other kinds of
perceived bias in all public and private workplaces, and much more.

At the same time Reagan's much-discussed plans for relief from *existing* intergovernmental regulations had modest results. Beginning in 1981
some two dozen rules judged burdensome to local governments were

reviewed.[16] In the end a number were corrected, but many were not. The Department of Transportation's initial untenable requirements for handicapped access in city transit systems, for example, were modified. However, efforts to release municipalities from Davis-Bacon regulations for contractors fell short.

## The Rise of Environmentalism

It strains credulity to suppose that the world suddenly became so utterly different after 1970 as to necessitate what figure 4-1 depicts: a doubling of statutory strictures directed at local governments. However, some fundamental changes did occur that helped justify the onslaught of federal activism or in any event set much of it in train.

### Sighting Spillovers

One was the nation's heightened awareness of environmental pollution. A substantial share of the intergovernmental mandates imposed in the past thirty years sprang out of this ferment. With Earth Day came greater public consciousness that the efforts of localities and states to protect the environment did not suffice, for the simple reason that pollution traverses jurisdictions. Certainly a forceful argument could be (and was) made for national enforcement of the Clean Air Act in 1970, 1977, and again in 1990.[17] Emissions of greenhouse gases and of sulfur dioxide are not local problems. Even the thick smog in urban air sheds does not simply dissipate at their borders; it can migrate far beyond them.

Once the transboundary properties of certain pollutants provided a plausible rationale for federal oversight, however, the case for nationalizing policy for many other kinds of environmental hazards, including those that are much less mobile, gained traction. One might think, for example, that the regulation of community drinking water ought to remain a local responsibility.[18] Yet, because persons who might imbibe impurities in a community's water supply are not *always* just local residents (out-of-town visitors, say, might drink the town's water, too), proponents of national programs such as the Safe Drinking Water Act were able to draw at least some parallels with precedents like the air quality statutes that regulated wide-ranging hazards.

### Environmental Politics

Some U.S. antipollution measures that began by aiming selectively at the right targets gradually became less discerning, not only when the extent of the problem they were meant to solve was characterized as multijuris-dictional but as the process of setting standards became politicized. Communities and interest groups would lobby to redistribute their burdens. The upshot commonly was not less federal regulation but more of it spread more widely. The original standards of the Clean Air Act of 1970 cracked down on utilities that burned high-sulfur coal, produced chiefly in West Virginia, Kentucky, Ohio, and Pennsylvania. To regain market share, these states prevailed on Congress to amend the law. After 1977 power plants across the land, regardless of the sulfur content of their fuel, were uniformly required to install smokestack scrubbers. Never mind that this coast-to-coast requirement was less a national public health imperative than an opaque cross subsidy to eastern coal producers.[19] Now, a relatively clean-burning municipal generating facility in Kansas or Colorado would have to be equipped no differently than a foul one in Georgia or New Jersey.

Another reason why regulators at the national level took charge of more localized pollution problems after 1970 was that advocates had learned to think and speak of pollution abatement as, in essence, a legal protection to which everybody was entitled.[20] The debate on the Clean Air Act exemplified this important development; its terms were framed from the outset as a matter of securing everyone's "*inherent right* to the enjoyment of a pure and uncontaminated air."[21] Akin to a civil right, a warrant to a clean environment ceases to be a mere aspiration that can be adjusted up or down according to community preferences; it tends to be absolute, universalistic, and noneconomic. There is, in other words, no such thing as attaching a price tag to an "inherent right" and allowing it to vary by locale. Because rights by definition belong to citizens equally, they imply nationally standardized commands and controls.

In 1994 the Supreme Court ruled in *City of Chicago* v. *Environmental Defense Fund* that the ash produced in Chicago's municipal incinerators had to be treated as hazardous waste. The Court not only shut down Chicago's waste-to-energy incineration plants (and thus impelled the city to truck its trash to outlying landfills) but implied that citizens of *every* community were entitled to the same remedy given the Clean Air Act's absolute ban on adverse health effects.[22]

Defining environmentalism in a rights-based fashion had other political implications. If environmental protection resembled a legal prerogative, plaintiffs naturally would lay claim to it in courts of law. The omnipresent prospect of litigation could lead vulnerable industries to seek shelter by widening the scope of government mandates. To forestall a

wave of lawsuits against asbestos manufacturers, for example, this industry joined the campaign for statutory asbestos-removal standards nationwide.[23] At least that way, the companies reckoned, they might know precisely what was expected of them everywhere, instead of remaining
wholly exposed to the case-by-case caprice of local juries.

Further, as environmental policy became more litigious, beleaguered
state and local officials, too, would be tempted to take cover under a
blanket of national standards. Invoking "the law of the land" is often a
safer defense than trying to explain nuanced exercises of local discretion.
In the proceedings that led to sweeping national directives for drinking
water the National Governors Association and various associations representing public water systems pressed for comprehensive standards that
might help insulate local administrators from incessant legal wrangles.[24]
Whether this tactic succeeded, or just left local officials with less flexibility and no real respite from legal troubles, was not clear.

There are at least two more explanations for why the post-1970 politics of environmental protection packed more and more specifications
into central statutes, which bore down heavily on states and municipalities. Especially during the 1980s and early 1990s, when Democratic
majorities in Congress faced Republican presidents, environmental policy
became the focus of intense distrust. The executive sought to slow the
pace of programs, whereas the legislative branch wanted to accelerate
them. Suspecting that Reagan and Bush appointees to the Environmental
Protection Agency would, if permitted, thwart the agency's mission,
Congress proceeded to micromanage it through detailed legislation. Thus
EPA administrators were required by law to resolve highly complex matters under grueling schedules. The Superfund Amendments and
Reauthorization Act of 1986 stipulated no fewer than 150 statutory
deadlines for rulemakings. Amendments to the Safe Drinking Water Act
that year identified eighty-three contaminants for which the EPA was to
set standards within tightly designated timeframes. Such pressure eventually made its way to local governments, as the EPA and the federal courts
pushed new targets and timetables for compliance down the line.

The dance of legislation occasionally seemed to go something like this:
skilled policy entrepreneurs, aided by frenzied media coverage, would
pivot on some supposed menace to the environment. The issue *du jour*
(asbestos in classrooms, say, or radon in tap water) might vary in severity from place to place. It might not move from one to another. And it
might be of fairly minor importance compared with other dangers (like

heat-trapping gas emissions, indoor air pollution, or the runoff from agricultural pesticides). No matter; through strong emotional appeals, mass opinion and lawmakers would be mobilized to purge the selected evil. Sponsors of bills would vie with one another for maximal impact; a process of "speculative augmentation" would develop, as Charles O. Jones observed in his definitive study of the 1970 Clean Air Act, where moderate bills were deemed sellouts and increasingly forceful alternatives gained legitimacy.[25] Thus some legislation seemingly sought to outlaw any margin of risk, no matter how small, at any price: no carcinogenic additives in food, zero discharge of pollutants into rivers, any ill-health effects from air pollution, and so on. That the price of outlawing any margin of risk at all might be prohibitive for local governments (as for many firms) was an afterthought.

In part a combination of scientific advances and continuing uncertainties has enabled alarmists to press such goals. Sophisticated technologies have enabled scientists to detect hazardous substances in smaller and smaller concentrations. A possible contaminant measured in parts per million might be noticed in only a handful of scattered sites. But if the same substance later is discerned in parts per *trillion*, it suddenly may be perceived as ubiquitous. Its presence, even if presenting a minuscule threat in most places, can frighten people everywhere—and turn the worries of a few localities into a wider panic, hence becoming cause for nationwide vigilance.

And the escalation becomes more likely if an excitable public is predisposed to discourage moderation. By the time Congress was debating the tough new amendments to the Clean Air Act in 1990, for example, a growing number of Americans had become convinced, erroneously, that the nation's air quality had steadily deteriorated and that "environmental improvements must be made *regardless of cost*."[26] In this charged atmosphere a raft of restrictive measures became law at the national level, often with lawmakers' minimal knowledge of whether the local public sector (let alone much private industry) could afford to comply.[27]

## The Age of "Low Politics"

When John F. Kennedy became president in 1961 his inaugural address contained a grand total of two words on domestic policy. (One sentence in his speech, about tyranny abroad, ended with a pledge to be "unwilling to witness or permit the slow undoing of those human rights to which this nation has always been committed, and to which we are committed *at home* and around the world.")[28] Foreign affairs were an overriding preoccupation of presidents, and the subject of great concern to congressional leaders, for most of the second half of the twentieth century.

By the time President Bill Clinton delivered his state of the union address in February 1997, however, international threats were receiving less than individual attention; the emphasis was overwhelmingly on the home front. Clinton turned to such issues as the enforcement of truancy laws, the advantages of school uniforms, the math tests of fourth graders, the need to connect hospitalized children to the Internet, the engagement of work-study students as reading tutors, the importance "for parents to begin talking, singing, even reading to their infants," the urgency of a $1,500 college tuition tax credit, the ability of medical insurance to cover annual mammograms, the appropriate hospital stay for women after a mastectomy, the utility of flex-time for employees, the revitalization of community waterfronts, the uses of community development banks, the record of Burger King and other businesses in creating jobs for welfare recipients, and so forth.[29]

Granted, at times the cold war had served to put the federal government's imprimatur on what were largely local projects. For example, it provided a national security pretext for underwriting certain local public works, like the building of bridges and roads under the National System of Interstate and Defense Highways (as the massive federal road program was formally titled in 1956). But for the most part the priorities of foreign policy and defense had distracted national politicians from fastening on the sorts of domestic details that cluttered Clinton's agenda. Such specifics had been the domain of state and municipal functionaries, if not private firms and households.

Inasmuch as the motifs of national politics during the post–cold war era have increasingly appropriated the routine responsibilities of governors, mayors, hospital administrators, or school boards, this novel twist did not represent just the Clinton administration's handiwork. The shift started earlier—and players from both political parties, and at both ends of Pennsylvania Avenue, participated.

## From Nanny State to Daddy State

Perestroika had lowered East-West tensions during the Reagan years. As the rest of the world looked less menacing, policymakers in Washington delved eagerly into more parochial matters. Indeed, with the exception of petty disputes about the balance of foreign trade with allies such as Japan, what little heed most members of Congress paid to international issues receded to the point that the Senate mustered more consensus on, say, legislation mandating special educational services for preschoolers than on a resolution to resist Iraq's invasion of the Persian Gulf.[30]

Republican legislators and presidents in the 1980s and 1990s paid lip service to local control, but as box 4-1 indicates, much "coercive federalism" transpired on their watch. Important initiatives had full bipartisan backing. It was with the Bush administration's firm support, for instance, that Congress contemplated the extraordinarily prescriptive Americans with Disabilities Act in 1990. Four years earlier just one lonely voice in the Reagan administration had dissented from the aforementioned preschool special education mandate. (Education Secretary William Bennett protested that it portended "serious encroachment" on local authority).[31] In general, judging from roll calls in the 98th through the 101st Congresses, Republicans, like Democrats, voted more often in favor of, than against, new mandates on local governments.[32]

On plenty of occasions the GOP did more than go along; it took the lead role. For Republicans, measures overriding local policies in crime prevention, welfare administration, "family values," and the regulation of business were favorites. So, through the 1990s, the same lawmakers that professed faith in decentralization scarcely hesitated to preempt, among other local determinations, the enforcement of child support laws, the eligibility standards of legal aliens for public assistance, and so many duties of local law enforcement that by 1998 Chief Justice William Rehnquist expressed grave doubts. "The pressure in Congress to appear responsive to every highly publicized societal ill or sensational crime," he wrote, needs to be weighed against "whether we want most of our legal relationships decided at the national rather than local level."[33]

As for business regulation, preemptive initiatives extended beyond sensible efforts to proscribe the most egregiously anticompetitive practices of some states and localities (their decisions to harbor trade sanctions, for example, or to countenance boundless tort litigation, or to cling to anachronistic banking regulations). One might think that how a community chooses to enforce its zoning ordinance falls squarely within the customary orbit of local administration. Not so, according to the House Republicans who passed a bill giving real estate developers additional recourse to litigate those decisions in federal court.[34]

Box 4-1. *Major New Enactments Regulating State and Local Government, 1981–91*

**1982**
*Surface Transportation Assistance Act.* Preempted local regulations of size and weight requirements for trucks on interstate highways.
*Voting Rights Act Amendments.* Extended and expanded coverage of 1965 Voting Rights Act to disabled voters and those needing language assistance.

**1983**
*Social Security Amendments.* Prohibited local withdrawal from Social Security coverage for local government employees; accelerated increases in payroll taxes paid by local governments.

**1984**
*Child Abuse Amendments.* Authorized "Baby Doe" regulations protecting handicapped newborns and requiring local governments to curb medical neglect.
*Hazardous and Solid Waste Amendments.* Strengthened scope and enforcement of the Resource Conservation and Recovery Act of 1968; partially preempted regulation of underground storage tanks in localities; and required EPA inspections of locally operated hazardous waste sites.
*Highway Safety Act Amendments.* Established uniform national drinking age of twenty-one.
*Voting Accessibility for the Elderly and Handicapped Act.* Mandated that local polling places be made accessible to the elderly and handicapped.
*Cable Deregulation Act.* Partially preempted local renewal standards and rate regulations.
*Math and Science Education Act.* Included a provision that required local schools to permit student religious groups to meet on premises before and after classes.
*Child Support Enforcement Act.* Mandated local enforcement of withholding of delinquent child support payments.

**1985**
*Consolidated Omnibus Budget Reconciliation Act.* Extended Medicare hospital insurance payroll taxes and coverage to all new local government employees.

**1986**
*Age Discrimination in Employment Act Amendments.* Outlawed mandatory retirement at age 70, with delay in coverage for police and firefighters.
*Asbestos Hazard Emergency Response Act.* Directs local schools to inspect and abate asbestos hazards.
*Commercial Motor Vehicle Safety Act.* Directs local governments to administer national license and testing standards for commercial and school bus drivers.
*Education of the Handicapped Amendments.* Expanded coverage and services for preschool children.
*Safe Drinking Water Amendments.* Mandated new national drinking water standards and new monitoring requirements for local public water systems.
*Water Resources Development Act.* Required local cost sharing for federal water resources projects.
*Emergency Planning and Community Right-to-Know Act.* Promulgated new national hazardous waste cleanup standards and timetables; required local notification of potential hazards.
*Handicapped Children's Protection Act.* Allowed recovery of attorneys' fees for both administrative and court proceedings for parents challenging school programs.

*Immigration Reform and Control Act.* Imposed service mandates on local public sector by granting legal status to certain illegal aliens.

## 1987
*Civil Rights Restoration Act.* Expanded institutional coverage of laws prohibiting racial, gender, handicapped, and age discrimination by local recipients of federal aid.
*Nursing Home Regulation.* Required local enforcement of federal quality and safety standards.
*Water Quality Act.* Required local control of non–point pollution; promulgated new requirements for permitting municipal storm sewers; authorized EPA to issue regulations for sewage sludge.

## 1988
*Ocean Dumping Ban Act.* Outlawed sea dumping of municipal sludge.
*Lead Contamination Control Act.* Required local school districts to replace lead-lined water coolers.
*Fair Housing Act Amendments.* Extends 1968 Civil Rights Act to cover handicapped and children.
*Drug-Free Workplace Act.* Requires all federal aid recipients to certify that their workplaces are drug-free.
*Family Support Act.* Required provision of jobs, child care, transitional Medicaid, and AFDC to unemployed parents; mandated workfare requirements and new child support enforcement.
*Medicare Catastrophic Coverage Act.* Mandated additional Medicaid coverage for poor elderly, new categories of children, pregnant mothers, and persons in nursing homes. (The law was repealed, but the FY 1989 Budget Reconciliation Act secured the added coverage for pregnant women and children to age six.)

## 1990
*Americans with Disabilities Act.* Established comprehensive national standards to prohibit discrimination in public services and accommodations to promote handicapped access to public buildings and transportation.
*Education of Handicapped Act Amendments.* Eliminated local sovereign immunity from parental suits seeking tuition reimbursements.
*Older Workers Benefit Protection Act.* Broadened Age Discrimination in Employment Act's prohibitions against discrimination in employee benefit plans.
*Clean Air Act Amendments.* Imposed new deadlines and requirements to control urban smog, acid rain, municipal incinerators, and local toxic emissions.
*Cash Management Improvement Act.* Created new procedures for managing the disbursement of federal aid, resulting in an overall reduction of interest earned on federal funds at local level.

## 1991
*FY 1991 Budget Reconciliation Act.* Extended Social Security coverage to all local employees not otherwise covered by public employee pension systems and mandated Medicaid benefits to all poor children between the ages of six and eighteen.

Sources: Adapted from U.S. Advisory Commission on Intergovernmental Relations, *Federal Regulation of State and Local Government: The Mixed Record of the 1980s* (Washington, July 1993), pp. 44–45; Timothy J. Conlan and David R. Bean, "Federal Mandates: The Record of Reform and Future Prospects," *Intergovernmental Perspective*, vol. 18 (Fall 1992), p. 8; Paul I. Posner, *The Politics of Unfunded Mandates: Whither Federalism?* (Georgetown University Press, 1998), pp. 233–37; and *Congressional Quarterly Almanac, 1989* (Congressional Quarterly, Inc., 1990), pp. 100, 171–75.

## The Delocalization of Domestic Politics

At least with regard to the overruling of local commercial controls, the main impetus has not been especially novel. Federal intervention has been urged by powerful corporate lobbies that normally prefer relatively uniform standards to a hodgepodge of local rules. In any event such corporations exert influence, particularly on the Republican regulatory agenda.[35] For the other kinds of national preemptions, however, the story is more involved.

In recent decades controversies of every kind have moved to the federal level because, simply put, Thomas P. O'Neill's aphorism ("all politics is local") is out of date. To a degree, increased integration of the national economy and interregional mobility of the population may have homogenized the country's expectations about appropriate public standards and services, encouraging the greater uniformity that only a central government can secure.[36] In addition, as links to local party organizations have weakened, the allegiances of senators and representatives have not remained confined to the concerns of their districts or states but frequently embrace the causes promoted by *national* issue advocates. These assertive actors have proved as capable as the traditional labor and industry associations of forging ties with key congressional committees and now successfully amplify what Jeffrey Berry has called "postmaterial" issues.[37] Whatever the challenges facing given communities—wetlands conservation, teenage smoking, school violence, carjackings, sex-abstinence education, "drunk driving"—lobbies in Washington exist to amplify the topic and make it the nation's business to address.

The amplification resonates in Congress thanks to the pattern of congressional campaign finance. Candidates, particularly for House seats, once depended primarily on the backing of local contributors and the local party hierarchy. Now the soaring cost of campaigns compels office seekers to rely more heavily on external sources. The winners of recent House elections have drawn upward of 40 percent of their contributions from political action committees—that is, the funding arms not only of unions and corporate donors but also of a lot of other well-financed interests with a national presence.[38] For many of these groups the laying on of federal hands is the solution to almost any problem.

The news media have contributed to this mind-set, heightening the profile of misfortunes in particular communities and depicting them as "trends" that seemingly afflict the country from coast to coast. Members of Congress do not want to seem uncaring about the latest reported tragedy, whether it happens to be a pervasive woe or not. Their response: enact a law. This was how, for example, the Anti-Car Theft Act, "Megan's law," and various other federal instructions to local law enforcement agencies sailed through, even as the war on crime in most municipalities and states was already being won by their own police and correctional institutions.[39] It was also how pressure mounted for a national blood-alcohol standard for motorists, even while alcohol-related accidents were nearing a low.[40] And it was how certain U.S. environmental prohibitions were rushed into law: the nationwide ban on ocean dumping of sludge, for example, followed the highly publicized appearance of trash slicks along the coastline of New York and New Jersey during the summer of 1988, even though the garbage that had washed onto the beaches that year had spilled from antiquated local sewers, not from dumping waste at sea.[41]

Finally, the public is now so accustomed to having local troubles gain national attention that partisans of the Right as well as the Left seem equally unconstrained in their urge to administer a federal remedy if core constituencies fancy it. Republicans started out in 1994 with a pledge to consolidate 350 rule-bound categorical grant programs into nine loose block grants. The idea, presumably, was to let local office holders attend to more of their own priorities. But the GOP-controlled 104th Congress then managed to enact only two such consolidations, covering fewer than twenty programs.[42] And for issues on which its base was vocal, even the block grants the GOP had contemplated tended to add, rather than subtract, instructions for local governments.

Consider the welfare reform package of 1996, which was heralded as a triumph of devolutionary block granting (on the whole, rightly). Although the new national legislation allowed states to experiment with various workfare plans, it also placed on them new restrictions. The House of Representatives insisted on a five-year cutoff of payments to any particular family, on denying support to women who bear children while on welfare, and on prohibiting cash assistance to unmarried parents under the age of eighteen. National prescriptions of such force and specificity may have seemed somewhat inconsonant with a program that subnational governments were meant to run according to their own tastes. But by the mid-1990s compunctions about selectively patronizing the states did not consistently restrain either political party. When the Republicans finally wrested control of Congress in 1995, they savored the chance to stamp their own partisan preferences onto some locally admin-istered programs, though for different purposes than those pursued by the Democrats.[43]

Crime legislation exhibited much the same pattern. As if the 1994 fed-eral anticrime bill (which swept dozens of new felonies into the grip of the federal penal code) had not gone far enough, House Republicans in 1995 strove to condition grants for local correctional and law enforcement functions on tougher sentencing requirements.[44] Many Democrats denounced this infringement on the independence of local courts. "We federalize everything that walks, talks, and moves," complained Senator Joseph Biden of Delaware.[45] But when the conversation turned to domes-tic violence, church burnings, or hate crimes the Democrats' reservations about "federalizing everything" seemed to vanish quickly.

## The Courts in Charge

As earlier chapters of this book repeatedly describe, court cases have become a prime instrument for attaching federal stipulations to the details of local administration. Indeed much, if not most, of the controversy over national mandates in the United States during the past forty years has centered on the bold orders of federal judges, which instruct local office holders on how to manage their schools, sanitation systems, prisons, fire departments, police forces, and so forth. This judicialization is another important force centralizing American intergovernmental affairs in mod-ern times.

### *Part and Parcel of the Political Culture*

Up to a point the judiciary's high profile in the American federal system is not surprising. For centuries foreign observers have marveled at the frequency with which Americans turn to the courts to rectify almost any imaginable injury or inequity. "There is hardly a political question in the United States which does not sooner or later turn into a judicial one," wrote Alexis de Tocqueville in 1835.[46] In the year the Constitution was written, J. Hector St. John Crevecoeur mused in his *Letters from an American Farmer* about how "our laws and the spirit of freedom . . . often tends to make us litigious."[47]

Whether a true "spirit of freedom" really requires incessant visits to the courthouse may be debatable. But that federalism, which divides power among governments, needs an arbiter is not debatable at all. The judicial branch has traditionally performed this service—all the more so because the Constitution delimits the powers of government in language that invites judicial interpretation: what concretely is meant by the injunctions against depriving any person of "liberty" without "due process" and against denying any person "equal protection of the laws"? And since these admonitions, however interpreted, were mainly intended to prevent abuses of power by the states, it is no wonder that judicial review has focused far less frequently on acts of Congress than on the laws or ordinances of the states and localities. As Martha Derthick explains, were it not for the existence of federalism, there would not be a Fourteenth Amendment. And without the Fourteenth Amendment's elastic terminology, the courts would have far less room to roam.[48]

Political traditions and constitutional design, however, cannot wholly explain the sheer extent of recent judicial involvement in the primary functions of local government. The judiciary, after all, did not begin fully engaging the potential of the Constitution's strongest mechanisms, including the Fourteenth Amendment and various other long-standing laws, until the latter third of the twentieth century.

## The Rights Revolution

Commencing in the 1960s, a basic legal transformation got under way: an expanding variety of social expectations sought, and increasingly attained, the status of rights that would be guaranteed by courts of law. New interest groups, emulating the civil rights movement, framed their grievances as pleas for constitutional justice. After African Americans had blazed a trail, additional minorities, women, the elderly, the disabled, and others joined the travelers.[49] Soon, to borrow Philip K. Howard's description, "Congress began handing out rights like land grants."[50]

The epic Civil Rights Act of 1964 marked the onset of this process. The Supreme Court's 1954 decisions in *Brown* v. *Board of Education* had called on the southern school districts to desegregate. Congress in 1964 forced them to do it. The Department of Justice was now authorized to sue to integrate public facilities of all kinds, and Title VI of the act barred federal aid to schools or any other grant recipients that practiced discrimination.[51] For all its breadth (for example, banning employment practices that discriminated on the basis not only of skin color but also religion, sex, and national origin), however, the original motivation of the 1964 Civil Rights Act was to redress a particular injustice: namely, centuries of state-sponsored enslavement of blacks, followed by a century of regional apartheid. That the success of this legislation would inspire many other kinds of pleaders to seek analogous legal status as repressed minorities meriting similar remedies was probably not foreseen. And in any case the act itself had accorded some immunities to the states and local governments: the proscription against discrimination in employment, for example, applied only to the private sector.

In the 1970s and at periodic intervals thereafter Congress added new layers to the foundation established by the 1964 law. In 1972, for example, prohibitions against job discrimination were extended to public employers at the state and local levels. In 1973 a bill was enacted that, in effect, deployed sanctions like those of the Civil Rights Act to protect individuals with handicaps. In 1974 older workers were added to the categories of persons protected from prejudice in the workplace, private or public. A year later handicapped children acquired protection from exclusionary treatment in public schools. During the 1980s and early 1990s legislation made sure that entire local governments, not just wayward units or programs therein, would be subject to sanctions if discriminatory behavior was detected in any program or unit. Legislation also made sure that even unintentional forms of bias (disparate impact) could be actionable. And, with passage of the Americans with Disabilities Act, the legislators ushered in many additional restitutions that persons with physical and mental impairments could claim as a matter of right.[52]

Inevitably federal dockets bulged as the courts began adjudicating charges from more plaintiffs that their newly minted rights had been abridged. In short order scores of cities were entangled in federal cases realigning the racial composition in schools, bettering prisons, providing special accommodations for disabled individuals, eliminating gender biases in police and fire departments, fashioning appropriate education for students with learning disabilities, increasing the numbers of indigents eligible for welfare payments, tenuring aging public employees (or impelling their employers to buy out retirements), securing freedoms from various environmental threats, and more.

### Judicial Activism

The courts did not bring all of this deluge of litigation upon themselves. As Supreme Court Chief Justice Warren E. Burger reflected in 1982, "Remedies for personal wrongs that once were considered the responsibility of institutions other than the courts are now boldly asserted as 'entitlements.'"[53] For this expansion of entitlements, acts of Congress were

instrumental; they supplied the statutory basis and much procedural facil-
itation. Frequently mistrustful of state and local agencies, and of federal
ones, too, Congress increasingly empowered citizens to sue government
to ensure its accountability. The ease with which complainants, including
those citizens challenging public agencies, could have their day in court
had long been a distinguishing feature of the U.S. legal system. By the
1980s it was hard to think of a major U.S. environmental law, consumer
protection measure, or antidiscrimination statute that did not extend this
opportunity.[54] Extensive standing to sue, combined with other time-
honored attributes of American law—ample fee-shifting and class-action
possibilities, for instance—kept the courts busy.[55] And more than ever
private parties would be taking state and city governments there for
alleged noncompliance with national regulations and suing the national
regulators if they appeared to cut state and city officials too much slack.[56]

Congress also activated the courts in another fundamental way: pivotal components of the laws it passed were vaguely worded—presenting
an open invitation for judges to, in effect, legislate from the bench.[57] The
civil rights laws, for example, outlawed discrimination "by reason of"
traits like race, color, religion, and national origin, but the laws did not
spell out how to ascertain whether discrimination had occurred, much
less what to do about it if the "reason" was not so simple. Thus the courts
would have to determine what, if any, "affirmative" remedial steps might
be "appropriate" in, say, the case of an underqualified job applicant who
claimed that his chances had been "adversely affected" because of his
ethnicity or origins. The judiciary also would be left to figure out at which
point disparate percentages of racial groups in a city's schools, for
instance, begot adverse impacts and what kinds of "relief" would presumably turn the adverse effects into propitious ones.

The urban busing decrees of the 1960s and 1970s were the consum-
mate products of this sweeping delegation to the federal courts. In dozens
of metropolitan areas judges were called on to do the work of legislators
and administrators. As Archibald Cox observed in 1975, the judicially
formulated desegregation plans took on "all the qualities of social legislation: they pertain to the future; they are mandatory; they govern millions of people; they reorder people's lives in ways that benefit some and
disappoint others in order to achieve social objectives."[58]

The judiciary was summoned to perform elaborate duties. Not infrequently, though, it also chose to engage in a good deal of what Judge
Learned Hand had once delicately termed "imaginative discovery" of

legislative intent.[59] An early rendition came in 1961, when the Supreme Court decided *Monroe* v. *Pape.* The case dusted off an act of Congress in 1871 that had entitled persons who believed they had been deprived of U.S. constitutional or statutory protections by anyone acting "under color of" a local ordinance or regulation to avail themselves of judicial remedies. From its inception this Reconstruction-era law (section 1983 of Title 42 of the U.S. Code) had been invoked infrequently. After *Monroe,* things changed.[60]

In *Monroe* the court held that victims of constitutional violations could recover damages in federal court directly, that is, without first exhausting all avenues of redress at the state level. More important, section 1983 would apply even when there had been no showing that the alleged constitutional violations had been authorized or encouraged by a state or local policy.[61] The impact of this now robust front-line remedy was unmistakable. In the year 1986 more than 40,000 civil rights suits went before federal courts, chiefly under section 1983. In 1961 such cases had numbered a few hundred.[62]

Federal judges pushed the envelope even more aggressively on fronts such as the transportation of students to integrate schools. In *Swann* v. *Charlotte-Mecklenburg Board of Education* a unanimous Supreme Court approved, in addition to an extensive busing operation, a system of attendance zones based on what Chief Justice Burger described as "frank—and sometimes drastic—gerrymandering." Never mind if some solutions for segregation might seem "awkward, inconvenient and even bizarre." In crafting "remedial adjustments" to eliminate "dual school systems," the court continued, a degree of "awkwardness and inconvenience" was unavoidable.[63]

Judicial rulings also set in motion political dynamics that eventually produced comprehensive legislated mandates. In 1972 a federal judge decided that the state of Pennsylvania had to provide free public education and training appropriate for mentally retarded children.[64] The following year a federal court ruled that all handicapped children in the District of Columbia were constitutionally entitled to such services, even if the city lacked money to pay for them.[65] By 1974 thirty-six similar lawsuits were pending or had been resolved in two dozen states, prompting many states to enact special education programs.

As the issue migrated from state to state and into the national consciousness—and as the expense of local programs began to increase—state education departments and local school boards looked to the federal government for assistance. The Education for All Handicapped Children Act of 1975 cleared Congress on votes of 404 to 7 in the House, 87 to 7 in the Senate. This overwhelming support was ensured in no small part by a strong endorsement from state and local officials who were promised federal money to pay for an entitlement that the courts had effectively created. What the state and local enthusiasts did not anticipate was that the authorized funding would never materialize—while the costs and legal complications of special education, now mandated nationwide, would only multiply.

## The Long and Winding Road to Restraint

Reflecting the judicial appointments of Republican presidents governing during twenty of the twenty-four years between 1969 and 1993, the Supreme Court and gradually the lower courts turned somewhat less expansive in the antidiscrimination arena. Signs of a shift could be discerned by the late 1970s, when the Supreme Court first began setting more limits on some of the remedies that had become commonplace in civil rights litigation. In 1978 the court narrowly sustained a claim that an explicit racial quota in state university admissions constituted reverse discrimination.[66] In cases decided in 1984 and 1986 a majority twice ruled that when municipalities laid off personnel, the seniority privileges of workers could not be overlooked to protect the jobs of minorities hired under affirmative action plans.[67] And in the 1989 case of *Wards Cove Packing Co.* v. *Atonio* five of the nine justices decided to place a greater burden of proof on plaintiffs who charged employers with racial discrimination: merely citing statistical underrepresentation in the work force, rather than an unambiguous intention to discriminate, would no longer suffice.[68]

To characterize these adjustments as a full about-face that shredded precedents and restored the status quo ante, however, would be an exaggeration. For one thing, the high court often seemed to tack between judgments that narrowed the scope of rights-based mandates and judgments that reaffirmed or even expanded these mandates. Two years after the court had questioned racial quotas in *Bakke,* for instance, they were upheld for set-asides in federally funded public works projects.[69] In a series of decisions between 1986 and 1987 the same court accepted minority quotas for union admissions, promotions in public employment, and other instances in which past discrimination was said to be in need of remediation.[70] Three years earlier the court had accepted federal limitations on local mandatory retirement policies for public safety officers.[71]

Further, Congress repeatedly stepped in to reinstate forceful judicial doctrines when the courts seemed to retreat from them. For example, the 1991 Civil Rights Act repudiated the *Wards Cove* test for discrimination and, in effect, resurrected the easier disparate-impact standard that the Supreme Court had introduced almost twenty years earlier.[72] Meanwhile, as we have seen, many district courts were kept busy supervising, and often elaborating, early consent decrees that persisted year after year.

It was not until fairly late in the 1990s that some of these remnants were allowed to wind down (judicially mandated plans for racial allocations in schools, for instance). By then the Supreme Court had chipped away again at some of their legal fundaments. The liberal use of racial classification schemes in government programs was challenged, especially when the schemes were not sufficiently "tailored" to further "a compelling governmental interest."[73] Later, in *Alexander* v. *Sandoval,* a 5-4 majority ruled that citizen suits triggering sanctions under Title VI of the Civil Rights Act would have to prove discriminatory intent, not just disparate results, on the part of a state or local agency.[74] And a Republican-controlled Congress generally signaled that, albeit selectively, judicial restraint was long overdue and now might even be reinforced legislatively.

The judiciary, at least in some disputes during the 1990s, edged back toward a narrower interpretation of federal authority over state and local governments. For example, the Supreme Court now found violations of the Tenth Amendment in cases in which local authorities had been commandeered to carry out federal laws for the disposal of radioactive waste and for the conduct of background checks on buyers of firearms. The court also rehabilitated the sovereign immunity of the states, arguing that the Eleventh Amendment shielded them from certain classes of federal suits arising under particular national labor and disabilities laws. And the court held that Congress had stretched the commerce clause with laws that essentially preempted state and local jurisdiction over guns in school zones and crimes "motivated by gender."[75]

Consequently, commentators sometimes feared that the pendulum of judicial opinions on intergovernmental relations was swinging back to where it had been three-quarters of a century ago. The reality is different. With most of its federalism cases decided by bare 5-4 majorities, considerable question remains about how many of the recent decisions will stand the test of time. Recall that in *National League of Cities* v. *Usery* a similarly split court had cited the Tenth Amendment to prevent the Fair Labor Standards Act from covering state and local employers—but then reversed its position in *Garcia* v. *San Antonio Metropolitan Transit Authority.*[76]

In any event plenty of verdicts have overridden local interests or concerns. In *City of Chicago* v. *Morales* a majority on the Rehnquist court struck down a municipal antiloitering ordinance that was aimed at preventing gang members from taking over neighborhood streets.[77] In *Davis* v. *Monroe County School Board* the court agreed that local schools could be subject to federal liability when one student harassed another—thereby prompting Justice Anthony M. Kennedy to write in dissent, "We can be assured that like suits will follow—suits, which in cost and number, will impose serious financial burdens on local school districts, the taxpayers who support them and the children they serve." In *Whitman* v. *American Trucking Association* the court unanimously upheld the EPA's charge to set higher standards for urban ozone and soot concentrations without considering local costs of implementation. While the court's reinstatement of these environmental regulations was never labeled, strictly speaking, a "federalism" case, its implications for cities—not only for their air sheds but their tax bases and budgets—were probably more momentous than any other of the decade's major judicial determinations.[78]

Finally, the high court is not the only locomotive in the judicial system. At the level of the lower courts new targets of federal litigation emerged, some with especially important consequences for what cities could or could not do to rebuild their economies. So-called environmental justice cases have loomed as one such potential source of new contention. When the state of New Jersey issued a permit to open a cement plant in a poor neighborhood of the perennially distressed city of Camden, a federal judge enjoined the project on grounds of a "prima facie case of disparate impact on race and national origin in violation of the E.P.A.'s regulations"—even though the plant was said to have satisfied air quality criteria.[79] Legal experts said this was the first time a state environmental permitting agency had been found in violation of civil rights law. (Whether it would be the last was hard to say. The appellate court for the Third Circuit recently reversed the Camden case. And at least for cases deploying Title VI, the Supreme Court has recently constricted the standing of private plaintiffs to sue state agencies for unintentional discriminatory impacts.)[80]

## Mandates without Money

As more federal policies enshrined rights and hence mobilized the courts, more of the federal government's stewardship naturally moved off-budget. If, for example, a public decision about the economic development of a depressed urban neighborhood turns not on how to underwrite investment there but on whether a given investment violates somebody's civil rights, juridical considerations eclipse financial ones. And if, say, a federal tribunal decides that citizens are owed municipal facilities that must operate virtually free of health risks (as the Supreme Court in essence ruled in 1994 with regard to city incinerators), the result is not an elective "program" to be aided; rather, it is a binding legal obligation that carries little or no federal budgetary responsibility. Federal authorities may police local compliance with the mandate, much as they enforce other constitutional rights, but these authorities do not ordinarily appropriate funds and distribute grants for that purpose.

Washington's unfunded demands on cities and states also increased in the late twentieth century as the national government's debt grew and Congress's capacity to sponsor direct action encountered budget constraints. "When its ability to make grants declined," observed Alice Rivlin in 1992, "the federal government turned increasingly to mandates as a means of controlling state and local activity without having to pay the bill."[81] Later in the decade, when the economy began expanding briskly in almost all regions of the country, federal office holders gained an additional excuse to allot less money to their mandates: locally raised revenues were on the rise. Some policymakers at the national level had long regarded as intergovernmental "subsidies" the deduction of local property taxes from the federal income tax and the exclusion of interest income earned from various forms of state and local debt. With many states and not a few municipalities now running surpluses in the context of a reasonably concerted effort to balance the federal budget, there was a case to be made for greater devolution of costs.

But a good deal of national mandating also became plainly opportunistic: it enabled politicians in Washington to claim credit by doing good—cleaning up the environment, protecting victims of bias, educating individuals with learning disabilities, increasing the mobility of persons with handicaps, and so forth—without incurring, in Princeton professor R. Douglas Arnold's term, "traceable" blame for the local tax increases that followed.[82] If more members of Congress were playing this card, part of the reason was that the objections of local officials seemed to be carrying less weight in the halls of the Capitol. As ties to local party organizations eroded, the allegiances of representatives moved increasingly beyond parochial realms to the agendas of national lobbies and pressure groups, many of which care, or know, little about the practicalities on the ground for local governments.

Thus members of the House of Representatives, who used to be especially sensitive to the concerns of mayors, county executives, and other local notables in their districts, now behaved more like senators or presidential candidates, pitching appeals to wider audiences, including Washington-based advocacy groups. During the run-up to the nationwide asbestos-removal requirement for schools, local administrators worried audibly about its looming costs. But Democratic representatives who led the charge for this mandate were undeterred. And Republican opposition never coalesced. Indeed the House Republicans enlisted in the asbestos campaign, incanting, "Everyone wants to do the same thing. We want to help children."[83] Despite misgivings at the local level, the House passed the asbestos bill unanimously.

The ability to mandate from above with such apparent ease, moreover, became all the greater because local misgivings were often feebly or belatedly expressed. Great expectations arise about the immediate benefits of many environmental statutes, for instance, but awareness of their costs frequently lags behind. Regulations based on the statutes take time to develop; their bottom line may not become visible for years. The Safe Drinking Water Act Amendments of 1996 passed with considerable state and local support. Only after the EPA's rulemakings emerged several years later, requiring specific (and enormous) local expenditures, did the law become a controversial intergovernmental issue.

## Summary

Whatever the future holds for American federalism after the seismic shock of September 11, there is little question that the politics of this country became increasingly centripetal through the better part of the twentieth century. Municipal governments saw a growing body of federal regulation head their way. Possibly, as this book's last chapter notes, the rising volume of what I broadly call federal mandates finally peaked a decade ago and has since leveled off. And certain acts of Congress in the 1990s (most notably the 1996 welfare reform law) were, on balance, bold devolutionary moves. Nevertheless, even if some recent signs may point to movement against the grain, a contemporary observer of local civic life in the United States cannot but remain awed by the concentration of regulatory powers over "the daily things" that, in Martin Diamond's phrase, "make up the vast bulk of a government's business"—and that used to be almost exclusively the business of states and localities.[84]

The accretion of central influence that commenced with the New Deal paused during various interludes thereafter but then resumed. The general trajectory at present remains much the same. Some periods—the 1960s and the 1970s—brought an exceptionally large quantity of new federal initiatives, mostly in the form of categorical grant programs. Distinctive attributes of this intergovernmental aid—its prescribed use for special purposes, extensive compliance rules, organized clients, and often failure to square actual appropriations with promised authorizations—effectively placed new regulatory constraints on municipal and state governments, including some constraints that came to be called "unfunded" mandates. These grew especially common during the decade of the 1980s with its persistent federal deficit. Though presently in greater check, their frequency eventually might increase (especially as federal budgets post-September 11 will again be spilling red ink in great quantities).

Republican presidents—Nixon, Reagan, the senior Bush—typically entered office pledging to relax regulations and restore greater local control. But at the end of the day, the devolutionary efforts fell far short of expectations. Why? Some realms of federal activism—environmental policy and employment law, for example—developed a centralizing tendency because they featured real or perceived issues of multijurisdictional coordination and strong lobbies invoking, with great fervor, nationwide standards of equity. Divided government also fueled mistrust between the legislative and executive branches, sometimes moving Congress to stiffen standards and ensure national compliance (as in the case of anti-pollution laws).

More generally, as the cold war faded, domestic issues of a parochial sort gained new prominence. Public opinion polls, interest group agendas, campaign finances, and news media coverage converged to support the trend. Republican lawmakers, no less than Democratic ones, frequently abandoned any principled restraint on political temptations to, in essence, insinuate the federal government into the management of local services, even if such federalization could often seem ill fitted to, as Abraham Lincoln might have said, "the majesty of the nation."[85]

Well before the Berlin Wall came down, the day-to-day work of cities and other local governments in the United States had drawn national scrutiny for another reason: a rising tide of federal laws and legal actions affirmed the existence of universalistic rights in pursuit of various public purposes. The rights revolution put the federal courts, long the central arbiters in the American federation, in the position of revising a wide range of municipal administrative practices. The national judiciary's uniquely active role has shifted appreciably in recent years but has not reconfigured the overall balance of power in today's intergovernmental relations.

# 5 | *Comparative Politics*

The picture of central authorities meddling in the administration of municipalities might seem more descriptive of the politics of foreign countries than of the United States. Certainly European welfare states, a number of which already had put down firm foundations in the nineteenth century, grew more imposing amid the worst crises of the twentieth—the Great Depression and the two world wars.[1] In his 1944 state of the union message Franklin D. Roosevelt had urged a "second Bill of Rights" that would have entitled citizens in every community to a decent home, adequate medical care, recreational facilities, and so forth.[2] Many European countries, digging out of the economic wreckage of the Second World War, etched such particulars into their constitutions or related statutes.

The postwar cities of Germany were required by law to administer everything from public assistance (*Sozialhilfe*) and special facilities for the aged, to housing, hospitals, and youth services.[3] In Italy national codes delineated the responsibilities of municipal government in the minutest detail—to ensure, for example, that inhabitants would receive a supply of properly processed milk.[4] In France so thorough were central checks on local land use decisions that theoretically a city "had to obtain the permission of Paris even to change a street name, cut down a tree or erect a public monument."[5]

Throughout Europe, as in the United States, the 1960s and 1970s launched waves of national programs that descended on local jurisdictions. By 1976 the federal government in Germany had passed hundreds of new laws guiding that country's state and local governments, to the point that, according to one observer, "There are hardly any functions left that the municipalities and counties can actually administer and develop on their own on the basis of their discretionary powers."[6] More than a few of the instructions dealt with antipollution requirements, for in Germany, and then elsewhere in Europe, green activism soon caught up with, and by some measures surpassed, the environmental agitation in America.[7]

More recently the European Union (EU) has become a prodigious source of regulatory initiatives most of which are broadly designed to dislodge impediments to a unified European market. Some of them also have impinged on local customs and preferences at a level seemingly so petty a critic might regard the "low politics" of the EU as second to none.[8] (One wonders what Charles de Gaulle, who originally coined the low politics phrase, would have thought of European institutions telling local authorities how to certify sausages, cheeses, or "bathing waters," for example). Why has the EU become a spirited regulator? Part of the answer has parallels with a simple explanation for the rise of insufficiently funded mandates in the United States: fiscal constraints.[9] Limited in its ability to tax and therefore to spend, Brussels (like Washington during the years budget caps were binding) fashions off-budget devices to work its will.[10]

Still, examined a little more closely, distinctions loom larger than the similarities in how municipalities have fared within the U.S. government's regulatory environment compared with that of other regimes.

## Fiscal Arrangements

To begin with, most of western Europe's political systems continue to make demands of local governments but also, for better or worse, to put more money into their hands. A time may come when this pattern will cease. (The impact of the EU's growing body of rules on intergovernmental finances is a work in progress.) But for now the prospect of city governments desperately scrambling for resources to cover mandated expenses—as has occurred in some of America's less auspicious urban places—remains generally remote.[11]

## Ways of Spreading the Wealth

The forms of compensation are varied. Intergovernmental grants in Germany, Britain, France, and Holland supplement locally raised revenues on a vast scale.[12] In some other parts of western Europe, notably Scandinavia, localities are required to spend their revenues on a long list of social services, but unlike the taxing and borrowing powers of U.S. cities, which tend to be tightly circumscribed by state law, Swedish and Danish municipalities traditionally have had far greater tax diversification.[13] Moreover, when locally sourced funds seem not to suffice, central assistance typically increases to fill the gap. In the late 1990s Sweden and Norway mandated waiting-time guarantees for patients entering local hospitals. The legal guarantees were backed up with large-scale grants.[14]

In much of Europe, furthermore, some of the most expensive items in local administration—teachers' salaries, for instance—are funded directly by national treasuries, thereby enabling local budgets to cover other costs more comfortably. In 1997 the local portion of overall expenditures on education (primary, secondary, and postsecondary) in the United States was more than twice as large as the shares borne by local governments in France, Italy, and Germany, and six to eight times the local share in the Netherlands and Spain.[15]

Not only are U.S. state and local governments more dependent on own-source revenues than are the subnational jurisdictions in most of Europe (Scandinavian countries being the exception), what federal funds do make their way to local governments tend to be in the form of categorical aid—that is, monies designated for certain purposes and hedged about with many qualifications and conditions. (Box 5-1 lists the breathtaking variety of specialized grants that trickled into one American city, Philadelphia, during a three-year period.) Less restrictive block grants that localities could use for broader assortments of activities exist, but as we have seen, efforts to reorganize federal intergovernmental aid from a welter of conditioned grants to a simplified block approach have repeatedly fallen short.[16] And the simplest type of transfer—namely, unfettered redistribution of tax revenues from the national to the local level—was briefly tried but abandoned in the United States: adopted in 1972, the State and Local Fiscal Assistance Act, also known as general revenue sharing, ended in 1986.[17]

Abroad, extensive sharing of revenue is common.[18] More than half of Germany's intergovernmental aid is in this mode. In Britain nearly two-thirds is, and in France, much more than that. Even in Canada, where fiscal federalism is somewhat more comparable to the American model, a so-called Fiscal Equalization Program automatically refunds a quotient of federal revenues to the provinces. The same holds for Australia.

## Micromanaging the Money

Why, when compared with other industrial nations, has intergovernmental cash flowed so differently in the United States? A system of selective grants, in contrast to permissive block grants and generalized revenue sharing, reflects the configuration of incentives in American political institutions. Such a system lends itself to the style of candidate-centered financing of elections for the national legislature and to the highly entrepreneurial role of its members.[19] In the United States to secure contributions and wage effective campaigns, each office seeker must maximize opportunities to cultivate particular political clients—by mining the rich lodes of high-income zip codes, appealing to contributors in business or labor, and as noted earlier, bonding with potential backers among professional advocacy groups. And members of the U.S. Congress are especially well situated to determine who gets what. No other democracy has developed a legislative committee structure that positions so many independent legislators in potentially pivotal command posts, and no other political system grants them a greater grip on the purse strings and policies of patron agencies in the executive bureaucracy.[20]

The party-centered parliamentary systems and electoral-financing arrangements of the German, British, or Canadian governments do not afford the same possibilities, nor the motivation, for lawmakers to tweak the targets and formulas of grants in the fashion of the American Congress. While many entrepreneurs on Capitol Hill can plausibly say to specific supplicants "From me to you" (or occasionally "Sorry, not this time"), backbenchers in Ottawa, Westminster, or Berlin are seldom in a position to exert comparable influence in crafting categories of spoils for selected constituencies. Besides, the constitutions of Germany, Canada, and various other democracies stipulate a national responsibility to level disparities in "living conditions" among communities, or at least to support among them "reasonably comparable levels of services"—in other words, to redistribute liberally large blocks of national revenues.[21]

Box 5-1. *Federal Grants-in-Aid to the City of Philadelphia, 1992–95*

| | | | |
|---|---|---|---|
| ATF | Training Assistance | DOL | Job Training Partnership Act |
| CNCS | Foster Grandparents Program | DOL | Senior Community Service Employment Program |
| DOA | Emergency Food Assistance | DOT | Airport Improvement Program |
| DOA | Food Distribution | DOT | Federal Transit Capital Improvement Grants |
| DOA | Matching Grants for Food Stamps | DOT | Federal Transit Technical Studies Grants |
| DOA | National School Lunch Program | DOT | Highway Planning and Construction |
| DOA | Summer Food Service Program for Children | DOT | State and Community Highway Safety |
| DOC | Economic Development | EEOC | Employment Discrimination, Title VII |
| DOE | Energy Conservation for Institutional Buildings | EPA | Air Pollution Control Program Support |
| DOE | Energy Task Force for the Urban Consortium | EPA | Environmental Justice Grants |
| DOE | Office of Policy and Financial Assistance | EPA | Solid Waste Disposal Research |
| DOE | Adult Education | EPA | Superfund Innovative Technology Evaluation |
| DOE | Drug-Free Schools and Communities—State Grants | EPA | Toxic Substances Research |
| DOE | Grants for Infants and Families with Disabilities | EPA | Wastewater Treatment Works Construction |
| DOE | Literacy for Incarcerated Adults | FEMA | Disaster Assistance |
| DOE | Special Education—Grants to States | FEMA | State and Local Emergency Management Assistance |
| DOI | Fish and Wildlife Management Assistance | HHS | Administration for Children, Youth, and Families |
| DOI | Historic Preservation Fund Grants-in-Aid | HHS | Adoption Assistance |
| DOI | Wildlife Conservation and Appreciation | HHS | AIDS Activity |
| | | HHS | AIDS Surveillance |
| DOJ | Criminal Justice Block Grants | HHS | Alcohol and Drug Abuse and Mental Health Services |
| DOJ | Drug Control and System Improvement | HHS | Child Care for Families At-Risk of Welfare Dependency |
| DOJ | Justice Research and Development Project Grants | HHS | Child Support Enforcement |
| | | HHS | Child Welfare Research and Demonstration |
| DOJ | Juvenile Justice and Delinquency Prevention | HHS | Child Welfare Services—State Grants |
| DOJ | Public Safety and Community Policing Grants | HHS | Childhood Immunization Grants |
| | | HHS | Childhood Lead Poisoning Prevention |
| DOL | Employment Services and Job Training | HHS | Community Development Block Grants—Entitlement Grants |

| | | | |
|---|---|---|---|
| HHS | Community Development Block Grants—Insular Areas, Technical Assistance | HHS | Independent Living |
| HHS | Community Mental Health Services | HHS | Injury Prevention and Control Research Projects |
| HHS | Community Mental Health Services—Technical Assistance | HHS | Job Opportunities and Basic Skills Training |
| HHS | Community Partnership Demonstration Grant | HHS | Low Income Energy Assistance |
| HHS | Community Services Block Grant | HHS | Maternal and Child Health Services |
| HHS | CSBG—Discretionary Awards - Demonstration Partnership | HHS | Medical Assistance Program |
| HHS | Drug Abuse Treatment Improvement | HHS | Mental Health for the Homeless |
| HHS | Drug Prevention and Education for Youth Gangs | HHS | Mental Health Planning and Demonstration Projects |
| HHS | Emergency Protection Grants— Substance Abuse | HHS | Mental Health Research Grants |
| HHS | Emergency Shelter Grants Program | HHS | Mental Health Services for Children with Serious Emotional Disturbances |
| HHS | Empowerment Zones Program | HHS | Model Comprehensive Drug Abuse Treatment Programs |
| HHS | Equal Opportunity in Housing | HHS | Opportunities for Youth— Youthbuild Program |
| HHS | Fair Housing Initiatives Program | HUD | Preventive Health and Health Services |
| HHS | Family Planning—Services | HUD | Primary Care Services— Resource Coordination and Development |
| HHS | Family Support Payments to States—Assistance Payments | HUD | Public Health and Social Services Emergency Fund |
| HHS | Foster Care—Title IV-E | HUD | Refugee and Entrant Assistance |
| HHS | General Clinical Research Centers | HUD | Section 312 Rehabilitation Loans |
| HHS | Health Care Financing Research, Demonstrations and Evaluations | HUD | Shelter Plus Care |
| HHS | Health Programs for Refugees | HUD | Social Security Administration—Research and Demonstration |
| HHS | Health Services to the Homeless | HUD | Social Service Block Grant |
| HHS | Healthy Start Initiative | HUD | Special Program for Aging— Title III Parts A, B, and C |
| HHS | HIV Care Formula Grants | HUD | Special Projects Program |
| HHS | HIV Demonstration Program for Children, Adolescents and Women | HUD | TB Control Programs |
| HHS | HIV Early Intervention Services | HUD | Urban Development Action Grants |
| HHS | HIV Emergency Relief Project Grants, Formula Grants | LOC | Books for the Blind and Physically Handicapped |
| HHS | HIV Prevention Activities | NARA | National Historical Publications and Records Grants |
| HHS | HIV/AIDS Mental Health Services Demonstration Program | | |
| HHS | HOME Investment in Affordable Housing | | |
| HHS | Housing Opportunities for Persons with AIDS | | |
| HHS | Immunization R and D, Public Information and Education | | |

An emphasis on special-purposes assistance, parceled out to particular interest groups at the perennial discretion of Congress, carries at least a couple of distinctive implications. One, of course, is that this form of grant giving involves a quid pro quo: compliance by local governments with rules to ensure, among other things, that the money gets spent on the intended clientele. A second implication is that what the grantors can give they can also take away. During the 1980s and first half of the 1990s, when federal deficits became a preoccupation, discretionary spending slowed and with it, so did the categorical transfers to state and local governments. Some programs that Congress had firmly implanted in city and state bureaucracies turned into burdens when their federal funds dried up. The uncertainties of funding led advocates of new programs to favor regulatory or judicially administered strategies over schemes dependent on budget cycles. Activists that framed the terms of the debate on the Americans with Disabilities Act, for example, did not lobby for a new bureau in Washington to assist the disabled; lacking confidence in the vagaries of the congressional appropriations process, they advanced instead an unfunded mandate to be enforced through the courts.[22] For city governments, costs often mounted when federal policies moved in these directions.

## Legalism

Federally authorized lawsuits, often resulting in complicated judicial edicts, are important levers of national power in America. From a European perspective this situation is eccentric. Surely it is hard to think of a major European city that spent decades dealing with anything like the court-ordered racial plans for schools and with suits over everything from alleged employment biases to special education services, patterns of practice in criminal justice, and investment in sewage lines—the kinds of legal altercations that put San Francisco, Baltimore, Philadelphia, and Los Angeles through the wringer.

To an extent U.S. city governments, along with corporations, other public institutions, and average citizens, are just one more group of defendants caught in the currents of America's famously litigious society. Tort suits per capita in the United States outpace the number in Germany by approximately 3 to 2; they exceed the United Kingdom's rate by more than 3 to 1.[23] Cross-national comparisons of the overall costs of such suits show the United States in a distant league of its own (figure 5-1). But

Figure 5-1. *Cross-National Comparison of Tort Costs as a Percentage of GDP, 1991*[a]

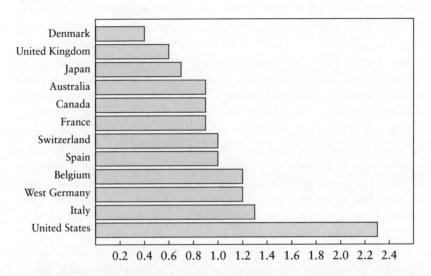

Source: *Tort Cost Trends: An International Perspective* (Tillinghast-Towers Perrin, 1992), pp. 8, 14. Reprinted with the express permission of Tillinghast-Towers Perrin.

a. Tort costs include first-party benefits (the cost of legal defense and claims handling), benefits paid to third parties (claimants and plaintiffs), and an administrative, or overhead, component.

as chapter 4 of this book suggests, a good deal of the coercive litigation into which American cities have been drawn occurs by design—central design. And the expanse of legal recourse that the central government has opened in the United States is *sui generis*.

## Exhibit A: Anti-Bias Policy

In job discrimination, to take a leading example, the national legal machinery is mightier than practically anywhere else. In most of the world there is no remedy at all for those who claim to be victims of bias in the workplace. Western Europe, Canada, and Japan do provide forms of relief. But the Civil Rights Act of 1991 moved U.S. law in unique directions.[24] Its approach, which requires employers (including public employers, if judged guilty) to reinstate workers with full back pay, and provides punitive damages awarded by juries, has no parallel in the legal systems of any other nation. The EU's "equal treatment directive" does not routinely remediate claims of indirect or unintentional bias (the statistically based disparate-impact concept that took root in American civil rights law). When European national courts award compensation, six months' back pay is typically the upper limit. Enforcement bodies like the Justice Department's Civil Rights Division and the U.S. Equal Employment Opportunity Commission are unusual; only the United Kingdom and Ireland have bureaus with faintly analogous investigative powers. According to a 1990 report of the International Labor Organization, nowhere is alleged discrimination in employment policed as closely by plaintiffs and prosecutors as in the United States.[25]

Thus American city officials have had to devote considerable time and resources to developing, for example, elaborate diversity programs, and to defending themselves against litigants who seemed to draw parallels between strength tests for police officers, sanitation workers, or firefighters with, say, the literacy tests of the old segregationist South.[26] Equivalents are hard to find in Europe. Antidiscrimination questions in Germany pose, at most, rare and minor perturbations for employers.[27] As far as municipal officials in France are concerned, matters are even simpler: American-style affirmative action that calls for "recruiting by ethnicity" is expressly forbidden.[28] There is one notable exception to German and French norms against preference programs in municipal workplaces: these countries have long imposed hiring quotas for the benefit of persons with physical disabilities.[29]

### Exhibit B: Environmental Policy

In the many domains of U.S. intergovernmental regulation, contemporary workplace regulation is not the only one bristling with punitive legalism. U.S. environmental programs have some similar attributes. While ambitious national standards, often sternly enforced through citizen suits and court orders, distinguish the American mode of fighting pollution, the regulatory styles of other industrial nations resort less commonly to legal injunctions, hard deadlines, and penalties.

Perhaps British, German, and Canadian regulators may be a bit less pliable today than they were reputed to be a couple of decades ago, but by most accounts, they still rely more than do their U.S. counterparts on negotiated accommodations, exercises in administrative discretion, and deference to local judgments. "The British make less use of legally enforceable quality or emission standards," concludes a well-known book comparing U.S. and UK environmental regulation.[30] Whether or not one is satisfied with their results, observes another comparative study, subnational governments in Canada, more than in the United States, "largely are free to respond to localized conditions and to pursue innovative, flexible approaches to environmental protection."[31] The German environmental policy apparatus also delegates control to local authorities, favors nonadversarial tactics, and is less given to "excessive rigidity" than the U.S. regime.[32]

What such contrasts can mean for municipalities is well demonstrated by a thumbnail sketch of recent British and American government policies governing one of the most mundane of municipal activities: waste management. On this side of the Atlantic, city governments have been jostled by the inclement decisions of various taskmasters: U.S. court rulings on waste disposal systems (incineration, for example), Congress's ban on sludge dumping, the Environmental Protection Agency's stipulations for lining landfills, state agencies acting on the EPA's orders, and so forth. Although the accretion of rules is legally binding for localities, questions of how or whether they can afford to comply are often shunted aside. Hence the usual grievances ring out: local officials regard their regulators as adversaries that pursue "one-size-fits-all thinking," solutions "too rigid and too costly," and "unwise priorities" without due compensation.[33]

In the United Kingdom, by contrast, a coordinated government program called "Waste Strategy 2000" extends financial incentives to local landfill operators to invest in improved reprocessing of waste and to meet standards for the reclamation of polluted land.[34] The program also works with various industrial associations to aid recycling with better methods of packaging. To lower the volume of nonessential waste the strategy includes explicit landfill-user fees levied on waste producers. And it has developed a tradable permits system for local authorities. Notably absent from the array of carrots and sticks in Britain's Waste Strategy 2000, it seems, are the hallmarks of many U.S. mandates: unshared fiscal burdens, rigid specifications and schedules, and the frequent threat of winding up in court.

## Other Elements of American Exceptionalism

The separation of powers, with its built-in potential for mistrust between the branches and its capacity for members of Congress to bid up the government's regulatory agenda, helps explain the militant tack taken by various U.S. environmental laws. (Recall the statutory timetables, inflexible goals, and invitations for citizen suits with which Democratic majorities in Congress armed much environmental legislation against Republican appointments to the EPA.) In Britain, where almost every important piece of legislation is drafted by the government's ministries and is then ordinarily adopted without modification—and where the executor is a respected civil service that regularly exercises discretion—the House of Commons is not in the independent business of dictating deadlines, ratcheting targets, or engaging private litigants to police administrators lest they ignore "legislative intent."[35] In the end it is partly for these reasons that Britain's environmental regulators are often freer to negotiate with local governments the terms of their compliance with national pollution controls.

## Modes of Jurisprudence

When local self-rule is made to give way to central authority in the United States, the federal judiciary is frequently a principal agent. In comparison with other countries this leading role of the courts is unique.[36] Almost nowhere else are courts so ready to decide questions that may contest the core values of communities and that force a commitment of their public funds—choices that other countries in varying degrees prefer to leave to elective office holders or administrative institutions elsewhere in the body politic.[37]

In France, perhaps because judges historically were identified, if not with feudal oppression, with retarding even moderate reforms in prerevolutionary times, ordinary civil courts are not permitted to review the legality of ordinances or administrative actions at any level; that responsibility is reserved for special administrative tribunals, led by the *Conseil d'État,* which acts as a watchdog. In the past quarter-century another body, the *Conseil Constitutionnel,* has come to occupy a position somewhat comparable to that of the U.S. Supreme Court—not only exercising some judicial review over the legislature but also protecting various individual rights and liberties. Parallels with the American judiciary, however, should not be overdrawn. For example, in France, one expert writes, "There are no instances—indeed, there is no possibility—of the judicial administration of public institutions such as schools or prisons in the name of protecting constitutional rights."[38]

Because, unlike France, Germany is a federation, its judiciary adjudicates a lot of intergovernmental disputes. But unlike U.S. federal courts, the German Constitutional Court seems to have been far more protective of the prerogatives of subnational jurisdictions. A verdict such as the one the U.S. Supreme Court handed down in the watershed case of *Garcia* v. *San Antonio Metropolitan Transit Authority* "would be unthinkable in Germany," concludes one assessment of German judicial review.[39]

To be sure, at times the courts in some European countries—most notably the United Kingdom—have vigorously reinforced national policies that groups of local officials opposed.[40] Not all local authorities in Britain welcomed, for example, Prime Minister Margaret Thatcher's plans to promote parental choice of schools. Parents gained standing to sue some of these authorities when they were deemed to obstruct school choice, and the courts generally sided with the plaintiffs (and the Thatcher government).[41] In Germany, where the constitution expressly denies federal authorities any jurisdiction over the education policies of the German state governments, the federal constitutional court has enjoined local practices when they are said to violate the most basic principles of the constitution (for example, the separation of church and state). In 1995 the court struck down a Bavarian ordinance that required crucifixes to be displayed in all classrooms.[42]

But by and large, whereas education issues of all kinds have been the object of continual conflict before the courts of the United States, nothing comparable has befallen the systems of primary and secondary education in any European country. Educational services for children with special needs exist throughout Europe. However, while legal actions have played a big part in expanding enrollments and local costs of U.S. special education policy, the program in Germany, for instance, remains relatively free of litigation. Perhaps that helps explain why the percentage of students classified as eligible for the equivalent of special education in Germany is less than half the U.S. percentage.[43] In any event the latter consideration is at least one of the factors behind the extraordinary per pupil costs of education in the United States: in 1997 overall expenditures per pupil at the local elementary level exceeded those in Germany by almost 40 percent—a statistic that hints at why many an American city dweller might regard the local school budget as ungainly.[44]

Much the same applies to environmental policy. Here is how the situation in Germany has been described:

> German . . . courts largely confine themselves to procedural issues, deferring to regulators on matters of substance. Under federal law, there are no provisions for private rights of action to force compliance with regulations, although environmental groups have had

standing to sue for damage to health or property in a number of German state courts. On the whole, the system is weighted against excessive litigation.[45]

One doubts, therefore, that any German city would incur the same legal risks that, say, Columbus, Ohio, faced when that city wanted to pave a small and forgettable patch of weeds and mud behind a municipal garage to park its police cruisers and sanitation trucks: when traces of chemicals were discovered in the dirt, the modest parking lot became an object of federal hazardous waste regulations, and, ipso facto, susceptible to action-forcing lawsuits.[46]

## The Rights Track

The prominence and considerable impact of federal litigants and judges in regulating local governments in the United States stems in part not only from the inherent exigencies of federalism but from the absence of a parliamentary regime. In most parliamentary systems the courts are usually more reluctant to make policy and to engage in matters of public administration at any level, because the rest of the government (the executive and the legislature) can promptly unite to overturn judicial interpretations of law.[47] A system of separated powers opens a larger policymaking space for the judiciary and offers it a less deferential role.[48] Besides these broad institutional contours, however, American public policies have increasingly given singular legal force to assertions of rights, thereby activating the courts. The importance of this element becomes all the more evident in a comparative context.

Rights-based litigation, it is safe to say, has exerted a greater centralizing influence in the United States than in Western Europe. At first glance this might seem paradoxical. Many of the cradle-to-grave welfare states of Europe have loaded their constitutions with lists of specific social and economic obligations, a range of commitments seemingly bolder than the basic constitutional protections in America's Bill of Rights. We might presume that such programmatic constitutions would only multiply the possibilities for actionable grievances by citizens whenever they felt that a nationally established "right" (to a municipal day care center, a local hospital bed, a living wage, an affordable housing unit, and so on) was being given short shrift. In fact no such flood of legal claims has occurred. There are two reasons.

First, not all rights are equal under European conceptions of constitutional law. The "basic rights" of the German constitution (that is, political protections such as freedom of speech, religion, association, and the like) are consistently enforceable in courts of law, but claims to social benefits (what continental lawyers sometimes call "programmatic" rights) are not necessarily accorded the same legal footing.[49] The American constitution is still uncluttered by explicit affirmations of welfare rights, but plenty of new entitlements of this sort have been introduced in this country, often because they are deemed implicit in the broad language (or "penumbras") of provisions like the Fourteenth Amendment. And when these interpretations are made, they are enforced. "Americans," explains Mary Ann Glendon, "take rights very seriously."[50]

Second, when social benefits are more extensively provided, there is simply less incentive to try to fashion them in the courts. Certainly America places an unusual reliance on tort litigation (both ordinary personal injury cases and constitutional tort actions) to meet social needs or wants that other advanced industrial nations handle with compensatory public programs—direct health insurance, for instance.[51] Why do German cities and companies rarely worry about, for example, asbestos suits? Germany's wide safety net "has the effect that many cases are not litigated."[52]

## Decentralization

City governments in the latter third of the twentieth century came under new central restrictions in almost every modern democracy. In Britain during the Thatcher years local councils had their discretion to tax and spend sharply "capped," their monopoly over local education curbed, and their transit systems, refuse collection, water utilities, and several other services privatized or placed under public bodies managed wholly or partly by appointees of the national government.[53] Cities in Germany also experienced considerable erosion of their discretionary powers. Under a postwar constitution that exhorts national politicians to promote "equivalence" among local governments their centrally defined "obligatory tasks" inevitably increased.[54] And so have their administrative costs, sometimes enormously. Mandatory child-care services, a 1995 federal dictum, is now a multibillion deutsche mark operation on the books of Germany's cities and towns.

But forms of decentralization in Europe could be discerned as well—and in some instances they have been remarkable even by American standards.[55] For example, in 1982 the quintessential *dirigiste* regime, France, initiated a significant reorganization.[56] The Napoleonic tradition of punctilious prefectorial supervision (*la tutelle*) of local governments was effectively discontinued. Mayors of municipalities in France had long enjoyed a good deal of informal leverage over national policy by way of their so-called *cumul des mandats,* or customary ability to hold municipal and national elective offices simultaneously.[57] Now the discretionary power of these local notables was formally enhanced. Significant decisions—over land use plans, permits, and "amenity control," for instance—were devolved. French city governments today are empowered to control their environs in ways that, if attempted in America, would probably swamp most big-city mayors in a sea of lawsuits.[58] (French law, for instance, enables city officials to protect small shopkeepers by obstructing the development of regional "hypermarkets.")[59]

Even in Britain certain acts of parliament that were widely deemed to usurp community control in the 1980s could just as easily be described as reforms that actually decentralized power, in some respects radically from an American vantage point. Thatcher's Education Reform Act of 1988 was a case in point:

> Under the act, power would be decentralized through "local management of schools," another name for what Americans call school-based management. Choice would be enhanced in important ways: by spelling out the rights of parents and students to choose their own schools, by giving schools the right to "opt out" of the local education authorities (LEAs), and by creating new kinds of schools—city technology colleges—for people to choose from. Finally, this population of more autonomous schools would be held accountable through a new national curriculum and a comprehensive battery of tests.[60]

Recently some writers have stressed that the scope of "subsidiarity" (or extent of local autonomy) has been shrinking under the European Union's detailed standards and "infringement proceedings" in fields such as environmental protection. Some perceive a drift toward a litigious style of regulation, so familiar to Americans, in which EU rules create in effect new legal rights for private parties (firms, individuals, and advocacy organizations) to enforce the European Community's laws through the national courts.[61] The powers of the Community are distributed among its several institutions (the European Parliament, the European

Commission, the Council of Ministers, which represents member states, and so forth), and inevitably they often distrust one another. As in America, private rights of action eventually might become for proactive players (the Commission, for example, and activist member states) an indirect means of pressuring recalcitrant ones.

The fact remains, however, that judicialization of the Community's policies, replete with U.S.-style private enforcement and micromanagement of local compliance through central court decrees, is still not even close to resembling the American model. Cases in which individual plaintiffs have managed to sue for alleged violations of rights are not unheard of under Community procedures, but to date such actions have been infrequent even in especially contentious realms such as environmental law.[62]

The influence of the EU has run in more than one direction—not just churning out new central precepts, but interestingly, also stirring significant devolution in some countries. Italy, for example, has long been a top-heavy unitary state, more so in many respects than France or the United Kingdom. To meet the Maastricht Treaty's fiscal standards for admission into the European Monetary Union, however, the Italian government was finally forced to lower its lavish deficit spending. It accomplished this improbable feat in part by decentralizing more routine functions to regional and municipal entities and ceding to them a greater capacity to raise their own revenues.[63] By the late 1990s the finances of a number of Italy's most important cities bore greater similarities to those of American cities: they administered more services directly and paid for most of their budgets with local taxes or fees. At the same time, to relieve pressure to overspend at the local level, the government seems to have imposed fewer new mandated expenditures on these municipalities.[64]

Apart from austerity measures, neoseparatist movements have contributed to the notable devolution in countries such as Italy, Spain, and most recently the United Kingdom. Nominally, Spain today is a unitary republic, but de facto it is a federation in which regions and cities effectively claim extensive home rule.[65] In Britain legislation introduced two years ago promises to strengthen local mayoralties and generally to restore greater independence for local governments.[66]

## Conclusions

The upshot of the political developments in Europe has been a surprising amount of independent local experimentation there. Chicago's attempts at reform of public housing, mired in regulatory disputes with the U.S. Department of Housing and Urban Development throughout the 1990s, had been at an impasse for years. City officials in Chicago might have been surprised to learn that cities in Britain had begun demolishing thousands of their worst public housing "estates" a decade ago.[67] The local council of Newcastle alone, a city less than one-twentieth the size of Chicago, has been taking down 6,000 units. For more than half a century the mayors of American cities have pondered how to turn their downtowns into districts dedicated to something other than cars, parking lots, and gasoline stations. Some of these mayors might wonder how Italian cities such as Florence or Bologna (where, at one time, prefects of the Interior Ministry presided over "every municipal act or decision," and often caused "the central government to stifle municipal initiatives") have managed to ban or drastically restrict traffic in large sections of their centers.[68] Similarly, local transportation planners in the United States might ask how Dutch cities—Amsterdam, Rotterdam, Utrecht, and the Hague—were able to install state-of-the-art systems of congestion pricing on urban roads, or how the German city of Bremen reduced congestion through a highly innovative rental car–sharing operation.[69]

The objective of these comparative observations is not to imply that urban governance in the United States is now, on balance, less autonomous, less flexible, or less inventive than in other parts of the industrialized world. What can be said about the path intergovernmental politics has taken in this country, however, is that U.S. city governments have met with no small share of federal mandates and legal sanctions, even in comparison with unitary polities abroad. At a minimum, some of these central constraints are distractions. "Are we going to wake up some morning and find that only 25 percent of city employees are working on city business?" asked the mayor of Omaha, Nebraska, a number of years ago.[70] At worst, the political dynamics underlying the national rules sometimes seem indifferent to the often limited resources of central cities subject to the American framework of fiscal federalism. Aspects of all this have been unusual from an international perspective.

# 6   *Conclusions*

After decades of decline the prospects of many American cities had brightened in the late years of the twentieth century, only to be dimmed again by the cataclysmic events of September 11, 2001. Even before that fateful day, however, there were signs of difficulties ahead. Between 1988 and 1997 the general revenues of cities had been increasing only about half as rapidly as the tax receipts of the federal government.[1] A national economy that began to stall three years later portended a return of old vulnerabilities for the financial health of local governments and for the well-being of many city dwellers. Then came September's devastating blow to the nation's peace and prosperity. The aftershocks would reverberate far beyond New York City, where the losses of life and property reached staggering proportions. To the familiar list of urban hardships and exigencies facing city governments, which were now entering a recession, was added an enormous unanticipated responsibility: organizing municipal services and budgets to cope with acts or threats of terrorism. A score of major central cities, which in the 1990s had expected their economies, coffers, and populations to bulge

through the following decade, had to revise their exuberant forecasts—
and to brace for harder times.[2]

Amid these sobering realities the chief implication of this book seems
all the more salient: a constructive system of federal regulation cannot
wade into every function that municipal governments exist to perform.
The federal government would do better to focus its attention on the core
priorities of securing the nation's overall defense and welfare. This means,
when practicable, sorting out which local activities are really worth preempting or supervising from on high. And it means deciding judiciously
what share of centrally mandated expenses local taxpayers rightfully
ought to shoulder, for in the United States the capacity of local authorities to tax, spend, and borrow is not only sensitive to economic down-
turns and to interjurisdictional competition but constrained by state constitutional strictures. In sum, if they are to discharge satisfactorily their
essential duties, neither the central government nor the nation's local
communities can handle policy portfolios filled with too many extraneous
pursuits.

## The March of Mandates

With each passing year in the 1990s a consensus among observers of
American federalism grew convinced that power at long last had begun
shifting back to the local level. The cold war, which gave Washington
politicians a national security pretext for launching local projects like the
building of bridges and roads, was history. Republican majorities, reput-
edly solicitous of state sovereignty, had gained control of Congress in
1995. They promptly enacted legislation (the Unfunded Mandates
Reform Act) that would supposedly kick the congressional habit of heap-
ing expensive obligations on state and local governments but not appropriating the money to help them comply. A year later Congress also put
the states in charge of the national public assistance program. "Welfare
reform," wrote one scholar, vividly exemplified the remarkable extent to
which authority was "cascading to lower levels of government."[3] The
Clinton administration not only signed off on this devolution but granted
state agencies more discretion in administering Medicaid and in managing some aspects of U.S. environmental policy. Much of the energy stirring domestic policy during the decade—from school reform to legal
attacks on tobacco—seemed to emanate from the statehouses.[4] Perhaps
most notable, according to those who viewed the federal government in

retreat, were a series of Supreme Court opinions that sought to shore up prerogatives of the states.

These developments were interesting and noteworthy. However, the importance of some of them has been exaggerated. Editorial writers and op-ed commentators seemed inconsolably frightened, for example, by the Supreme Court's affirmations of states' rights—which made "a kind of fetish out of state sovereign immunity," opined one in the *Washington Post,* or even harked back to "racist precedents of the 1880s," declaimed another in the *New York Times.*[5] In truth neither the recent body of court decisions nor of legislative initiatives was likely to reverse, dramatically and durably, the accretion of federal prescriptions and proscriptions bearing down on local governments.

## Congressional Restraint

First let us contemplate Congress's main effort at self-limitation—the Unfunded Mandates Reform Act of 1995 (UMRA). This law has tried to interpose new procedural hurdles for legislation aimed at local governments. The Congressional Budget Office (CBO) was instructed to calculate the local costs of proposed statutory mandates. Those that were estimated to exceed $50 million could be subjected to a point of order that could prompt an explicit vote on whether federal financial support would have to be forthcoming. Another section of the reform law required federal agencies to prepare "written statements" spelling out the financial arrangements for rulemakings that might result in expenditures of $100 million or more by state and local governments. The idea has been to add transparency to lawmaking and to the formulation of agency rules that follow.

The 1995 reform did go farther than had earlier attempts. Unlike, for instance, the essentially toothless State and Local Cost Estimate Act of 1981, UMRA may have made it somewhat less tempting for members of Congress to quietly tuck costly mandates into broad pieces of legislation. Because at least some categories of bills are now routinely scored by the Congressional Budget Office, and parliamentary challenges can expose them to visible up-or-down votes, the law may have deterred lawmakers from sponsoring too many new proposals priced wildly in excess of $50 million.

Still, assessing the significance of UMRA has been frustrating. The CBO's estimations for complex regulatory projects cannot easily foretell the costs of technical standards and rules promulgated years after authorizing legislation has been enacted. No crystal ball would display, for instance, the eventual multibillion dollar price tags of all the "hammers" wielded by the Environmental Protection Agency pursuant to the Clean Air Act Amendments of 1990. The CBO reported that the number of bills containing intergovernmental mandates (above the $50 million threshold) declined by as much as two-thirds between 1996 and 2000.[6] However, the quantity of new administrative rules affecting local governments dipped the year that UMRA was passed but inched up steadily thereafter, from 410 in 1995 to 453 in 1999.[7] The number of new EPA rules that were said to have a direct impact on localities was higher in 1999 (173 rules) than in 1994 (157). The increases reflected the fact that UMRA tries to circumscribe legislative mandating rather than affect bureaucratic rulemaking.

Beyond that, what to make of bean counts like these is hard to say. Certain bills and rules are more important than others, and sometimes the actual costs of the important ones have remained unknown, or when roughly determined, surprisingly large. No sooner was UMRA on the books than Congress enacted, for example, the Mental Health Parity Act (a bill promising employees with psychiatric disorders the same insurance coverage available to persons with other medical conditions) and an increase in the federally mandated minimum wage—two new laws with costs in the billions of dollars.

Further, because UMRA defines a "mandate" rather narrowly as an "enforceable duty" that is distinct from a condition of federal aid, huge regulatory programs that were accompanied by some quotient of federal funding could fly under the radar screen.[8] The 104th Congress's first deficit reduction initiative in fiscal year 1995, for instance, cut $1.3 billion in previously appropriated federal wastewater treatment grants, leaving local authorities to make up the difference. To municipal water systems managers Congress had violated the spirit, if not the letter, of the mandate reform act.[9] Arcane semantics about whether this action was an underfunded mandate or technically an "appropriations rescission" of a "voluntary" grant-in-aid must have seemed beside the point. Similarly, when Congress added a ream of new local requirements to the Safe Drinking Water Act in 1996, the mandates marched through because, as a technical matter, they were called conditions-of-aid instead of direct orders.[10]

The scope of UMRA was further narrowed by excluding the large category of legislative action that widened the civil rights of individuals or groups.[11] In other words, Congress could continue, if it wanted to, enacting more laws resembling, say, the Americans with Disabilities Act without ever having to examine closely the intergovernmental fiscal implications.

At the end of the day many local officials contended that Congress had not provided enough relief. As one mayor told the chairman of a Senate committee in 1999, despite the Unfunded Mandates Reform Act of 1995 the "pile" of federal regulations facing his city remained "taller than you, Senator, taller than the rest of the Senators on your Committee, and taller than myself on an annual basis."[12]

## Centripetal Politics

For power to "cascade" to lower levels of government in the United States the political changes in this country would have to run deeper than a mere shift in the partisan composition of Congress and the executive. As chapter 4 notes, both political parties in their own ways give precedence to national rules and laws even when local ones suffice. Certainly at numerous intervals the Left campaigned doggedly to drive the federal legal apparatus deeply into the regulation of local workplaces, educational institutions, pollution programs, and much more. But commonly the Right has been eager to reverse, and nationalize, local decisions, too: what was the reaction to ballot initiatives that liberalized marijuana laws in Arizona and California in the mid-1990s? Conservative representatives called for federal countermeasures. How did the conservatives react to a 1996 Hawaii court decision that legalized a same-sex union? They proposed a national "Defense of Marriage Act."

And the *pas de deux* goes on. Who were the policymakers that advanced what has been described as "the largest and most far-reaching mandate on elementary and secondary schools in 25 years"?[13] The answer is: a Republican administration with bipartisan support. Whence came the latest proposal to preempt health insurance standards, much to the dismay of many state officials?[14] This was the sausage Republican lawmakers had to produce to parry relentless Democratic pressure to legislate patients' "rights." Which politicians, Democrats or Republicans, favored mandating the use of ethanol in California? Plenty of members on both sides endorsed this "clean air" commandment with equal enthusiasm.

Of course, not every proposed increment to the federal agenda would stick. Much was posturing and symbolism. Symbols and postures can matter, however. At a minimum, they signaled how readily players across the spectrum of American politics are prepared to game federalism, fluidly invoking or abandoning its principles on an ad hoc basis. Hence, often enough, talk of devolution yielded contradictory outcomes: yes, the Environmental Protection Agency granted more so-called Performance Partnership Agreements that have enabled local authorities to customize their means of attaining various environmental ends. No, state and local air quality regulators would get no reprieve from a U.S. ethanol mandate. Evidently, national environmental initiatives could run in opposite directions—sometimes permitting more local leeway, or, today like yesterday, slavishly serving bureaucratic dictums and potent lobbies with an interest in top-down control.

Centralist compulsions remained powerful among other movers and shakers of the nation's intergovernmental politics. The media, for example, have exhibited in recent decades a penchant for portraying localized misfortunes, mistakes, or misdeeds as national faults requiring comprehensive correctives. A typical illustration was the story of what the *New York Times* decided to call in the spring of 2001 "Patterns of Police Violence." After covering various episodes of rights abuses by local police departments, the nation's leading newspaper not only began perceiving pervasive "patterns" but also editorializing that their "brutality aimed disproportionately at minorities has become *a national problem.*"[15]

Never mind how sparse was the systematic evidence of such *patterns* of police brutality. Indeed in all probability the contemporary behavior of most city police forces was less abusive, and more sensitive, toward communities of minorities than it had been in years past. The received wisdom now was that a new supposed "problem" existed, that it was "national," and by implication, that it urgently needed to join the lengthy list of federal regulatory responsibilities. According to this logic, it seems, an action like the U.S. government's shakeup of the Los Angeles Police Department should be regarded not as a strained digression but a necessary and proper prelude to similar federal intervention in cities from coast to coast (see chapter 3).

## Whither Federalism Jurisprudence?

It is not entirely clear how consistently the Supreme Court has countervailed the many political reflexes that tend to centralize policy. To be sure, on and off throughout American history the high court had held federal hegemony in check, and the Rehnquist court could be considered part of that tradition. Here and there its deliberations not only lubricated the rusty Tenth Amendment but even braked some of the commerce clause's all-purpose propulsion of national legislation. The court during recent years also departed, at least in some kinds of cases, from precedents that liberally enlisted private advocacy groups to litigate on behalf of the constituencies Congress intended to benefit.[16]

These were significant moves, but they were not the court's only ones of consequence for intergovernmental relations. "States' rights" decisions got big headlines, but the cases in which the justices overturned state policies governing everything from child-visitation rights and oil-tanker safety training to the sale of personal databases by motor-vehicle bureaus did not.[17] And when local governments gained little or no judicial relief from rigid provisions of important U.S. environmental statutes like the Clean Air Act, critics of the court's federalism jurisprudence scarcely seemed to take into account the strong affirmation of congressional authority. The lower courts did not back away from the enforcement of key national rights-based statutes that imposed costs on municipalities. One study of claims by local governments that the Americans with Disabilities Act caused them "undue burdens" found the federal courts rejecting such pleas more than two-thirds of the time during the first half of the 1990s.[18]

In the aftermath of September 11, anyway, a bit of the so-called federalism revolution that the Supreme Court was said to spur may have been overtaken by events. Local control usually wanes while central power waxes in times of national crisis. In the months ahead a number of federal agencies might intrude into more than just management of airport screeners. If such intrusions are in the offing, will the judiciary stand in the way? Some court watchers now wondered aloud whether precedents like *United States* v. *Lopez* might be deemed luxuries of a bygone era.[19] (In my judgment, an abrupt about-face on such precedents is unlikely. At the same time, it would surprise me if the court were to question, say, the federalization of airport security, and ponder why Congress did not leave that job, if not to private companies, to local public authorities.) Conversely, as I suggest at the end of this book, September 11's force of gravity could pull the federal government back to a more focused set of exertions, allowing it to drop tasks that state and local governments can carry out adequately.

## Too Much of a Good Thing

Despite some intermittent contrary currents, the ebb and flow of the central government's role in determining what local jurisdictions can or cannot do in this country, as in many others, has flowed more than ebbed.

To put forth this conclusion is not to imply that the federal role has been mostly reckless or even inappropriate. Few would contend that our states and cities, nor those in any other federation, can function efficiently and fairly without a good many national standards. Activities in one place that injure many others plainly merit regulation by higher orders of government. There is no question that certain kinds of industrial pollution, for example, meet this criterion. Nor could localities be allowed to trample on the venerable rights of citizens. The framers of the Constitution, after all, duly worried about local despotism and were at pains to counteract it even before they annexed a Bill of Rights. That is why, for instance, a necessary (though not sufficient) national mandate— the stipulation that every state in the union have "a republican form of government"—was prescribed in the Constitution's fourth article.

Moreover the diverse policy pursuits, and downward pressure on taxation, inherent in a system of competing local entities carries risks as well as rewards. Such a system can stimulate innovations and cut wasteful public spending overall, but might it also suppress various essential expenditures to levels that are simply too penurious? Certainly that possibility has been on the minds of skeptics eyeing the devolution of programs that redistribute income. Local administration of workfare, they fear, may be successful during a sustained economic expansion but less viable when the economies of states and cities contract. Issues like this invite ongoing discussion about the limits of localism and the importance of national safeguards.

But so do other questions. If local governments were confronted solely with national legal requirements that spoke to large concerns like those just mentioned, local objections to the requirements would be hard to justify. In practice, however, much federal law pokes into domains that quite possibly do not warrant a federal presence. This reality remains to be reckoned with, despite the rehabilitation of certain local immunities by the Supreme Court, and the handoff of considerable jurisdiction for some programs by Congress to the states, during the past decade.

Federal policy can expect a municipal water system to be monitored for grave dangers, including deadly contamination by terrorists. But in a world besieged by these real menaces, what justifies stern central directives that effectively also order the local taxpayers to execute green mandates so risk averse they must all but wipe out even commonplace impurities that can cause little harm to the community, much less its neighbors? Federal paternalism loses legitimacy when it commandeers local resources to fuss with localized imperfections that pose no great hazard to society at large.

Federal law properly gives legal recourse to persons who are victims of bigotry. Should the law, though, also encourage social engineers to sue into submission a city agency that, without any intention of discriminating against anyone, did not fulfill some formulaic goal of "diversity"? Local public servants have grounds to be bewildered by the amount of litigation in federal as well as state courts that hangs over local administrative life—particularly when the lawsuits seem to move under cover of rather contorted constitutional claims.

In an economic slump, national standards and support might be bolstered to prevent county welfare offices from letting thousands of indigents fall through a civilized society's safety net. But what justification is there for perpetuating, say, nationwide rules that prop the wages of already well-paid workers in local public works contracts? Some federal regulations seem to institutionalize, more than militate against, the distorted local power of particular interest groups.

In sum, there has been reason to be perplexed by an assortment of centralized sanctions that not only strain local fiscal and administrative capacities but simply appear to lack a persuasive rationale.

## Nostrums

To think through the possibilities for easing this conundrum, it helps to start with some sense of what most likely is not promising. Consider three notions that periodically make their way into proposals to improve American fiscal federalism: the idea that systemic imbalances can be rectified by elaborating legislative and bureaucratic procedures; the idea that all centrally mandated expenditures ought to be reimbursed; and the idea that, more generally, the efficacy of local government is necessarily enhanced by a greater measure of "cooperative federalism."

### A Federalism Accountability Act?

In 1999 congressional hearings were held on a bill that would have supplemented the Unfunded Mandates Reform Act: a so-called Federalism Accountability Act.[20] Under this scheme, for example, federal agencies would be required to operate "in cooperation with" state officials when the agencies were preparing performance measures for states that were administering grants received from Washington. Rules promulgated by agencies or bills clearing congressional committees would require impact assessments—that is, reports on how the measures might affect intergovernmental relations. These would be buttressed by independent evaluations from the Congressional Budget Office and biannual reports from the Office of Management and Budget and the Congressional Research Service. Any federal statute or rule effectively aggrandizing state and local policies would have to state its intent clearly or risk nullification by judicial review.

These suggestions had deep roots. Their inspiration could be traced to executive orders in the 1980s and 1990s and to the critical work of the Advisory Commission on Intergovernmental Relations over several decades. The main departure the "accountability act" made from these earlier efforts was that it no longer relied on mere exhortation; state and local authorities could now go to court to challenge, among other omissions, federal laws that fail to mention explicitly what state statutes were being subordinated.

Lurking here was the possibility of extensive litigation as the courts wrestled with whether this or that federal bureau adequately "cooperated" with local officials, whether the language of the *Federal Register* was "explicit" enough, and so on. And the additional reporting requirements, if seriously enforced, would join the many others already tying up the time and talents of understaffed government agencies. Granted, these steps might delay, if not derail, at least some federal usurpations. But opening yet another avenue for legal wrangles in America's amply adversarial administrative proceedings, and burying federal administrators in more red tape, seemed like inelegant remedies at best.

Most important, reforming parts of the process by which national policies displace those of states and localities does not automatically impart to the displacements a legitimate purpose. Put another way, as the scope of federal authority is enlarged, policymakers can be made to perform fuller disclosures, file more reports, and generally follow more intricate procedures. But all this monitoring still does not hold anyone answerable for whether each enlargement makes sense in the first place.

## Pay-as-You-Go

Maybe a surer way to force politicians and bureaucrats in Washington to delineate with greater precision the proper extent of federal regulatory jurisdiction would be to embrace (somehow) a seemingly straightforward proposition: no lower-level government should be obligated to comply with any new mandate from a higher-level government unless compensated by the latter. The logic in this instance is based on a simple principle of fiscal accountability: presumably, when a government is compelled to pay for its dictations out of its own tax collections, it will dictate less, or at least dictate for clear and convincing reasons. If this seems far-fetched, we might note that a number of state governments have enacted constitutional amendments or statutes purporting to ensure such accountability: in sixteen states, theoretically, state mandates on municipalities are conditioned on adequate compensation.[21] From time to time, proposals for ground rules along these lines have come before Congress as well.[22]

The attempted solution, however, turns out to be largely unworkable. In the first seven years after Illinois passed a law forbidding uncompensated state-imposed mandates on cities and towns, it was overridden twenty-five times by the state legislature. Fifteen years after Michigan amended its constitution to require that the local costs of major mandates be reimbursed, no reimbursements followed.[23] California has been among the handful of states that has tried somewhat harder to honor its commitments. Despite receiving at times hundreds of millions of dollars in reimbursements, local officials have continued to claim that they are being shortchanged.[24] At the federal level, whatever the accomplishments of the Unfunded Mandates Reform Act, it has hardly converted Congress to a pay-as-you-go norm for intergovernmental regulation.

To a considerable extent the politics of blame avoidance explain these outcomes.[25] The irresistible political charm of regulatory federalism often lies in the opportunities it affords to shift tax burdens away from the top tiers of government and down toward the bottom. Decentralizing the incidence of taxation, but not necessarily the application of the federal system's laws and rules, enables elective office holders to take credit for broad policies while distancing themselves from their tax bills, which, conveniently, are sent elsewhere.

A disinclination to compensate for each and every mandate, however, is based on more than just these calculations. Under certain circumstances compensation would be a mistake. A city that grossly fouls the atmosphere or rivers far beyond its borders should mostly be expected to reduce with its own revenues the effluents it disgorges. To hand out a national remittance in a case of this sort would be to condone the polluter's apathy or free riding.

Even where generous burden sharing plainly seems called for—as when federal regulators impose, say, a water treatment regimen on a city that emits little downstream pollution—circumspection is still in order. For a time, most of the expense of constructing municipal water treatment facilities in the United States was financed by the federal government. As a result state and local governments had little incentive to control the cost of their abatement projects. Working under budgets flush with federal cash, local construction companies, unions, and auditors may not have prevented part of the heavy investment in water pollution abatement from being wasted.[26] Prudence would seem to require that, while localities ought not carry the full cost of satisfying a fastidious federal standard, neither should they always be succored to attain a modest and feasible one.

### Cooperative Federalism

Taken to the next notch, the concept of compensatory payments to local governments graduates to a generalized redistribution of revenues—which is to say, a model of fiscal federation closer to that of Australia, Canada, and Germany. The German system, for instance, pools the proceeds from the nation's principal taxes (those on personal and corporate income as well as on value added) and then not only allocates the money between the federal and subordinate governments but among the latter in a fashion that moves money from prosperous to depressed regions. The German constitution recognizes that each level of government has its own competences but also that the states (*Länder*) and localities have to administer certain federal statutes and regulations. How the states and localities perform these tasks may be largely "their own affair" (article 83 of the Basic Law), but the financial affairs of some places are a lot weaker than others, and so, the argument goes, the weak ones deserve an extra boost.

An irony of this model is that in its zeal to shore up local fiscal capabilities by lessening their disparities, it occasions no small degree of intergovernmental friction. The heavily taxed donors, so to say, in Germany's massive revenue-sharing process resent the takers, whose dependency on the system's subventions often seems less deserved (or "cooperative") than parasitic.[27] How is the conflict managed? The German approach, its skeptics say, has been to mollify parties by growing the public sector as a whole.[28] Whatever else the growth of government might achieve, one consequence is predictable: the larger the pot of revenue sloshing around, the higher the overall rate of taxation has to be.

The extensive equalization grants or revenue-sharing arrangements of democracies abroad are akin to mechanisms for "across-the-board mandate reimbursement"—that is, general methods of offsetting the uneven compliance costs any central government's rules and regulations, rightly or wrongly, lay at the feet of local jurisdictions.[29] As chapter 5 suggests, these methods apparently give municipalities in various European countries a fiscal cushion that American municipal governments lack. That may be their good news. The bad news, though, is that expansive sharing of revenue potentially sacrifices a basic axiom of sound public finance: namely, fiscal equivalence. The more the expenses of government in your community are defrayed by taxable income from somewhere else, the less incentive your community has to operate cost effectively. Simply stated, the concept of fiscal equivalence holds that as much as possible each jurisdiction should pay its bills from its own taxable income.

Lest we think that this maxim is mainly of theoretical rather than practical interest, countries that have strayed from it have had unhappy experiences, ranging in scale from small to very large. At one point the city of Hamburg created special parking bays in front of bus stops on busy streets so that buses picking up and discharging passengers would not obstruct the regular flow of traffic. Later the Green Party, a member of the local governing coalition, insisted on eliminating these recently constructed facilities.[30] Evidently the Greens favored bus-stop designs that would deliberately snarl traffic so as to discourage the use of private motor vehicles. Under Germany's cooperative federalism the taxes collected in Hamburg were not the only revenues that would pay to build the bus stations (at a cost of 175,000 deutsche marks per bay) and then to remove them. In effect, the taxpayers of other Länder as well had to underwrite the whims of Hamburg's politicians.

A fiasco of far greater proportions attended the muddled fiscal relations among the strata of government in Italy. In the Italian system, at least until the last decade, the collection and distribution of revenues was progressively centralized on the theory that the national government could thereby overcome inequalities in the tax bases and administrative burdens of subnational units (regions, provinces, and municipalities). The result for many years was that these units neither knew nor cared to know the costs of the services they were obligated to administer. Local overspending and debt swelled—irresponsibility made worse by the willingness of the central government to bail out the most debt-ridden municipalities.[31] France, another practitioner of grand compensatory transfers of tax revenue, experienced some similar symptoms of local fiscal reck-lessness during the 1980s.[32]

So severe were the public spending and indebtedness problems in Italy, however, that they were likely to impede that country's participation in the European monetary union. With a series of measures starting in 1990, the Italian government at last succeeded in establishing a degree of disci-pline. How? The answer, in large part, lay in restoring a semblance of fis-cal equivalence: many municipalities and other local bodies now are expected to meet a more substantial portion of their costs with own-source taxes.[33]

## Making Progress

Thus what might be called, for lack of a better label, the European approach—guaranteeing that local governments are funded to handle everything they are told to do—may seem like an uncomplicated solution. In practice it is one with potentially disagreeable side effects. Faltering regions or disadvantaged urban centers should not be left to sink or swim amid a torrent of centrally generated demands on local budgets and agen-cies. But neither should relieving these local areas come at the price of public profligacy. Indeed, with precisely this concern in mind policymak-ers in some of Europe's most centralized regimes have begun taking steps to devolve to their regions and municipalities additional concurrent tax authority.

A better way of bolstering hard-pressed communities would rely not just on giving them money to help support the extra workloads they are assigned, but more basically, on disencumbering local government from some of the assignments. What might this mean in concrete terms?

### UMRA-Plus

In an ideal world each decision to wedge federal authority into the work of local governments would be weighed carefully for whether the federal interventions genuinely serve a compelling national interest. Ideally, in other words, policymakers would conduct a routine inquiry, as impartial and rigorous as possible, into whether the proposed interventions are likely to yield appreciable net gains to society: are major or merely trivial perils to the public health and welfare being addressed, how effectively, and at what cost? A device like the Unfunded Mandates Reform Act falls short of doing this job—though at least UMRA accepts the principle that the financial liabilities Congress imposes on local budgets ought to be independently estimated and publicly displayed.

Frequently, foretelling the costs of a public policy, let alone determining whether it is worth pursuing, is impossible without knowing how it is likely to be implemented in rules or standards that will be promulgated at a later stage.[34] Alas, it is hard to envision how UMRA or any other institutional mechanism can be perfected to handle even this pedestrian practicality.

The most that can be hoped for is that as new regulatory statutes are authorized or old ones reauthorized, more of them will direct (and trust) agencies to formulate their rules and standards on the basis of risk assessments and cost-benefit evaluations.[35] No one should be under the illusion that these activities will ever rise to an exact science. Still, they endeavor to ask the right questions, regardless of whether their answers are at best mere educated guesses. Even a crude picture of what social payoff regulators can plausibly expect from their regulations is preferable to no picture at all. And the exercise just might help restrain a bit of the ordinary urge in Washington to shout "there ought to be a law" in the face of almost any local controversy.

Congress also might consider taking the spirit of UMRA a step or two further. For all practical purposes, conditions attached to many federal aid programs are mandates. There should be no blanket dispensation for large congressional grant authorizations that abound with instructions but not with promised appropriations. These acts of Congress especially should be viewed as coercive rather than "voluntary" from the standpoint of local authorities and thus ought to fall within UMRA's scrutiny when reauthorizations are due. The Individuals with Disabilities Education Act is an example. As chapter 3 discusses, this perennially underfunded "grant-in-aid" has placed the school systems of cities like Baltimore under unforeseen stress. A worthy aim of UMRA has been to inform congressional debates by furthering reasonably systematic and transparent appraisals of costly programs. Laws such as IDEA, so grueling for city school budgets, should be no exception.

Indeed perhaps not all legislation that affirms *rights* should be entitled to automatic exemption. When such legislation is at bottom a congressionally mandated benefit program, paid for by conscripting the resources of state and local governments, its costs probably ought to be "scored" much like those of any other new federal entitlement. In the words of the *Economic Report of the President*, "Requiring owners of public buildings to install access facilities for handicapped persons, for example, is equivalent to the government installing those facilities with revenues from a tax on building owners. If the latter program were counted in the budget, it would increase both spending and revenue figures."[36] Congress in the end may craft social policies in whatever style it sees fit. But to enact these policies without obtaining first a respectable approximation of their bottom line for the taxpayer sometimes seems too politically commodious.

### Legal Issues

If the stack of regulations that mayors protest consisted only of congressional mandates and rules from federal bureaus, it would be less tall and less costly than it actually has been. The reason, as I have noted more than once, is that in the pile are also a lot of requirements resulting from lawsuits. Many, maybe even most, of these serve socially fruitful purposes and should not be choked off. But something seems amiss with the wheels of a legal system that also ushers into the federal courts plaintiffs who complain that, say, enforcing a seat-belt ordinance intended for the protection of motorists discriminates against people with claustrophobia, or who complain that a strength test is discriminatory because it requires applicants for a local fire department to simulate the real world by carrying a heavy weight through an obstacle course.[37]

And some of the court-approved remedies seem increasingly out of touch with exigencies on the ground. However laudable the intention, there is something faintly naive about a court order that, for example, bars border patrol agents from considering the ethnic "appearance" of individuals as a factor in deciding which motorists to stop for questioning near the nation's borders.[38] The same goes for aspects of consent decrees like the one that governed Philadelphia's detention of suspects until a few years ago, or maybe even the plans imposed on the Los Angeles Police Department to eradicate any trace of racial or ethnic profiling when officers stop vehicles or passersby. The fact is that city police forces are stretched to their limits coping with terrorist threats on top of countless other law enforcement needs.[39] Under the circumstances, how realistic—indeed, how smart—is it to have as a pressing priority the diversion of departmental resources into complex record-keeping projects aimed at penalizing the cops for "prejudging" anybody?[40]

It is in respects like these that city governments abroad, especially in most of Europe, are decidedly less weighed down—and the contrast offers valuable lessons. Paris has some 21,000 police officers, or roughly one per 100 residents, compared with one per 270 inhabitants in New York.[41] No doubt the dense police presence in Paris helps keep that city's homicide rate below New York's. Sheer numbers, however, are not the only advantage of the Parisian police. Its legal and political environment is less adversarial; hence problems of morale and recruitment are not what they have become for many municipal police departments in the United States.

Here, according to a recent account, "Many officers from the lowest to the highest rank are questioning their occupation." At least part of the explanation, reportedly, is that many are now "discouraged by seemingly constant public and news media criticism about police brutality and racial profiling."[42] How might some rank and file adapt to this climate? "Parking under a shady tree to work on a crossword puzzle is a great alternative to being labeled a racist and being dragged through an inquest, a review board, an FBI and U.S. attorney investigation and a lawsuit," explains a patrolman in Seattle.[43] And how rattled are some of their superiors ? "The politics of being police chief have become so insane no one wants the job," says an assistant chief in the same city.[44]

It is not too much to say that the public managers of most "street-level bureaucracies" in the United States, not just those in local law enforcement agencies, go about their business with an ominous sense of being perpetually at risk of legal run-ins they cannot readily prevent or minimize, no matter how honestly they try.[45] Inasmuch as the vagaries of federal litigation (or perceived trajectories thereof) have contributed to this discomfort, it could be lowered somewhat if all three branches of the national government made a few changes. "See you in court" is the prospect that national laws almost inevitably raise when, among other complexities, legislation defines unmet social needs or wants as actionable deprivations of rights, or when its wording is potentially open ended, or when it deliberately deputizes private litigators for the purpose of enforcement. To expect the political process to shed every such source of disputation is wishful thinking, but surely at least a couple could get better attention.

Take legislative interpretation. What precisely does it mean to mandate "safe and complete" inspections for asbestos fibers in school buildings? At what point do incidents of alleged bias amount to a "pattern or practice"? Which "related services" qualify as "appropriate" in special education? Exactly how must a workplace accommodate an employee who makes a case that he or she is "substantially" limited from engaging in a "major life activity"? When, if ever, can a city prove conclusively that fulfilling Washington's wishes causes the local taxpayers an "undue" hardship? Language like this is bait for lawsuits, with the result that responsibility for ironing out the ambiguities is continually offloaded to the judiciary.[46]

There may come a time when the courts will simply decline to take in so much of Congress's laundry. (Not long ago, Justice Antonin Scalia warned, "If you have a legislature that is eager to push the envelope you should expect a higher percentage of invalidations.")[47] But short of that, the legislative and judicial branches need to bridge more of the gaps between their respective deliberations. At the very least, steadier lines of communication would enable "judges to alert legislators to statutory drafting problems identified in the course of adjudication," as Chief Justice William H. Rehnquist has suggested.[48] The conversation might even regularly remind both institutions that flinging open the courthouse doors to litigants, and emboldening them to extract broad remedies on the basis of pliant statutory expressions, is often tantamount to legislating by proxy—that is, with too little toil by the elective office holders to whom the Constitution entrusted the central power to tax and spend.

The executive, too, can help turn down some of the litigious heat on state and local governments. Many U.S. regulatory statutes, in sharp contrast to those of most other countries, send individuals or organizations to sue local authorities over questions of compliance, even when a competent federal enforcement agency exists and its labors ought to suffice. The double-barreled approach to enforcement—coming from agencies *and* private plaintiffs—sometimes subjects local officials to no end of legal headaches, especially when terms of federal statutes are vague and officials are unsure what is required of them. By the mid-1990s the Advisory Commission on Intergovernmental Relations had come to regard this problem as severe enough to justify an audacious recommendation: "Only the federal agency responsible for enforcement of a law should be permitted to sue state and local governments."[49] The ACIR's proposal is drastic and perhaps unwise, but some lesser measures would not be.

Pruning the payment of legal fees or the fee-shifting provisions for citizen suits under certain conditions (as Congress and the Supreme Court have occasionally contemplated in recent years) may be one option.[50] Another is that executive agencies need not make a habit of joining these suits. A tilt toward more selective and limited engagement may already be under way. Federal administrators, like their local counterparts, worry when, in the words of a former EPA chief, "Litigation is essentially setting the priorities."[51] But last year, for example, the Justice Department pulled out of a case in which a local transportation agency in Pennsylvania was accused of administering an overly rigorous aerobics test for applicants to its security force.[52]

## Retrenchment

Of the names and places that were etched into the nation's consciousness on September 11 the Emma E. Booker Elementary School in Sarasota, Florida, is not one of the first that comes to mind. But perhaps it should be. For there was where President George W. Bush happened to be when United Airlines Flight 175 slammed into lower Manhattan. On that morning Bush was abruptly forced to interrupt the sort of presidential pastime that had become fashionable in the 1990s—including duties like sitting in on a second-grade classroom a thousand miles away—and get back to more serious business in the capital.[53]

The point of relating this incident is not so much to predict with any certainty that from now on what passes for national leadership will no longer include dabbling in the minutiae of education programs, municipal staffing practices, sanitation standards, criminal justice, and countless other issues customarily of local interest. In fact, for some spheres the post-"9/11" world will probably deepen the federal involvement. (No small assortment of central initiatives might make headway under the broad banners of counterterrorism, homeland security, economic stimulus packages, and so on.) Rather, the point is that federal policymakers are at a crossroads: they may well become more engrossed in the particulars of local public administration, or conceivably, they could retrench. At least an *opportunity* to elevate and clarify the respective roles of central and local institutions is at hand.

Of course, clarifications have been attempted before. At the height of the cold war, when American cities were thought to be in imminent danger of nuclear attack, the Eisenhower administration struggled to sort out the proper confines of national and local policies. A 1955 report, titled *Civil Defense and Urban Vulnerability*, concluded that "intergovernmental responsibilities" were "inappropriately defined and assigned," but then drew no simple road map for how to define and assign those responsibilities, and wound up recommending solutions such as more "national financial assistance to states and cities."[54]

During an earlier era, the latter third of the nineteenth century and the first third of the twentieth, the Supreme Court strove repeatedly to parse activities that Congress could constitutionally regulate and activities that would remain under the aegis of the states and localities. The result was a welter of seemingly arbitrary distinctions: federal laws governing the movement of lottery tickets, liquor, prostitutes, and harmful foods and drugs were upheld, while other basic functions—including manufacturing, insurance, and farming—were classified as *intra*state commerce, hence left to state regulators. By the 1940s the Court had all but given up trying to sustain such differentiations. Some would persist, however. For example, according to the Court, the commerce clause duly empowered Congress to instruct the city of San Antonio how to pay its transit system operators, but somehow the same clause did not give Congress the power to direct the local police to perform background checks on prospective gun purchasers.

A clean and stable division of labor between the levels of government has proved impossible to demarcate over time. Still, there ought to be some middle ground between either persevering stubbornly with futile theories of dual sovereignty or throwing up one's hands and accepting the proposition that the concerns of federal and local authorities can only be randomly distributed. The messy and frustrating debate over federalism must continue, for much is at stake.

## Cities Back in Trouble

At the municipal level the turn of events last fall inflicted extensive damage. Whereas the preponderance of jobs in U.S. metropolitan areas had been clustered close to city centers before the Second World War, less than a quarter of urban jobs were situated there by 1996.[55] This hollowing out of the urban core had barely started to diminish when the nation was suddenly reminded that cities are high-profile targets, vulnerable to extreme violence and disruption. Central locations that had become safer and more inviting for firms and workers by the late 1990s now looked dangerous and costly again. Many companies would almost certainly resume their outward trek—their exit now increasingly facilitated by the Internet, new teleconferencing media, and other new technologies of the advanced digital age.[56]

The balance sheets of more than just a couple of front-line cities took a hit in the weeks and months following the terrorist assaults on New York and Washington. Boston found itself spending $100,000 a week on police overtime alone.[57] Baltimore disbursed an unexpected $2.6 million for security costs in just over a month and feared the bill could run to almost $16 million by the end of the fiscal year.[58] Year-end predictions for Dallas were $6 million, and for New Orleans $10 million. These and other unplanned expenses arrived as local economies were already deteriorating. By year's end, the flagging economy had shriveled tax revenues in at least forty-three states. Facing shortfalls totaling about $36 billion, they were in no position to salve quickly the widespread budgetary bruises of cities and counties.[59]

All of this fell on top of preexisting liabilities that had rendered tenuous the revival of many central cities before the current crisis. The gains in New York, Chicago, Los Angeles, and various other major centers in the 1990s had been aided by a dramatic reduction in urban crime. But in New York homicides were up by 9 percent in 1999 over the previous year.[60] There and elsewhere the uptick in crime seemed more likely to continue than abate in the aftermath of September 11. Redeployments of manpower to investigate bomb threats, guard buildings, improve airport security, protect water supplies, respond to anthrax mailings, and countless other antiterrorist exigencies have left fewer police on the street for ordinary patrols.

Central city tax rates had continued to repel prospective urbanites, especially in light of the fact that essential city services failed to compete in quality with those in the suburbs. Despite its relatively high taxes, for instance, New York City's teachers have been earning up to 20 percent less than their suburban counterparts, with the result that recruitment is harder and the percentage of uncertified teachers too high.[61] The average total tax burden for a resident of the District of Columbia was recently estimated to be $10,881 a year, which was higher than the average in all of the city's adjoining suburban counties (about $1,000 higher than in all but one).[62] Immediate prospects for leveling this very uneven playing field seemed doomed after September 11. A combination of emergency spending and revenue reductions (worsened by, among other pressures, a prolonged closing of Reagan National Airport) quickly carved a sizable hole in the District's shaky finances.[63]

When this urban panorama might begin to look less bleak again was anybody's guess at the end of 2001. But even if a recovery would start sooner rather than later, the circumstances served as a reminder that local officials have had their hands full securing the bare essentials of public health and safety. To keep requiring of city governments a lot of additional exertions, many of which have little bearing on the basics, is to overstep, so to speak, the city limits.

## *Simplify, Simplify, Simplify*

Much as we wonder whether, for example, chasing car thieves, medicinal marijuana users, unwitting wetlands trespassers, and deadbeat dads are a suitable preoccupation of federal law enforcement these days, a variety of municipal agencies ought to have their own bedrock functions simplified. For a conspicuous illustration, ponder once again the unwieldy modern missions of local public schools.

America's public school systems have been juggling more than a few extracurricular activities: they have had to create correct racial balances in enrollments; clear asbestos; offer bilingual-bicultural instruction for students with limited proficiency in English; perform recycling; offer special education options; serve lunches; ensure "gender equity"; use standardized achievement tests (but mind their possible "disparate impacts" on minorities); delead the water coolers; prepare to be held liable when expelling certain students for disciplinary reasons; face liability when one student harasses another; and accept the possibility of receiving the medical bills of still others.[64] As if the list did not suffice, for a time the Clinton administration considered adding other requisite services, so that schools would be monitoring such matters as Medicaid coverage of matriculants. Buried somewhere under all these items, and more, is the primary purpose of public education: to impart to pupils at least a basic level of literacy.[65]

It is interesting to compare this complex undertaking with the systems abroad—Germany's, for instance. The provision of basic instruction is just about the sole order of business for German elementary schools. Auxiliary requirements, including such tasks as supplying transportation and meals, are not considered the responsibility of schools. "The school has never assumed its role to be in loco parentis," writes one observer, and hence it does not double as a multipurpose social service agency.[66] The typical school board in the United States invests substantially in things like athletic programs and facilities, and by law it must attend to whether they are equitably utilized. German primary and secondary schools commonly offer no organized athletic programs at all. (Sports are left to amateur athletic associations and municipal gyms.) While the typical American high school is heavily staffed with full-time administrators, counselors, health specialists, and the like, such specialized staff are rare in the German equivalent. Even the principal (called a director, leader, or rector) in a German grade school is a teacher.

Although the German model may be too austere, the American way is overwrought, expensive, and, particularly in urban districts, substandard.[67] The contrast drops some useful hints. What our city schools need is not just another consignment of intergovernmental aid to better match their wide-ranging responsibilities. The responsibilities should be narrowed. In the long run, for instance, local oversubscription of federally mandated special education services will only be relieved by improving intergovernmental funding formulas *and* narrowing the near-boundless clientele that school districts are presently led to accommodate under the law.[68]

The agendas of our urban school systems, loaded with legal intricacies and tangential policy demands, are not the only ones in need of a trim. Various other operations of city government, too, might run more smoothly if some of their extra freight were downsized. The importance of this adjustment bears emphasizing. Whatever the other prerequisites for a sustained revitalization of America's central cities, these places need to lower their tax rates in relation to those of surrounding suburbs and to devote undivided attention to bettering the delivery of traditional local services. Intergovernmental regulations that lose sight of these fundamentals and that fixate on accessories do the cities no favor.

## A Matter of Trust

A final thought: for local governments to get their job done, they need to be accorded the trust they deserve—and that the public increasingly believes they have earned. In 1964 three-quarters of respondents in opinion polls expressed confidence in the ability of the federal government to do the right thing most of the time.[69] State and local authorities were viewed less favorably. By the mid-1990s the roles had been reversed. Now states and localities were held in higher regard than the national government. In 1997, for instance, 40 percent of citizens put little or no stock in the ability of the federal government to handle their problems, whereas only 21 percent held so dim a view of their local governments.[70] Although the federal establishment has since improved its image, a striking fact of contemporary public attitudes toward government in the United States—a fact that policymakers in the capital have yet to fathom fully—is the degree to which trust in local institutions has been restored.[71]

Some of this restoration, ironically, might be credited to national more than to local initiatives. Suppose, for instance, that notable national environmental laws of recent decades had never been adopted. Quite a few cities and states would almost certainly be more polluted today, lowering people's respect for their local officials. But there is also a simpler consideration. The public is not blind; it sees that not all the successes of government spring from Washington, and not all of the failings can be blamed on City Hall. In the hours and weeks following the destruction of the World Trade Center, Americans watched their federal and municipal officials in action—and were impressed by the dedication, courage, and sacrifices of the firefighters and police officers of New York, New York.

# Notes

## Chapter 1

1. U.S. Department of Housing and Urban Development, *The State of the Cities 1999: Third Annual Report* (Government Printing Office, 1999), p. 3.

2. See Bruce Katz and Jennifer Bradley, "Divided We Sprawl," *Atlantic Monthly,* December 1999, pp. 26–42.

3. Atlanta was illustrative: it gained 12,300 residents in the 1990s and was able to reverse the population losses it had experienced in the 1980s. But the city's gains were trivial compared with those of its surrounding counties, which expanded by 647,100 people. Brookings Center on Urban and Metropolitan Policy, *Moving Beyond Sprawl: The Challenge for Metropolitan Atlanta* (Brookings, 2000), p. 9.

4. Brookings Center on Urban and Metropolitan Policy, *Housing Heats Up: Home Building Patterns in Metropolitan Areas* (Brookings, 1999), p. 3.

5. The estimate is based on an analysis of ninety-two large metropolitan areas by John Brennan and Edward W. Hill, *Where Are the Jobs? Cities, Suburbs, and the Competition for Employment* (Brookings Center for Urban and Metropolitan Policy, November 1999), p. 1.

6. Bruce Katz, "Enough of the Small Stuff! Toward a New Urban Agenda," *Brookings Review*, vol. 18 (Summer 2000), p. 5.

161

7. While poverty had declined in central cities in absolute terms, urban rates of poverty were still twice as high as suburban poverty rates, 18.8 percent as against 9 percent in 1997. In 1989 suburban median income was 58 percent higher than the median income in central cities. By 1996 the gap had widened to 67 percent. See Katz, "Enough of the Small Stuff!" p. 8. The proportion of the nation's welfare families that live in the one hundred largest U.S. cities went from 48 percent to 58 percent between 1994 and 1999.

8. "Mean Streets," *Economist*, July 22, 2000, p. 31.

9. Brookings Center for Urban and Metropolitan Policy, *A Region Divided: The State of Growth in Greater Washington, D.C.* (Brookings, 1999), p. 3.

10. Leslie Eaton, "Big Job Losses Add to New York Economic Gloom," *New York Times*, November 16, 2001, p. A1; and Spencer S. Hsu, "Forecast Is Gloomy for District Economy," *Washington Post*, November 16, 2001, p. B1.

11. By the end of September 2001, the twelve-month forecast for economic growth in Miami suddenly plunged from 2.44 percent to -0.65 percent. San Francisco's outlook went from 2.72 percent to -0.36 percent. The situation in the rest of the country changed dramatically almost everywhere as well. Mary William Walsh, "Urban Pain, From Sea to Sea," *New York Times*, September 30, 2001, p. C2.

12. Edward I. Koch, "The Mandate Millstone," *Public Interest*, no. 61 (Fall 1981), p. 13.

13. Dennis R. Judd, *The Politics of American Cities: Private Power and Public Policy*, 3d ed. (Scott, Foresman, 1988), p. 201.

14. See Hartmut Haubermann, "The Relationship between Local and Federal Government Policy in the Federal Republic of Germany," in Chris Pickvance and Edmond Preteceille, eds., *State Restructuring and Local Power: A Comparative Perspective* (London: Pinter Publishers, 1991), pp. 92, 93, 99.

15. "Local Difficulties," *Economist*, May 9, 1998, p. 55; and Manfred Konukiewitz and Helmut Wollman, "Physical Planning in a Federal System: The Case of West Germany," in David H. McKay, ed., *Planning and Politics in Western Europe* (St. Martin's Press, 1982), p. 75.

16. Clyde Wayne Crews Jr., *Ten Thousand Commandments: An Annual Policymaker's Snapshot of the Federal Regulatory State, 2000 Edition* (Washington: Competitive Enterprise Institute, 2000), p. 48.

17. U.S. Advisory Commission on Intergovernmental Relations, *Federal Regulation of State and Local Governments: The Mixed Record of the 1980s* (July 1993), p. 7.

18. Cities in general bear a disproportionate burden for poverty-related public expenditures, including police, fire, courts, and administrative functions. See, for instance, Janet Rothenberg Pack, "Poverty and Urban Public Expenditures," *Urban Studies*, vol. 35, no. 11 (1998), pp. 1995–2019.

19. Bridgeport's formal bankruptcy in 1991 was imputed to the impact of unfunded mandates emanating largely from the state of Connecticut, not the federal government. However, the state itself had been hammered by Washington's mandates. Residents of Connecticut, more than taxpayers in any other state, have been paying more in federal taxes than they receive back in federal spending. Inevitably, much of the pressure from this imbalance passes down from the state to the local level. States in the Northeast and Great Lakes regions have experienced intergovernmental deficits more commonly than states in the Sun Belt and Great Plains. See Jay H. Walder and Herman B. Leonard, *The Federal Budget and the States, Fiscal Year 1997* (Harvard University, John F. Kennedy School of Government, September 30, 1998), p. 1.

20. Michael A. Pagano, *City Fiscal Conditions in 1998* (Washington: National League of Cities, June 1998), pp. 1–2.

21. The rate of growth in city revenues was approximately 30 percent less than the growth rate of the nation's gross domestic product during the period 1988–97. Pagano, *City Fiscal Conditions.*

22. Stephen Goldsmith and others, *Markets Not Mandates: A Request to Congress for a New Contract with America's Cities* (Washington: Cato Institute, 1998), p. 1.

23. The figures are in 1996 dollars and include SRF capitalization, plus annual local operations and maintenance costs. See Association of Metropolitan Sewerage Agencies, *The Costs of Clean* (Washington, March 1999).

24. Office of Management and Budget, *Preliminary Ten-Year Capital Strategy: Fiscal Years 2002–2011* (New York, January 24, 2001), p. iii.

25. In 1997 New York City's bond rating was just slightly better than Philadelphia's, no better than Detroit's, and worse than that of St. Louis and Baltimore. New York had $42 billion in loans outstanding as of early 2002. This debt burden was much larger than that of the entire state of California ($25 billion). Richard Pérez-Peña and James McKinley Jr., "A Mountain of Boom-Time Debt Looms as New York Feels Pinch," *New York Times,* February 21, 2002, p. A1. Until Mayor Rudolph Giuliani managed some reductions, the overall tax rates had reached the point that further increases were likely to yield diminishing returns. For a careful analysis comparing New York's precarious position to that of several other cities, see Andrew Haughwout and others, "Local Revenue Hills: A General Equilibrium Specification with Evidence from Four U.S. Cities," *National Bureau of Economic Research,* Working Paper 7603 (Cambridge, Mass.: National Bureau of Economic Research, March 2000). Although the Giuliani administration scaled back a number of the city's manifold taxes (including most notably the commercial rent tax), others, including the personal income tax, did not seem to come down much below the level prevailing at the end of 1989.

26. See Pietro S. Nivola, *Laws of the Landscape: How Policies Shape Cities in Europe and America* (Brookings, 1999), p. 81.

27. Tom Loveless and Diane Ravitch, "Broken Promises: What the Federal Government Can Do to Imrpove American Education," *Brookings Review*, vol. 18 (Spring 2000), p. 20.

28. "Coming Up $80 Million Short," *Washington Post*, September 8, 2001, p.A20. Cost overruns in special education caused the program's expense for the city to jump 41 percent from 1998 to 2001.

29. Kalman R. Hettleman, "Special-Ed Funding Isn't Fair to All Students," *Baltimore Sun*, May 17, 1998, p. 1L.

30. Paul G. Vallas, "Saving Public Schools," *Manhattan Institute Civic Bulletin*, no. 16 (March 1999), pp. 1–2, 9.

31. Paul T. Hill, Christine Campbell, and James Harvey, *It Takes a City: Getting Serious about Urban School Reform* (Brookings, 2000), chap. 2.

32. A large body of work has attempted, with mixed success, to evaluate the effects of federal urban programs. To pay full homage to that literature would require a footnote of unwieldy length. For an early, and thorough, compendium that reviews methodological complexities, as well as some particular programs, see Norman J. Glickman, ed., *The Urban Impacts of Federal Policies* (Johns Hopkins University Press, 1980). The "urban impacts" of several federal regulatory activities I discuss later in this volume are not the ones that have been widely studied.

33. See, for example, Helen F. Ladd, "Big-City Finances," in George Peterson, ed., *Big-City Politics, Governance, and Fiscal Constraints* (Washington: Urban Institute Press, 1994).

34. See Pietro S. Nivola, "Apocalypse Now? Whither the Urban Fiscal Crisis," *Polity*, vol. 14 (Spring 1982), pp. 371–94.

35. Steven Greenhouse, "Transit Contract Raises Pay by 18%," *New York Times*, December 16, 1999, p. A1.

36. *Trenton v. New Jersey*, 262 U.S. 192 (1923). Emphasis added.

37. James Madison, "The Federalist No. 45," in Edward Mead Earle, ed., *The Federalist* (Random House, 1937), pp. 298–304.

38. See more generally E. Blaine Linder, *A Decade of Devolution: Perspectives on State-Local Relations* (Washington.: Urban Institute Press, 1989).

39. See Demetrios Caraley, "Washington Abandons the Cities," *Political Science Quarterly*, vol. 107, no. 1 (1992), p. 14.

40. On a more complete definition of federal paternalism, see Lawrence M. Mead, "The Rise of Paternalism," in Lawrence M. Mead, ed., *The New Paternalism: Supervisory Approaches to Poverty* (Brookings, 1997), chap. 1.

41. As the U.S. Advisory Commission on Intergovernmental Relations observed some years ago, there "is no universally accepted definition of a federal mandate and surprisingly little consensus on the matter." U.S. Advisory

Commission on Intergovernmental Relations, *Federally Induced Costs Affecting State and Local Governments* (September 1994), p. 3. Undoubtedly, there will be lawyers and scholars of intergovernmental jurisprudence that will be unhappy with my (and the ACIR's) frequently nontechnical use of terms such as mandates and preemptions. Strictly speaking, to legal experts a federal "preemption" prohibits local governments from doing x or y, whereas, technically, a "mandate" tells local governments to do x or y. The concepts may seem straightforward and distinct, but, alas, sometimes they are not. Suppose, for instance, that the prohibition on x or y is part of a grant-in-aid program (that is, "Once you receive a federal grant that you cannot do without, you are prevented from doing x or y"). This common condition is ordinarily called a mandate, but for all practical purposes it is also a preemption. Or suppose that a federal grant program, as a condition of receipt, requires local government to do x or y. Suppose, also, that funding for the program languishes over time, but the conditional requirements persist (because some token funds remain available), so that it becomes hard, or even impossible, for the locals to pay for x, y, or—for good measure—z. How should this constraint be labeled? If a federal intervention effectively impedes a community from accomplishing x, y, or z, as a practical matter local priorities have been displaced or preempted—though not in a formal sense. Here and there, this book uses the terminology of federalism more loosely than is customary in legal formulations, chiefly because the formulations sometimes seem to draw distinctions without a practical difference.

# Chapter 2

1. For a full account of the Tulsa riot on which this paragraph is based, see Brent Staples, "Unearthing a Riot," *New York Times Magazine*, December 19, 1999, pp. 64–69.

2. See Paul E. Peterson, *City Limits* (University of Chicago Press, 1981), chaps. 10, 11.

3. See David Goldberg, "Heads Up, Atlanta: Cities Are Scrambling to Comply with the Clean Air Act's Strict New Rules," *Planning*, vol. 64 (July 1998), pp. 20–23.

4. James Fallows, *More Like Us* (Houghton Mifflin, 1989), p. 169.

5. Racial violence, sparked by alleged black rapes, exploded in Omaha, Kansas City, Knoxville, Rosewood, Fla., Longview, Tex., and Washington, D.C., among other towns, at about this period.

6. Nearly all the PCBs flowing into the Great Lakes originate from the air. An estimated quarter of the nitrogen in the Chesapeake Bay derives from polluted air drifting from at least four neighboring states. Mary Graham, *The Morning after Earth Day: Practical Environmental Politics* (Brookings, 1999), p. 80.

7. Susan Rose-Ackerman, "Does Federalism Matter? Choice in a Federal Republic," *Journal of Political Economy*, vol. 49, no. 1 (1981), pp. 152–63. See also John H. Cumberland, "Interregional Pollution Spillovers and Consistency of Environmental Policy," in M. Siebert and others, eds., *Regional Environmental Policy: The Economic Issues* (New York University Press, 1979), pp. 255–81.

8. James Madison, "Federalist No. 10," in Pietro S. Nivola and David H. Rosenbloom, eds., *Classic Readings in American Politics*, 3d ed. (St. Martin's, 1999), p. 34.

9. *Budget of the United States Government, Fiscal Year 1993*, table 12.1, part 5, pp. 164–65.

10. This was reflected in the nearly static level of aid to state and local governments between 1980 and 1995, excluding federal assistance for Medicaid. Timothy Conlan, *From New Federalism to Devolution: Twenty-Five Years of Intergovernmental Reform* (Brookings, 1998), pp. 204–06, 219.

11. Conlan, *From New Federalism to Devolution*, p. 204.

12. James Q. Wilson and John J. DiIulio Jr., *American Government: Institutions and Policies*, 7th ed. (Houghton Mifflin Company, 1998), p. 70.

13. Bernard J. Frieden and Marshall Kaplan, *The Politics of Neglect: Urban Aid from Model Cities to Revenue Sharing* (MIT Press, 1977).

14. As early as 1994, the states were enjoying surpluses that totaled more than $17 billion.

15. On how devolution has been a cost-controlling mechanism for social programs such as Medicaid, see James R. Tallon Jr. and Lawrence D. Brown, "Who Gets What? Devolution of Eligibility and Benefits in Medicaid," in Frank J. Thompson and John J. DiIulio Jr., *Medicaid and Devolution: A View from the States* (Brookings, 1998), p. 237.

16. See generally, on the efficiency gains from interjurisdicational competition within federal systems, Michael S. Greve, *Real Federalism* (Washington: American Enterprise Institute Press, 1999). For the leading analysis of its disadvantages, see Paul E. Peterson, *The Price of Federalism* (Brookings, 1995).

17. Paul C. Light, *The True Size of Government* (Brookings, 1999), p. 32.

18. In 1995, for instance, California collected $1.2 billion in federal disaster relief, much of it to compensate questionable "victims." Dan Morgan, "Governors Bit Helping Hand in Mandates Fight," *Washington Post*, January 22, 1995, pp. A1, A6.

19. Demetrios Caraley, "Washington Abandons the Cities," *Political Science Quarterly*, vol. 107, no. 1 (1992), p. 13.

20. For the subsidy argument, see James R. St. John, "Unfunded Mandates: Balancing State and National Needs," *Brookings Review*, vol. 13 (Spring 1995), pp. 12–15.

21. *South Carolina v. Baker*, 485 U.S. 505 (1988).

22. *Garcia* v. *San Antonio Metropolitan Transit Authority,* 469 U.S. 528 (1985). Nine months later Congress responded by amending the Fair Labor Standards Act (FLSA), extending it again to all public sector employees. Public Law 99-150, November 13, 1985.

23. *National League of Cities* v. *Usery,* 426 U.S. 833 (1976).

24. On the impact of Davis-Bacon, see U.S. Advisory Commission on Intergovernmental Relations, *The Role of Federal Mandates in Intergovernmental Relations* (January 1996), p. 13.

25. See Walter Olson, *The Excuse Factory: How Employment Law is Paralyzing the American Workplace* (Free Press, 1997), p. 185.

26. For instance, *Tinker* v. *Des Moines Independent Community School District,* 393 U.S. 503 (1969); *Goss* v. *Lopez,* 419 U.S. 565 (1975). See Abigail Thernstrom, "Where Did All the Order Go? School Discipline and the Law," in Diane Ravitch, ed., *Brookings Papers on Education Policy, 1999* (Brookings, 1999), p. 213. In a North Carolina school district, for instance, a student who broke a teacher's arm was given a mere two-day suspension.

27. In *Bethel School District No. 403* v. *Fraser,* 478 U.S. 675 (1986) and several ensuing decisions, the court sought to nudge the balance of authority back from students to school officials. However, lower courts have tended to restrict removals and even suspensions of special-ed students.

28. According to the so-called "2-in, 2-out" procedure, at least two employees have to remain outside the site of an "interior structural fire" when two go inside (Standard Number 1910.134 (g) (4) (i) through (iii)). OSHA , *Regulations (Standards - 29 CFR): Standard Number 1910.134.* The rule may apply to many fire departments that have federally approved occupational safety and health (OSH) plans in effect. Section 18(b) of the Occupational Safety and Health Act of 1970 (Public Law 91-596) stipulated that states operating under their own OSH plans are required to provide OSH protection to public as well as private sector workers. And the standards of each state OSH plan have to be at least as stringent as those of the federal OSHA program, which covers all private sector workers. See U.S. Department of Labor, Office of Inspector General, *Evaluating the Status of Occupational Safety and Health Coverage of State and Local Workers in Federal OSHA States* (February 2000). Some two dozen states operate under federally approved OSH plans. Thus, California, as an example, follows the federal OSHA firefighting guideline verbatim. How much, if any, flexibility localities might have in such states is not entirely clear. A note attached to paragraph (g) of the OSHA regulations, however, adds this proviso: "Nothing in this section is meant to preclude firefighters from performing emergency rescue activities before an entire team has assembled."

29. Motor Carrier Safety Administration, Federal Highway Administration, Regulation no. 393.90.

30. Paul R. Portney, "Environmental Policy in the Next Century," in Henry J. Aaron and Robert E. Reischauer, eds., *Setting National Priorities: The 2000 Election and Beyond* (Brookings, 1999), p. 379.

31. Paul I. Posner, *The Politics of Unfunded Mandates* (Georgetown University Press, 1998), p. 64.

32. See, for instance, Pietro S. Nivola, *The Urban Service Problem* (D.C. Heath, 1979), pp. 145–46.

33. Olson, *The Excuse Factory*, p. 185.

34. See Fred Siegel, "The Social Democratic City," *Public Interest*, no. 139 (Spring 2000), p. 89. It was estimated that when New York City's full- and part-time municipal work force was at its peak, this bloc of voters, and their relatives, represented nearly a third of the city's entire active voting age population. Unlike the rest of the voting age population, this constituency is intensely motivated to turn out, hence its influence in local elections was disproportionate. See Edward M. Gramlich, "The New York City Fiscal Crisis: What Happened and What Is to Be Done," *American Economic Review*, vol. 66 (May 1976), p. 415.

35. Some would argue, however, that the effects are far from neutral. The difficulty with preference programs for police forces, for example, is not that they add minorities to a force, but that the programs may lower a department's *overall* recruitment standards for new minority and new nonminority officers alike. See John R. Lott Jr., "Does a Helping Hand Put Others at Risk: Affirmative Action, Police Departments, and Crime," *Economic Inquiry*, vol. 38 (April 2000), pp. 239–77.

36. I owe the Beverly Hills joke to James Q. Wilson and John J. DiIulio Jr., *American Government: Institutions and Policies* (Boston: Houghton Mifflin Company, 1998), p. 68.

37. The ensuing discussion is drawn from Pietro S. Nivola and Jon A. Shields, *Managing Green Mandates: Local Rigors of U.S. Environmental Regulation* (AEI-Brookings Joint Center for Regulatory Studies, 2001).

38. San Francisco concluded that it was simpler in the long run to build an oceanside secondary treatment plant than to count on obtaining periodic waivers. This city's experience illustrates the kinds of local complications that arise, even under EPA policies intended to increase local flexibility. San Francisco had obtained a waiver in the early 1980s, but it was only good for five years. If, one day, the city would have to build a second treatment plant, a particular site was preferred. Rather than risk that subsequent waiver applications might be turned down, and that by then the land at the site might not be available, the city broke ground for the new facility in the late 1980s and opened it in September 1993.

39. At one time, however, the product in question had been in use near Columbus as well. For a breezy account of this and other incidents, see Thomas J. DiLorenzo, "Federal Regulations: Environmentalism's Achilles' Heel," *USA Today Magazine*, vol. 123 (September 1994), p. 48.

40. Mike Allen, "Connecticut Joins Lawsuit over Pollution in Sound," *New York Times*, March 24, 1998, p. A24.

41. Robert A. Katzmann, *Institutional Disability: The Saga of Transportation Policy for the Disabled* (Brookings, 1986), p. 189.

42. The phrase is from Lawrence M. Friedman, *Total Justice* (Russell Sage Foundation, 1988).

43. Edward I. Koch, "The Mandate Millstone," *Public Interest*, no. 61 (Fall 1980), p. 45.

44. Representative Charles Vanik, quoted in Timothy Clark, "Access for the Handicapped," *National Journal*, October 21, 1978, p. 1673. The Congressional Budget Office estimated that section 504 of the 1973 Rehabilitation Act would require $6.8 billion to equip buses with wheelchair lifts, install elevators in subway systems, and take other measures to expand access to public transit systems for the physically disabled. Congressional Budget Office, *Urban Transportation for Handicapped Persons: Alternative Federal Approaches* (Washington, 1979), p. xi.

45. For a definitive treatment of this initiative see Thomas F. Burke, "On the Rights Track: The Americans with Disabilities Act," in Pietro S. Nivola, ed., *Comparative Disadvantages: Social Regulations and the Global Economy* (Brookings, 1997).

46. Stephen L. Percy, "ADA, Disability Rights, and Evolving Regulatory Federalism," *Publius,* vol. 23 ( Fall 1993), p. 87.

47. *Hearings on the Americans with Disabilities Act* before the Subcommittee on Surface Transportation of the House Committee on Public Works and Transportation, 101 Cong. 1 sess. (Government Printing Office, 1989), p. 2721.

48. James H. Matteson, "Americans with Disabilities Act Requirements: Community Sidewalks and Curbs," *City Council Report*, City of Phoenix, January 24, 1997, pp. 1–2.

49. Percy, "ADA," p. 104.

50. Pursuant to the Clean Air Act amendments of 1990, "Standards of Performance for New Stationary Sources and Emissions Guidelines for Existing Sources," *Federal Register*, vol. 60, no. 243 (December 19, 1995), pp. 65378–436.

51. City of Tampa, *Mayor's Strategic Initiatives* (January 1999), pp. 51–52.

52. Medical Research Council, *Health Effects of Waste Combustion Products* (Leicester, UK: Institute for Environment and Health, 1997).

53. U.S. Environmental Protection Agency, *Mercury Study Report to Congress: Volume II* (December 1997).

54. Katherine N. Probst and others, *Footing the Bill for Superfund Cleanup: Who Pays and How?* (Brookings and Resources for the Future, 1995), p. 1995.

55. Cleaning up urban waste sites, rivers, air sheds, and so on, by 90 percent may be practicable, but erasing the remaining 10 percent can be prohibitive.

Stephen Breyer, *Breaking the Vicious Cycle: Toward Effective Risk Regulation* (Harvard University Press, 1993), pp. 11–12, 29.

56. Tom Arrandale, "A Guide to Environmental Mandates," *Governing,* vol. 7 ( March 1994), p. 73.

57. Association of California Water Agencies, *National Primary Drinking Water Regulation for Radon-222* (Sacramento, February 2000), p. 1.

58. John D. Spengler and others, *Summary of Symposium on Health Aspects of Exposure to Asbestos in Buildings* (Harvard University, John F. Kennedy School of Government, Energy and Environmental Policy Center, August 1989). A 1989 article in the *New England Journal of Medicine* found no excess cases of cancer from low exposure levels. See Brooke T. Mossman and J. Bernald I. Gee, "Asbestos—Related Diseases," *New England Journal of Medicine,* vol. 320, no. 26 (1989).

59. W. Kip Viscusi has estimated the risk of cancer there to be 0.09 per million, or a death rate of under one per 10,000,000. "The low levels of these risks," Viscusi notes, "have led some risk analysts to call into question the ambitious asbestos removal programs that may increase the risk by disrupting the asbestos now in place." W. Kip Viscusi, "Alternative Institutional Responses to Asbestos," *Journal of Risk and Uncertainty,* vol. 12 (May 1996), p. 149.

60. Robert N. Stavins, "Environmental Protection: Visions of Governance for the Twenty-First Century," Working Paper (Harvard University, John F. Kennedy School of Government, June 1998), p. 22. The figure is in 1994 dollars.

61. National School Boards Association, *A Survey of Public Education in the Nation's Urban School Districts* (Alexandria, Va., 1995).

62. Olson, *The Excuse Factory,* p. 17.

63. James Rutenberg, "Long Weight's Over," *New York Daily News,* March 5, 1998, p. 8.

64. Olson, *The Excuse Factory,* p. 253.

65. Rene Sanchez, "LAPD Reeling as Corruption Cases Multiply," *Washington Post,* February 12, 2000, pp. A1, A14.

66. James Sterngold, "Los Angeles Police Officials Admit Widespread Lapses," *New York Times,* February 17, 2000, p. A12.

67. Olson, *The Excuse Factory,* pp. 64, 82. Municipalities in fair or poor fiscal condition are the ones that seem to have experienced the sharpest increases in liability expenditures. Susan MacManus, "Municipal Liability: The Impact of Litigation on Cities," *Syracuse Law Review,* vol. 44, no. 3 (1993), p. 834.

68. Charles Epp, "Litigation against Local Governments: Expenditures on Legal Services, 1960–1995," paper presented at the annual meeting of the American Political Science Association, 1997, p. 5.

69. Allen R. Myerson, "Soaring Liability Payments Burdening New York," *New York Times,* June 29, 1992, p. B1.

70. Epp, "Litigation against Local Governments," p. 5.

71. See, for instance, *Monell* v. *New York City Department of Social Services,* 436 U.S. 658, 56 2d 611, 98 S Ct. 2018 (1978); *Owen* v. *City of Independence,* 445 U.S. 622, 633n.,13m 100 S Ct. 1398, 1406–1407 (1980); and *Maine* v. *Thiboutot,* 448, 100 S Ct. 2502 (1980).

72. Richard A. Posner, *The Federal Courts: Challenge and Reform* (Harvard University Press, 1996), pp. 57, 60–61.

73. Don Vannatta Jr., "U.S. Judge Says Removing Alarm Boxes Discriminates against the Deaf," *New York Times,* February 14, 1996, pp. B3.

74. Greg B. Smith, "City Asks for End to Jail Regs," *New York Daily News,* May 30, 1996, p. 22.

75. "MTA Officials Admit Violating Federal Court Order to Reduce Overcrowding, Report Says," Associated Press State and Local Wire, September 9, 1998.

76. See Sarah B. Vanderbraak, "Why Criminals Would Rather Be in Philadelphia," *Policy Review,* no. 71 (Summer 1995), pp. 73–75.

77. See Charles R. Epp, "Litigation Stories: Official Perceptions of Lawsuits against Local Government," paper prepared for the 1998 annual meeting of the Law and Society Association, Aspen, Colorado, pp. 9–11.

78. The frivolous suit, though appealed, was thrown out. Pat Morrison, "Snapshots of Life in the Gold State," *Los Angeles Times,* May 24, 1996, p. A3; and "Lawyer's Fine over Unisex-Restroom Suit Upheld," *Associated Press,* December 7, 1998.

79. *Allied Signal, Inc.* v. *City of Phoenix,* 182 F. 3d 692 (9th Cir. 1999)

80. Act to Enforce the Fourteenth Amendment, April 20, 1871, *U.S. Statutes at Large,* vol. 17, p. 13 ff. See Henry Steele Commager, ed., *Documents of American History,* 9th ed. (Prentice-Hall, 1973), p. 502.

81. Michael B. Katz, *In the Shadow of the Poorhouse: A Social History of Welfare in America* (Basic Books, 1986), p. 283.

82. For a forceful critique of this development, see Michael S. Greve, "Private Enforcement, Private Rewards: How Environmental Citizen Suits Became an Entitlement Program," in Michael S. Greve and Fred L. Smith Jr., eds., *Environmental Politics: Public Costs, Private Rewards* (Praeger, 1992), pp. 105–27.

83. Antonio Olivo, "Carwashes Get Huge Bill from Superfund Site," *Los Angeles Times,* October 19, 1998, p. A1.

84. *City of Chicago* v. *Environmental Defense Fund,* 522 U.S. 328 (1994). Charles Wise and Rosemary O'Leary, "Intergovernmental Relations and Federalism in Environmental Management and Policy: The Role of the Courts," *Public Administration Review,* vol. 57 (March–April 1997), pp. 150–59.

85. Yong S. Lee, "Civil Liability of State and Local Governments," *Public Administration Review,* vol. 47 (March–April 1987), p. 160.

86. Koch, "Mandate Millstone," p. 53.

87. Roger Clegg, "Lee Loves Quotas, Just as the Senate Feared," *Wall Street Journal*, December 14, 1998, p. A19.

88. White student enrollment in Milwaukee stood at 58.9 percent in 1976. After the city's desegregation plan took effect, the percentage dropped to 45.3 percent by 1980. White students had been leaving city schools all along, but the annual rate of departures accelerated by almost 62 percent as the desegregation process unfolded. Paul E. Peterson, Barry G. Rabe, and Kenneth K. Wong, *When Federalism Works* (Brookings, 1986), p. 185. Forced busing in Charlotte-Mecklenburg had been in effect for decades. As of the late 1990s, it had still to achieve racial balance. In fact, forty-two of the district's schools were not in balance as of 1998, compared with only seven in 1979. Busing in Denver began in 1974. Parents responded by moving away to suburban districts, sharply reducing the number of white students in city schools. In 1995 a federal judge finally ordered the busing to stop. "Stopping the School Bus," *Economist*, May 29, 1999, pp. 25–26. Boston's busing program also began in 1974. Today, only 15 percent of the city's public school students are white, compared with 60 percent in the early 1970s. Carey Goldberg, "Busing's Day Ends: Boston Drops Race in Pupil Placement," *New York Times*, July 15, 1999, p. A1.

89. National School Boards Association, *Survey of Public Education in the Nation's Urban Districts* (Alexandria, Va., 1995), pp. 130–32.

90. Clegg, "Lee," p. A19.

91. For an excellent chronicle of this program's evolution, see R. Shep Melnick, *Between the Lines: Interpreting Welfare Rights* (Brookings, 1994), chaps. 7 and 8.

92. Peterson and others, *When Federalism Works*, p. 127.

93. Roberta Weiner and Maggie Hume, *And Education for All: Public Policy and Handicapped Education* (Alexandria, Va.: Capital, 1987), cited in Paul I. Posner, *The Politics of Unfunded Mandates: Whither Federalism* (Georgetown University Press, 1998), p. 132.

94. *Smith v. Robinson*, 468 U.S. 992 (1984); and *Dellmuth v. Muth*, 491 U.S. 223, 230 (1989).

95. See *Congressional Quarterly Almanac* (Washington: Congressional Quarterly, Inc., 1990), p. 616.

96. Lisa Gubernick and Michelle Conlin, "The Special Education Scandal," *Forbes*, February 10, 1997, p. 66.

97. Urban school systems naturally have disproportionate numbers of pupils in special education because learning disabilities are closely correlated with poverty. Jay Gottlieb and others, "Special Education in Urban America," *Journal of Special Education*, vol. 27, no. 4 (1994), pp. 453–65.

98. See Wade F. Horn and Douglas Tynan, "Revamping Special Education," *Public Interest*, no. 144 (Summer 2001), p. 38.

99. Under the wide-ranging category of students said to suffer a "specific learning disability" (SLD) are those who may have trouble listening, speaking, reading basic words, comprehending what they read, expressing themselves in writing, problem solving in mathematics, or doing mathematical calculations. According to the director of the University of Minnesota's National Center on Educational Outcomes, more than 80 percent of all schoolchildren in the United States could qualify as having SLD under one definition or another. Horn and Tynan, "Revamping Special Education," p. 38. See also Joseph P. Shapiro and others, "Separate and Unequal," *U.S. News & World Report*, December 13, 1993. Some diagnosed afflictions seem to have burst onto the scene in epidemic proportions. In the years 1994–99, for instance, the number of children considered autistic increased by 153.6 percent. David Brown, "Autism's New Face," *Washington Post*, March 26, 2000, p. A1.

100. The 6.1 million figure was for 1999–2000 and included children and youth ages three to twenty-one. In 1976–77 the number of children receiving special education services and accommodations had been 3.7 million. Horn and Tynan, "Revamping Special Education," p. 36. Jeffrey L. Katz, "Policy on Disabled Is Scrutinized over Discipline Problems, Cost," *Congressional Quarterly Weekly Report,* May 11, 1996.

101. *Congressional Quarterly Almanac, 1975*, vol. 31 (Congressional Quarterly Inc., 1976), p. 651.

102. Tom Loveless and Diane Ravitch, "Broken Promises: What the Federal Government Can Do to Improve American Education," *Brookings Review,* vol. 18 (Spring 2000), p. 20.

103. U.S. Advisory Commission on Intergovernmental Relations, *The Role of Federal Mandates in Intergovernmental Relations* (January 1996). Loveless and Ravitch, "Broken Promises," give a more current 12 percent estimate. See also Jeffrey L. Katz, "Policy on Disabled Is Scrutinized," p. 1297.

104. Norm Fruchter and others, *Focus on Learning: A Report on Reorganizing General and Special Education in New York City*, New York University, Institute for Education and Social Policy, 1995; Sam Illon, "Special Education Absorbs School Resources," *New York Times*, April 7, 1994, p. A1; Scott Miner Brook, "The Cratering of New York," *U.S. News & World Report*, May 27, 1991, p. 31.

105. This distortion in New York was far worse than in the rest of the state. (Spending on special education grew much less rapidly elsewhere in New York State, and did not squeeze the resources available for regular students as badly.) Mark Lankgord and James Wyckoff, "The Allocation of Resources to Special Education and Regular Instruction," in Helen F. Ladd, ed., *Holding Schools Accountable: Performance-Based Reform in Education* (Brookings, 1996), p. 231. In the District of Columbia, as much as $49 million of the city's proposed

$125 million special education budget in 1998 may have been claimed by the 17 percent of special education students that had to be sent to private schools. Beset by litigation, the District's program also anticipated paying between $6 million and $8 million in legal fees to plaintiffs' lawyers. Doug Struck and Valerie Strauss, "D.C. Special Ed System Still in Disarray, Report Says," *Washington Post,* July 20, 1998, p. B1.

106. Struck and Strauss, "D.C. Special Ed System." At times, reports of the costs of the private school option, preceded by litigation, have been dismaying. A California school district reportedly wound up paying half a million dollars for three years of private schooling, plus legal expenses for both sides, all for just one student. Gubernick and Conlin, "Special Education Scandal."

107. Posner, *Unfunded Mandates*, p. 148.

108. Charlotte J. Fraas, *Preschool Programs for the Education of Handicapped Children* (Congressional Research Service, March, 1986), cited in Posner, *Unfunded Mandates*, pp. 137, 157.

109. Loveless and Ravitch, "Broken Promises," pp. 20–21.

110. Melnick, *Between the Lines*, pp. 165–66.

111. Horn and Tyman, "Revamping Special Education," p. 45.

112. Peter Applebome, "Push for School Safety Led to New Rules on Discipline," *New York Times,* May 14, 1997, p. B8.

113. See Abigail Thernstrom, "Where Did All the Order Go? School Discipline and the Law," in Diane Ravitch, ed., *Brookings Papers on Education Policy, 1999* (Brookings, 1999), p. 301.

114. For a broad treatment of the problem, see Chester E. Finn Jr., Andrew J. Rotherman, and Charles R. Hokanson Jr., eds., *Rethinking Special Education for a New Century* (Thomas B. Fordham Foundation and the Progressive Policy Institute, 2001).

115. Diane Ravitch, "Student Performance: The National Agenda in Education," in Marci Kanstoroom and Chester E. Finn, eds., *Federal Education Policy in the Twenty-First Century* (Thomas B. Fordham Foundation, 1999), p. 143.

116. Among the advocacy groups guarding the law are the National Association of Retarded Children, the Children's Defense Fund, and the Council for Exceptional Children—an association composed of more than 70,000 special education professionals. Special education promoters at the local level, such as the National Association of State Directors of Special Education (an organization funded in part by the federal government), often have closer links to their counterparts in Washington—including the Department of Education's Office of Special Education, the Department of Justice's Office of Civil Rights, and the corresponding legislative committees in Congress—than to the rest of the education bureaucracy in their respective states or districts.

117. Roger Clegg, "The Bad Law of 'Disparate Impact,'" *Public Interest*, no. 138 (Winter 2000), p. 80.

118. Hugh Davis Graham, "The Origins of Affirmative Action: Civil Rights and the Regulatory State," *Annals of the American Academy of Political and Social Science,* vol. 523 (September 1992), pp. 50–62.

119. By 1984 approximately 44 percent of government employees in the United States were represented by labor organizations and 36 percent were members of unions, compared with 18 percent in the private sector. See Richard B. Freeman, "Unionism Comes to the Public Sector," *Journal of Economic Literature,* vol. 24 (March 1986), p. 41.

120. "Behind the Scenes Politics: Teacher's Pet," *Economist,* April 1, 2000, p. 28. It should be stressed that public employee unions are hardly monolithic or necessarily like-minded. The smaller American Federation of Teachers, for instance, has proved more amenable to a variety of educational reform measures.

121. On these barriers, see Nivola, *Urban Service Problem.* pp. 103–09; and Olson, *Excuse Factory,* p. 172.

122. *Bombrys v. City of Toledo,* 849 F. Supp. 1210 (1993). See August J. Jones Jr., "Federal Court Responses to State and Local Claims of 'Undue Burden' in Complying with the Americans with Disabilities Act," *Publius,* vol. 25 (Summer 1995), p. 52.

123. Olson, *Excuse Factory,* p. 127.

124. The estimate is in James Allen and others, *Without Sanctuary* (Twin Palms Publishers, 2000).

125. On the general problem of intergovernmental bureaucracies as, in effect, cartels, see Aaron Wildavsky, "A Double Society: Federalism as Competition," in Aaron Wildavsky, ed., *Federalism and Political Culture* (Transaction, 1997), pp. 74–76. See also William H. Niskanen, "The Peculiar Economics of American Bureaucracy," *American Economic Review,* vol. 58 (May 1968), p. 293.

126. The watershed Personal Responsibility and Work Opportunity Reconciliation Act was finally signed into law on August 22, 1996.

127. Olson, *Excuse Factory,* p. 181.

128. U.S. Conference of Mayors, *Recycling America's Land: A National Report on Brownfields Redevelopment,* vol. 3 (February 2000), pp. 9–11.

129. Epp, "Litigation Stories," pp. 6–7.

130. Paul T. Hill, "Supplying Effective Public Schools in Big Cities," in Diane Ravitch, ed., *Brookings Papers on Education Policy, 1999* (Brookings, 1999), pp. 422–23.

131. Ross Sandler and David Shoenbrod, "Government by Decree—The High Cost of Letting Judges Make Policy," *City Journal,* vol. 4 (Summer 1994).

132. Allen R. Myerson, "Soaring Liability Payments Burdening New York," *New York Times,* June 29, 1992, sec. B, p. 1.

133. Congressional Budget Office, *Federalism and Environmental Protection: Case Studies for Drinking Water and Ground-Level Ozone* (GPO, November 1997), pp. 25–30.

134. Great variations in the intermediary roles of state governments translate into widely divergent federal impacts. The U.S. special education program does not pose the same financial complexities for the cities of Florida, say, as for the municipalities of New York. (Local districts in Florida are responsible for only 2 to 3 percent of special education spending.) Peterson, *When Federalism Works,* p. 156.

135. Brookings Center on Urban and Metropolitan Government, *A Region Divided: The State of Growth in Greater Washington, D.C.* (Brookings, 1999), p. 3.

136. For a general analysis of this unbalanced pattern in metropolitan areas, see Janet Rothenberg Pack, "Poverty and Urban Public Expenditures," *Urban Studies,* vol. 33, no. 11 (1998), pp. 1995–2020.

137. U.S. General Accounting Office, *District of Columbia Government: Overtime Costs Exceed Those of Neighboring Governments* (September 1997), pp. 21, 32. The GAO found the District paying more in overtime as a percentage of municipal salaries than did any of the city's surrounding counties. For some poverty-related services (corrections, for instance) nearly 18 percent of the District's salary base went to overtime, compared with 0.2 percent in Maryland's Prince George's County.

138. Posner, *Unfunded Mandates,* p. 64.

139. "School Accountability: How Are States Holding Schools Responsible for Results?" *Education Week,* vol. 20 (January 11, 2001), p. 80.

140. See, more generally, the delightfully readable Jonathan Rauch, *Government's End: Why Washington Stopped Working* (New York: Public Affairs, 1999), especially chap. 6.

141. Association of Metropolitan Sewerage Agencies and Water Environment Federation, *The Cost of Clean: Water Quality in the New Millennium,* March 1999.

142. Michael A. Pagano, *City Fiscal Conditions in 1998* (National League of Cities, June 1998), p. 8.

143. See Frank J. Thompson, "Federalism and the Medicaid Challenge," in Frank J. Thompson and John J. DiIulio Jr., eds., *Medicaid and Devolution: A View from the States* (Brookings, 1998), pp. 270–71. A number of states were still running deficits at the start of the twenty-first century, despite a booming economy. Michael Janofsky, "In Time of Plenty, Some States Facing Plenty of Shortfalls," *New York Times,* February 16, 2000, pp. A1, A14.

144. See John J. DiIulio Jr. and Donald F. Kettl, *Fine Print: The Contract with America, Devolution, and the Administrative Realities of American Federalism* (Brookings Center for Public Management, March 1, 1995), p. 10.

145. This was certainly the case in New York, for instance, a city that is a net loser in the federal system: more money leaves the city in tax dollars than is returned in the form aid. John Marks, "New York, New York," *U.S. News &*

*World Report*, September 29, 1997, p. 54; and Thomas Carroll, "Waking Up to Taxes," *New York Times*, February 9, 2000, p. A29.

146. Posner, *Unfunded Mandates*, p. 165. Stephen Goldsmith and others, *Markets Not Mandates: A Request to Congress for a New Contract with America's Cities* (Washington: Cato Institute, 1998), p. 4.

147. Michael J. Pompili, "Environmental Mandates: The Impact on Local Governments," *Journal of Environmental Health*, vol. 57, no. 6 (January–February 1995), p. 6.

148. Brett Snyder and others, *The Municipal Sector Study: Impacts of Environmental Regulations on Municipalities* (Environmental Protection Agency, September 1988), p. ii.

# Chapter 3

1. "Delivering services, little or big, is just what Camden's city government has been unable to do," recounts a recent report. This city "has been functionally bankrupt for more than a decade, kept afloat with cash from Trenton, which now pays for 70 percent of the municipal and public school budget." Iver Peterson, "Stricken Camden Is to Become a Ward of the State," *New York Times*, July 17, 2000, p. A1.

2. Data from the Baltimore Metropolitan Council (www.baltometro.org/. [April 19, 2002] ).

3. David Rusk, *Baltimore Unbound* (Baltimore: Abell Foundation, 1996), p. xiv.

4. Although Baltimore still held 56 percent of Maryland's entire welfare caseload, by 1999 the absolute volume of welfare cases in the city had been cut in half.

5. Francis X. Clines, "Baltimore Gladly Breaks 10-Year Homicide Streak," *New York Times*, January 3, 2001, p. A8.

6. City of Baltimore, *The Mayor's Plan to Dramatically Reduce Crime in Baltimore* (April 5, 2000).

7. Government of the District of Columbia, *Tax Rates and Tax Burdens in the District of Columbia—A Nationwide Comparison, 1997* (July 1998), p. 9.

8. The ensuing figures are based on data provided directly by the city of Baltimore, Department of Public Works, Bureau of Water and Wastewater, June 2000.

9. *Vaughn G. v. The Mayor and City Council of Baltimore,*117 F. 3d 1415 (4th Civ. 1997).

10. Kalman R. Hettleman, "Special-Ed Funding Isn't Fair to All Students," *Baltimore Sun*, May 17, 1998, p. 1L.

11. State of Maryland, Department of Education, *Maryland Special Education Census Data* (Annapolis, 1999), table 7.

12. Based on State of Maryland, Department of Education, *The Fact Book: 1998–1999* (Annapolis, 1999), pp. 28–29. See also Maryland State Department of Education, *Maryland Special Education Census Data* (Annapolis, May 1999), table 4.

13. State of Maryland, Department of Education, *Selected Financial Data—Part 4, 1997–98* (Annapolis, 1999), table 10.

14. State of Maryland, Department of Education, *Selected Financial Data—Part 1 (Revenue, Wealth, and Effort), 1997-98* (Annapolis, 1999), tables 1, 7, 8, 9; and State of Maryland, Department of Education, *The Fact Book, 1998–1999* (Annapolis, 1999), p. 3.

15. The local effort estimate is drawn from State of Maryland, Department of Education, *Selected Financial Data—Part 1 (Revenue, Wealth, and Effort), 1997–98* (Annapolis, 1999), tables 1–9.

16. The figures in table 3-1 provide conservative estimates of comparative per pupil expenditures for the instruction of regular students. Depending on the cost items included, other sources have ranked Baltimore dead last *in the entire state* in spending per pupil for regular education. See, for instance, the report in Debbie M. Price and others, "Special Ed: A Decade of Bloat and Failure," *Baltimore Sun,* September 20, 1998.

17. Teachers' salaries in Baltimore were the lowest in the state. State of Maryland, Department of Education, *Selected Financial Data—Part 3 (Analysis of Costs), 1997–98* (Annapolis, 1999), table 3.

18 Philadelphia City Planning Commission, *City States: General Demographic and Economic Data* (April 2000), p. 1.

19. Mark Alan Hughes, "Dirt Into Dollars: Converting Vacant Land into Valuable Development," *Brookings Review*, vol. 18 (Summer 2000), p. 38.

20. Lynne Duke, "A City Trying Hard to Shine," *Washington Post*, July 30, 2000, p. M3.

21. U.S. Conference of Mayors, *Recycling America's Land: A National Report on Brownfields Redevelopment—Volume III* (February 2000), pp. 21–27.

22. Mark Alan Hughes and Rebekah Cook-Mack, *Critical Issues Facing Philadelphia Neighborhoods: Vacancy Reassessed*, December 1999.

23. Deirdre A. Gaquin and Katherine A. DeBrandt, *2000 County and City Extra: Annual Metro, City, and County Data Book,* 9th ed. (Bernan Press, 2000), pp. 602–03.

24. U.S. Department of Commerce, Bureau of the Census, *State and Metropolitan Area Data Book, 1997–98* (1998), p. 149.

25. Philadelphia City Planning Commission, *City Stats*, p. 7.

26. Robert P. Inman, "How to Have a Fiscal Crisis: Lessons from Philadelphia," *American Economic Review,* vol. 85 (May 1995), pp. 378–83.

27. Scott Quehl, "The Bottom Line and Beyond: Financial Plans Guided Philadelphia and New Haven to Recovery," *Brookings Review*, vol. 18 (Summer 2000), p. 34.

28. Quoted in Duke, "A City Trying Hard, " p. M3.

29. In October 25, 2000, the city's teachers' union was again threatening to go on strike. Debbie Goldberg, "Philadelphia Teachers May Go on Strike Friday," *Washington Post,* October 25, 2000, p. A2.

30. Government of the District of Columbia, *Tax Rates and Tax Burdens in the District of Columbia—A Nationwide Comparison, 1997* (July 1998), p. 9.

31. Fred Siegel and Kay S. Hymowitz, "Why Did Ed Rendell Fizzle Out?" in Myron Magnet, ed., *The Millennial City: A New Urban Paradigm for 21st-Century America* (Ivan R. Dee, 2000), p. 26.

32. U.S. Department of Commerce, Bureau of the Census, *State and Metropolitan Area Data Book, 1997–98* (1999), p. 165. See also Nicholas Lehman, "No Man's Land," *New Yorker,* June 5, 2000, p. 42.

33. *Kinney* v. *Yerusalim,* 9 F 3d 1067 (3d Cir 1993). "In Settling Suit, City Agrees to Accelerate Installation of Curb Ramps," *Disability Compliance Bulletin,* vol. 7 (January 18, 1996).

34. "Curb Ramps at Center of ADA Controversy," *Disability Compliance Bulletin,* vol. 7 (February 15, 1996).

35. City of Philadelphia, *Five-Year Financial Plan: Fiscal Year 2000–Fiscal Year 2004 (including Fiscal Year 1999),* January 26, 1999, p. 469.

36. According to the city's *Five-Year Financial Plan, 2000–2004,* p. 469, between fiscal years 1990 and 1999, city departments forked out $36.6 million to make municipal facilities more accessible to people with disabilities.

37. The 1998 figure is conservative because, according to the Philadelphia Comptroller, the Philadelphia Police Department may have underreported between 13,000 and 37,000 offenses that year. Philadelphia Comptroller's Office, "Saidel Releases Evaluation of 1998 Police Crime Statistics: Undercounting of Serious Crimes Found," press release, September 13, 2000.

38. U.S. Department of Commerce, Bureau of the Census, *Statistical Abstract of the United States, 1994* (1994), p. 200; and Federal Bureau of Investigation, *Uniform Crime Reports, 2000* (Washington, 2001).

39. The following discussion of the Philadelphia decrees draws extensively on the account by William D. Hagedorn and John J. DiIulio Jr., "The People's Court? Federal Judges and Criminal Justice," in Martha Derthick, ed., *Dilemmas of Scale in America's Federal Democracy* (Woodrow Wilson Center Press and Cambridge University Press, 1999), especially pp. 339–48. For up-to-date details, see Judge Norma L. Shapiro, "Memorandum and Order," *Harris* v. *City of Philadelphia,* August 30, 2000, 47 F. 3d 1342 (3d Cir. 1995).

40. Crime and Justice Institute, *An Alternative-to-Incarceration Plan for Philadelphia: Findings and Proposed Strategies* (Philadelphia, November 1992), pp. 20–21.

41. Sarah B. Vandenbraak, "Bail, Humbug!" *Policy Review* (Summer 1995), pp. 22–25.

42. Testimony of the Honorable Lynne Abraham, Hearings before the House Committee on the Judiciary, Subcommittee on Crime, Concerning H.R. 3 and H.R. 554, 104 Cong. 1 sess. (Government Printing Office, 1995).

43. "After 18 Years, Shapiro 'Emancipates' City Prisons from Federal Oversight," *Legal Intelligencer,* September 5, 2000.

44. Barbara Stewart, "Garbage Transfer Stations Spur Civil Rights Complaint," *New York Times,* July 25, 2000, p. A24.

45. Laura Mansnerus, "New York Is Failing People with AIDS, a U.S. Judge Rules," *New York Times,* September 20, 2000, p. A27.

46. "Bias Charges at the Parks Department," *New York Times,* February 15, 2001, p. A30.

47. Benjamin Weiser, "New York Police Accused of Bias," *New York Times,* October 5, 2000, p. A1.

48. Richard Pérez-Peña, "U.S. Judge Blocks 25¢ Fare Increase: Sees Possible Bias," *New York Times,* November 9, 1995, p. A1.

49. Joyce Purnick, "Board Says Fees for School Case Pass $250,000," *New York Times,* June 14, 1982, p. B1.

50. Joseph P. Fried, "Women Win Ruling on Fire Dept. Test," *New York Times,* March 6, 1982, p. A1.

51. Hamilton Lankford and James Wyckoff, "The Allocation of Resources to Special Education and Regular Students," in Helen F. Ladd, ed., *Holding Schools Accountable: Performance-Based Reform in Education* (Brookings, 1996), p. 230.

52. See Council of Urban Boards of Education, *A Survey of Public Education in the Nation's Urban School Districts* (Alexandria, Va.: National School Boards Association, 1995), p. 102; and Sam Dillon, "Comptroller Report Faults Special Education," *New York Times,* June 27, 1994, B3.

53. Joseph P. Viteritti, "Find Alternatives to Failing Schools," *New York Post,* September 14, 2000.

54. New York City Independent Budget Office, *Analysis of the Mayor's 1998 Executive Budget* (May 27, 1997), pp. 20, 50.

55. Note, however, that the projected cost of the 70,000 liability claims that were in the pipeline as of 1996 ran much higher—perhaps totaling $2.1 billion. Richard Miniter, "Under Siege: New York's Liability Ordeal," *Civil Justice Memo,* no. 23 (New York: Manhattan Institute for Policy Research, January 1996), p. 1.

56. John Marks, "New York, New York," *U.S. News & World Report,* September 29, 1996, p. 54.

57. Leslie Eaton, "Hot Economy Cooling Down? Not New York's," *New York Times,* December 7, 2000, pp. A1, C19.

58. See David Leonhardt, "New York Area Has a Cushion, Economists Say," *New York Times,* January 25, 2001, pp. C1, C15.

59. New York City Independent Budget Office, *Analysis of the Mayor's Executive Budget for 2001*, p. 1.

60. Justin Gillis and Robert O'Harrow Jr., "A $90 Billion Hole in N.Y.," *Washington Post*, October 13, 2001, pp. E1, E8.

61. Leslie Eaton, "Only Certainty to Economists Is Dire Outlook," *New York Times*, October 4, 2001, p. B1.

62. Jennifer Steinhauer, "Finances of New York City Are Staggered by Emergency," *New York Times*, October 3, 2001, pp. A1, B9.

63. New York City Independent Budget Office, *Analysis of the Mayor's 1998 Executive Budget*, p. 20.

64. See Steven G. Craig and D. Anderson Austin, "New York's Million Missing Jobs," in Myron Magnet, ed., *The Millennial City* (Ivan R. Dee, 2000), p. 297.

65. U.S. Department of Commerce, Bureau of the Census, *Finances of Municipal and Township Governments: 1997* (September 2000).

66. Craig and Austin, "New York's Million," p. 295.

67. Andrew Haughwout and others, *Local Revenue Hills: A General Equilibrium Specification with Evidence from Four U.S. Cities* (Cambridge, Mass.: National Bureau of Economic Research, March 2000). More significant than the depth of Mayor Giuliani's tax cuts were some of the targets of those cuts—the self-defeating commercial rent tax, for instance. In general, writes James Traub, Giuliani succeeded in convincing New Yorkers that "New York City isn't on an endless tax-increase spiral." James Traub, "Giuliani Internalized," *New York Times Magazine*, February 11, 20001, p. 100. Overall, the Giuliani administration's tax reductions may have generated tens of thousands of additional jobs in the city between 1997 and mid-2001. For econometric estimates, underscoring the positive effects of the tax relief, see the Manhattan Institute's Edmund J. McMahon, "What New York Has Gained from Tax Cuts," *Civic Report*, no. 20 (New York, September 2001).

68. City of New York, Office of the Comptroller, *Fiscal Year 2001 Annual Report of the Comptroller on Capital Debt and Obligations* (November 2000).

69. New York City Independent Budget Office, *Analysis of the Mayor's Executive Budget for 2001*, p. 20.

70. *United States v. City of New York*, 179 FRD 373, 379 (EDNY 1998).

71. Interview, John R. Murray, assistant director, Office of Management and Budget, New York City, November 19, 1999.

72. Watershed Agricultural Council, *New York Water Supply Facts* (Walton, New York).

73. Rutherford H. Platt, Paul K. Barten, and Max J. Pfeffer, "A Full Clean Glass? Managing New York City's Watersheds," *Environment* (June 1, 2000), p. 8.

74. See New York City Department of Environmental Protection, *Protecting Water Quality in the Catskill/Delaware and Croton Watersheds* (September 17, 1997); New York City Department of Environmental Protection, *New York City's*

*Water Supply System: Watershed Agreement Overview;* and Watershed Agricultural Council, *Watershed Agricultural Program of New York City's Water Supply Watersheds* (Walton, New York, July 2001).

75. Andrew C. Revkin, "Troubled Waters: Billion Dollar Plan to Clean New York City Water at Its Source," *New York Times,* August 31, 1997, p. 1.

76. U.S. Environmental Protection Agency, *Assessing New York City's Watershed Protection Program: The 1997 Filtration Avoidance Determination Mid-Course Review of the Catskill/Delaware Water Supply Watershed* (May 2000), pp. 1–3.

77. Total obligations for the watershed preservation program (not including the cost of filtration plants) currently stand at more than $1.2 billion. Stephen L. Kass and Steven M. Brautigam, "New York City Attempts Watershed Experiment," *National Law Journal,* December 1, 1997, p. C12.

78. U.S. Environmental Protection Agency, Region 2, "Needs Survey, 1996." See also U.S. Environmental Protection Agency, *Long Island Sound Study: Phase III Actions for Hypoxia Management* (July 1998), p. 14.

79. In 1989, for instance, 1.4 billion gallons of sewage poured into the New York harbor. Bruno Tedeschi, "Depth of Sewage Woes Surfaces for N.J., N.Y.," *Bergen Record,* February 23, 1997, p. A1.

80. New York City Department of Environmental Protection, *Nitrogen Control Action Plan—6th Semi Annual Report* (December 31, 1998), p. 6.

81. New York City Office of Management and Budget, "New York State Revolving Fund (SRF) Programs and New York City" (2000).

82. Mike Allen, "Connecticut Joins Lawsuit over Pollution in Sound," *New York Times,* March 24, 1998, p. A24.

83. New York City Municipal Water Finance Authority, *Water and Sewer System Revenue Bonds, Fiscal 2001 Series A* (November 9, 2000), p. 33.

84. The estimate is derived from civilian labor force and unemployment figures for 1990 and 1998 in Deirdre A. Gaquin and Katherine A. DeBrandt, eds., *2000 County and City Extra: Annual Metro, City, and County Data Book,* 9th ed. (Bernan Press, 2000), p. 964.

85. U.S. Department of Commerce, Bureau of the Census, 1990, and City Comptroller's Office, *Comprehensive Annual Financial Report, 1999;* and Joseph Weber and others, "Chicago Blues," *Business Week,* October 16, 2000, p. 162.

86. David Roeder, "Moves Don't Signal Flight to Suburbs," *Chicago Sun-Times,* October 2, 2000, p. 46.

87. Illinois Department of Revenue, *Illinois Property Tax Statistics, 1997;* and City of Chicago, City Comptroller's Office, *Comprehensive Annual Financial Report, 1999.*

88. Eric Ferkenhoff, "Chicago Slayings Decline Slightly in 2000, Reaching a 33-Year Low," *Chicago Tribune,* January 3, 2001.

89. Robert E. Pierre, "Chicago May Surpass New York Homicide Total," *Washington Post,* December 31, 2001, p. A2.

90. Raoul V. Mowatt, "Crime in State Continues to Fall," *Chicago Tribune,* June 25, 2000.

91. Metropolitan Water Reclamation District, "Major Issues, Policy, and Program Changes" (Chicago, Ill.: Metropolitan Water Reclamation District of Greater Chicago, 1997).

92. Metropolitan Water Reclamation District of Greater Chicago, *2000 Budget*; and Metropolitan Sanitary District of Greater Chicago, *1980 Budget.*

93. Metro Chicago Survey Report, 1997, www.mcic.org/htmls/metrosurvey/ metrosur5.htm. (April 19, 2002).

94. G. Alfred Hess Jr., "Changes in Student Achievement in Illinois and Chicago, 1990–2000," paper presented for the Brookings Brown Center Report National Tour, Washington, September 7, 2000.

95. National School Boards Association, *A Survey of Public Education in the Nation's Urban Districts, 1995* (Alexandria, Va., 1996), pp. 118, 120.

96. Board of Education of the City of Chicago, *Chicago Public Schools FY 2001 Final Budget,* p. 83.

97. *Corey H. v. Chicago Board of Education,* 995 F. Supp. 900 (N.D. Ill.1998); and see Stephanie Banchero, "Special Ed Teachers under State Pressure," *Chicago Tribune,* November 13, 2000.

98. Flynn McRoberts, "CHA Gets OK to Raze High-Rises," *Chicago Tribune,* March 12, 1995, p. 1-1. As of 1998, the CHA had demolished ten high-rise buildings and planned to knock down twenty more. "High-Rise Brought Low at Last," *Economist,* July 11, 1998, p. 31. Chicago has sometimes seemed at odds with HUD officials on its public-housing demolition plans. In the fall of 1999, the department seemed to call into question the scope of the operation (it targets a total of 17,000 housing units, with plans to build or rehabilitate 24,000). The disputes with HUD drew sharp criticism from Mayor Richard M. Daley—"Locally, we should be able to handle this. It's not a Washington problem"—and from the CHA's vice chairman, Rahm Emanuel, who exclaimed, "This is a sham. You cannot defend public housing in Chicago." See Robert D. Novak, "HUD vs. Chicago," *Washington Post,* November 1999, p. A35.

99. City of Chicago, "Putting Federalism to Work for America: Tackling the Problems of Unfunded Mandates and Burdensome Regulations," November 19, 1992, p. 63.

100. John McCarron, "HUD and the Public Housing Mess," *Chicago Tribune,* June 5, 1995. In February 2000, HUD finally approved a plan granting the Chicago Housing Authority substantially more waivers of federal housing regulations. See Melita Maria Garza, "CHA Gives Go-Ahead to $1.5 Billion Overhaul of Public Housing," *Chicago Tribune,* January 7, 2000, p. 1-1.

101. "A City Hall May Be for Hire: Philadelphia Considers Plan That Would Pay for Overhaul," *Washington Post,* December 17, 2000, p. A20.

102. Christopher Farrell and others, "Brighter Lights for Big Cities," *Business Week,* May 4, 1998, pp. 89, 95.

103. Deidra A. Gaquin and Katherine A. DeBrandt, *2000 County and City Extra: Annual Metro, City, and County Data Book,* 9th ed. (Bernan Press, 2000), p. 151; and U.S. Department of Commerce, Bureau of the Census, *County and City Data Book, 1983* (1983), pp. 50, 64.

104. Gaquin and DeBrandt, *2000 County and City Extra,* pp. 148–49.

105. In the first three months of 2001, however, the commercial vacancy rate more than doubled, to 18 percent. Evelyn Nieves, "With New Economy Chilling, San Francisco's Party Fizzles," *New York Times,* March 26, 2001, p. A1.

106. Brian C. Anderson and Matt Robinson, "Willie Brown Shows How Not to Run a City," in Myron Magnet, ed., *The Millennial City: A New Urban Paradigm for 21st-Century America* (Ivan R. Dee, 2000), p. 43.

107. Bill Kisliuk, "Fire Department Consent Decree Should Be Extended, Says Special Master," *Recorder,* May 5, 1995, p. 4.

108. Gregory Lewis, "City Asks End to Consent Decree," *San Francisco Examiner,* June 14, 1997, p. A1.

109. Edward Epstein, "Court Ends Decade of Oversight of S.F. Fire Department," *San Francisco Examiner,* December 3, 1998, p. A25.

110. Figure cited in Epstein, "Court Ends Decade of Oversight," p. A25.

111. Maitland Zane, "White Male Fighters Union Official Says Fire Dept. Morale Low," *San Francisco Chronicle,* October 4, 1989, p. A3.

112. Reynolds Holding and Clarence Johnson, "S.F.'s Still-Troubled Fire Department: Court Has Forced Minority Hiring but Discord Continues," *San Francisco Chronicle,* June 1, 1995, p. A1.

113. "Political Smoke Clouds the S.F. Fire Department," *San Francisco Chronicle,* April 20, 2000, p. A26.

114. Jonathan Curiel, "Probe Sought of Demeaning Newsletters," *San Francisco Chronicle,* August 24, 1999, p. A15.

115. Waldemar Rojas, *Benefits of the SFUSD Consent Decree* (San Francisco Unified School District, 1999), p. 3.

116. *Johnson v. San Francisco Unified School District,* 500 F 2d 349 (9th Cir. 1971).

117. Gary Orfield and others, *Progress Made, Challenges Remaining in San Francisco School Desegregation,* report of the Consent Decree Advisory Committee to the Federal District Court, San Francisco, January 1999, p. 12.

118. *San Francisco NAACP v. San Francisco Unified School District,* 59F. Supp. 2d 1021 (N.D. Cal. 1999).

119. Lisa Davis, "Bus to Nowhere: Why San Francisco Byzantine School Desegregation Plan Systematically Fails the Students It Was Designed to Help," *San Francisco Weekly*, April 2, 1997.

120. According to the 1999 California "Academic Performance Index," Lowell High School ranked third in the state. Nanette Asimov and others, "Ranking In on California School Tests," *San Francisco Examiner*, January 26, 2000, p. A1; and Elaine Woo, "Caught on the Wrong Side of the Line?" *Los Angeles Times*, July 13, 1995, p. A1.

121. Quoted in Anderson and Robinson, "Willie Brown," p. 42.

122. *Ho v. San Francisco Unified School District*, 965 F. Supp. 1316 (N.D. Cal. 1997).

123. *Adarand v. Peña*, 93-1841, 515 U.S. 200 (1995).

124. Orfield, *Progress Made*, p. 54.

125. Rojas, *Benefits of the SFUSD Consent Decree*, pp. 5–7.

126. Orfield, *Progress Made*, p. 45.

127. *Desegregation and Educational Change in San Francisco* (1992), reported in Orfield, *Progress Made*, p. 22.

128. Orfield, *Progress Made*, pp. 92–98.

129. Ibid., pp. 85, 97.

130. Ibid., pp. 84–85.

131. Rojas, *Benefits of the SFUSD Consent Decree*," p. 7.

132. Orfield, *Progress Made*, pp. 96–97.

133. Mary Ann Zehr, "Calif. Settles Battle over LEP Testing," *Education Week*, November 22, 2000, p. 1.

134. On the dismal case of Kansas City, see, for instance, Raad Cawthon, "The Failure of a School District," *Philadelphia Inquirer*, August 24, 2000; and Paul Ciotti, "Money and School Performance: Lessons from the Kansas City Desegregation Experiment," *Policy Analysis*, no. 298 (Washington: Cato Institute, March 1998).

135. Todd S. Purdum, "Washington Tries to Right a Stumbling Los Angeles," *New York Times*, May 15, 2000, p. A12.

136. D'Arlynn Carey, chief administrative analyst, "Effect of Mandatory Social Security Coverage on City of Los Angeles Employees," communication to author, March 22, 1999; *Kimpel et al. v. Willie Williams*, W.L. 638580 (D.C. Cal. 1999); *Huff v. Parks*, no. 98 Civ. 10245 (D.C. Cal. 2001); *Cleveland v. City of Los Angeles*, no. 99 Civ. 9175 (C.D. Cal. 2002); "MTA Officials Admit Violating Federal Court Order to Reduce Overcrowding, Report Says," *Associated Press State and Local Wire*, September 9, 1998; Keith Comrie, city administrative officer, "Bond Measure for Sidewalk Improvements Required by the Americans with Disabilities Act," Ad Hoc Committee on Capital Improvements, City of Los

Angeles, December 11, 1998, p. 1; and Joe Domanick, "Can the LAPD Reform Itself?" *Los Angeles Times*, September 24, 2000, p. M1.

137. City of Los Angeles, *Budget: Fiscal Year 1979–80*, p. 134 and *Budget: Fiscal Year 1997-98*, pp. 191–92.

138. *Los Angeles v. Santa Monica Baykeeper*, 254 F. 3d 882 (9th Cir. 2001).

139. Department of Public Works, City of Los Angeles, "City of Los Angeles Official Criticizes Federal Lawsuit," January 9, 2001, p. 1.

140. Marla Cone, "EPA Sues to Demand That City Prevent Spills from Sewer Lines," *Los Angeles Times*, January 9, 2001, p. A1.

141. The L.A. sewer system serves 3.7 million people with over 6,500 miles of sewer lines, making it the nation's largest system. The spill rate, calculated in spills per sewer mile, in this immense system is 30 percent lower than the national average. Marla Cone, "So Far, LA Is Spared Sewage Spills," *Los Angeles Times*, March 1, 2001, p. B-3.

142. Association of California Water Agencies, *National Primary Drinking Water Regulation for Radon-222*, p. 8.

143. Peter J. Boyer, "Bad Cops," *New Yorker*, May 21, 2001, p. 77.

144. Letter from Bill Lann Lee, acting assistant attorney general, Civil Rights Division, U.S. Department of Justice, to James K. Hahn, city attorney, City of Los Angeles, May 8, 2000.

145. *USA v. Los Angeles*, W.L. 649190 (9th Cir. 2002).

146. See U.S. Department of Justice, "Justice Department Reaches Agreement with City of Los Angeles," press release, November 2, 2000.

147. Quoted in Tina Daunt, "Panel to Urge Wide Internal Reform of LAPD Probes," *Los Angeles Times*, October 13, 2000, p. B1.

148. U.S. Department of Commerce, Bureau of the Census, *Statistical Abstract of the United States, 1992* (1992), p. 182; and *Statistical Abstract of the United States, 1999* (1999), p. 217.

149. L.A.'s police force has averaged about 7,000 officers; hence it can deploy only 15 per square mile. New York's 40,000-strong force deploys 129 officers per square mile. Boyer, "Bad Cops," pp. 63–64.

150. When Lou Cannon queried residents of the Rampart district in the summer of 2000, he "found residents far more worried about emboldened gangs than police misconduct." Lou Cannon, "One Bad Cop," *New York Times Magazine*, October 1, 2000, p. 62.

151. Boyer, "Bad Cops," pp. 65–70.

152. Beth Shuster and Vincent J. Schodolski, "Poor Morale Rife in LAPD, Survey Finds," *Los Angeles Times*, September 8, 2000. It is impossible to discern how deep this dissatisfaction ran. The Report of the Rampart Independent Review Panel, *Survey of Los Angeles Police Department Officers* (Pricewaterhouse, 2000), noted that 12.7 percent of police lieutenants on the force indicated that

hiring standards needed to be raised. Although this percentage seems modest, only one other item of the sixteen listed in this portion of the questionnaire—holding Police Chief Bernard C. Parks accountable—drew a larger response among the officers.

153. The population of Los Angeles expanded by almost 5 percent during the 1970s and by more than 17 percent from 1980 to 1990. Between 1990 and 2000 the city grew almost another 29 percent. City of Los Angeles, Office of Administrative and Research Services, *City of Los Angeles 2000: Economic and Demographic Information* (November 21, 2000), pp. 1–2.

154. Figure is for civilian employment. Deirdre A. Gaquin and Katherine A. DeBrandt, eds., *2000 County and City Extra: Annual Metro, City, and County Data Book,* 9th ed. (Bernan Press, 2000), p. 920.

155. In fact, even during the period 1980 through 1995, L.A.'s general revenues increased more than 60 percent (in 1995 dollars). U.S. Department of Commerce, U.S. Bureau of the Census, *Statistical Abstract of the United States, 1982–83* (1983), p. 300; and U.S. Department of Commerce, Bureau of the Census, *Statistical Abstract of the United States, 1998* (1998), p. 328.

156. Gaquin and DeBrandt, *2000 County and City Extra,* p. 925.

157. See generally Michael A. Shires, "Changes in State and Local Public Finance since Proposition 13," *Research Brief,* no. 18 (San Francisco: Public Policy Institute of California, March 1999); and J. Fred Silva and Elisa Barbour, "Should Local Fiscal Authority Be Strengthened?" *Research Brief,* no. 28 (San Francisco: Public Policy Institute of California, December 1999).

158. Thomas P. Parrish and others, *State Special Education Finance Systems, 1994–95* (Palo Alto, Calif.: Center for Special Education Finance, June 1997), p. 36.

159. "Still Worst in U.S., California's Air Is at Cleanest Level in 40 Years," *New York Times,* October 31, 1996, p. A20.

160. James Q. Wilson, "Cars and Their Enemies," *Commentary,* vol. 104 (July 1997), pp. 17–21.

161. Keith Comrie, city administrative officer, "Impact of Federal and State Unfunded Mandates and Recommendations for Action," *Report to the Mayor,* June 17, 1994, p. 5, and Exhibit G.

162. Keith Comrie, city administrative officer, "Impact of Federal and State Unfunded Mandates and Recommendations for Action," *Report to the Mayor,* June 17, 1994, p. 1.

163. City of Los Angeles, *1997-98 Budget Summary.*

164. L.A.'s business tax rates (per employee) have towered above those of various surrounding communities in the region. See Joel Kotkin, *Can the Cities Be Saved?* (Santa Monica.: Milkin Institute, 1997), p. 62.

165. Cannon, "One Bad Cop," p. 62. At the end of 2001, a letter by the president of the patrolmen's union to its 9,000 members called the police department

"increasingly dysfunctional." "Crime rates, the bottom line of any police agency, are up dramatically, arrests are declining and officer morale is at an all-time low," the letter added. "No-Confidence Vote to Be Called against Los Angeles Police Chief," *New York Times,* December 29, 2001, p. A7.

166. Michael Specter, "Sea-Dumping Ban: Good Politics, but Not Necessarily Good Policy," *New York Times*, March 22, 1993, p. A1. While ocean dumping may not be pretty, arguably dropping it to the bottom of the ocean more than one hundred miles from shore may be less hazardous than most of the disposal methods that have since replaced the practice.

167. Quoted in William C. Smith, "Taking a Jab at Judges," *ABA Journal*, vol. 84 (September 1998).

168. One assessment found that detainees released under the consent decree committed crimes at more than twice the rate of defendants released under state-court bail programs. Sarah B. Vandenbraak, "Bail, Humbug!" *Policy Review,* no. 73 (Summer 1995), pp. 22–25.

169. In 1992 Philadelphia received $125,232 in criminal justice block grant monies. The next year it got $20,788. Then in 1994 and 1995, no funds were reported.

170. "San Francisco Adds Adults but Loses Children," *New York Times,* October 21, 2001, p. A23.

171. Melita Maria Garza, "CHA Gives Go-Ahead to $1.5 Billion Overhaul of Public Housing," *Chicago Tribune,* January 7, 2000, p. 1-1.

172. Stephen Henderson, "Schools Seek Millions More for Disabled," *Baltimore Sun*, March 23, 1999, p. 1A.

## Chapter 4

1. I begin this discussion with the New Deal, but arguably a better starting point is the Progressive period. See Martha Derthick *Keeping the Compound Republic: Essays on American Federalism* (Brookings, 2001), chap. 8.

2. *Hammer* v. *Dagenhart,* 247 U.S. 251 (1918).

3. *Wickard* v. *Filburn,* 317 U.S. 111 (1942); and *United States* v. *Darby Lumber Co.,* 312 U.A. 100 (1941).

4. For an excellent summary, on which I draw at various points in this section, see John D. Donahue, *Disunited States* (Basic Books, 1997).

5. *Brown* v. *Board of Education of Topeka, Kansas,* 347 U.S. 483 (1954). In no southern state did the percentage of African American school children attending desegregated schools exceed 6 percent as of 1964. See David C. Nice, *Federalism: The Politics of Intergovernmental Relations* (St. Martin's, 1987), p. 104.

6. I am indebted to Michael S. Greve for emphasizing to me that the constitutional basis for federal mandates on state and local governments derives more

often from Congress's spending power than from the commerce clause. Affirmation of that basis by the Supreme Court came early in the twentieth century. See, for instance, *Commonwealth of Massachusetts* v. *Mellon,* 262 U.S. 447 (1923).

7. See Daniel P. Moynihan, *Maximum Feasible Misunderstanding: Community Action in the War on Poverty* (Free Press, 1969).

8. See, in general, James L. Sundquist and David W. Davis, *Making Federalism Work: A Study of Program Coordination at the Local Level* (Brookings, 1969), p. 11.

9. Harold J. Laski, "The Obsolescence of Federalism," *New Republic,* vol. 98 (May 3, 1939). I credit the idea of recalling Laski's prediction to Donahue, *Disunited States,* p. 26.

10. Derthick, *Keeping the Compound Republic,* p. 151.

11. On this and the following points, see John E. Chubb, "Federalism and the Bias for Centralization," in John E. Chubb and Paul E. Peterson, eds., *The New Direction in American Politics* (Brookings, 1985), pp. 279–86.

12. Ibid.

13. On preemptions, see Joseph F. Zimmerman, *Federal Preemption: The Silent Revolution* (Iowa State University Press, 1991).

14. See Arnold M. Howitt, *Managing Federalism: Studies in Intergovernmental Relations* (CQ Press, 1984), p. 13.

15. The phrase is from David R. Beam, "On the Origins of the Mandate Issue," in Michael Fix and Daphne A. Kenyon, eds., *Coping with Mandates: What Are the Alternatives?* (Washington: Urban Institute Press, 1990), p. 23.

16. See Timothy Conlan, *From New Federalism to Devolution: Twenty-Five Years of Intergovernmental Reform* (Brookings, 1998), pp. 197–98, 211. Reagan appointees, and the work of the administration's regulatory relief task force, however, did manage to block some *new* rules that would have abridged local prerogatives. In 1983, for instance, the Department of Transportation declined to preempt local airport noise restrictions despite demands by the airline industry for more uniform regulations. In the environmental arena, the administration successfully resisted such legislative initiatives as an effort to preempt local pesticide regulations.

17. As of 1970, only twenty-one states had submitted implementation plans in accordance with the Air Quality Act of 1967, which had left responsibility for air pollution control to the states but called on them to develop appropriate plans. The initial demand for federal help in improving air quality came from cities that were unable to act effectively on an individual basis or were dissatisfied with the efforts in adjoining states.

18. The externality rationale for nationalizing public policy can become a reductio ad absurdum. Consider an entirely different subject: education. A nationalist could argue that externalities plague this sphere, too. Federal control of higher education might be justified on the grounds that the system of state

universities presumably gives some states an incentive to free-ride—that is, to underfund their institutions of higher education because the benefits of superior institutions in other states spill over their jurisdictional boundaries.

19. See Bruce A. Ackerman and William T. Hassler, *Clean Coal/Dirty Air: Or How the Clean Air Act Became a Multibillion-Dollar Bailout for High-Sulfur Coal Producers and What Should Be Done about It* (Yale University Press, 1981).

20. Cass R. Sunstein, *After the Rights Revolution: Reconceiving the Regulatory State* (Harvard, 1990), pp. 28–29.

21. These were the words of the bill's sponsor, Senator Edmund Muskie (D-Maine). *A Legislative History of the Clean Air Amendments of 1970,* Committee Print, Senate Committee on Public Works, 93 Cong. 2 sess. (Government Printing Office, 1974), pp. 227, 231. Emphasis added. Not to be outdone, President Richard Nixon proclaimed, "Clean air, clean water, open spaces—these should again be the birthright for every American." Quoted in Sunstein, *After the Rights Revolution,* p. 29.

22. *City of Chicago* v. *Environmental Defense Fund,* 511 U.S. 328 (1994). See generally Charles Wise and Rosemary O'Leary, "Intergovernmental Relations and Federalism in Environmental Management and Policy: The Role of the Courts," *Public Administration Review,* vol. 57 (March-April 1997), pp. 150–59.

23. Paul L. Posner, *The Politics of Unfunded Mandates: Whither Federalism?* (Georgetown University Press, 1998), p. 87.

24. Ibid., p. 84.

25. Charles O. Jones, *Clean Air: The Policies and Politics of Pollution Control* (University of Pittsburgh Press, 1975).

26. See James Q. Wilson and John J. DiIulio Jr., *American Government: Institutions and Policies,* 7th ed. (Houghton Mifflin, 1998), p. 655. Emphasis added. The attitudes persist. According to recent opinion polls, more than two-thirds of the public subscribe to the statement: "Despite the Clean Air Act and Clean Water Act, air and water pollution seem to continue to get worse." Jonathan Rauch, "There's Smog in the Air, but It Isn't All Pollution," *Washington Post,* April 30, 2000, p. B4.

27. The Congressional Budget Office estimated that the 1986 Safe Drinking Water Act amendments, for example, would yield benefits costing in the range of $0.5 million to $4.3 *billion* per cancer case avoided, depending on the contaminant in question. Because the law provided no federal funds to cover these costs in local water systems, it was an ill-considered mandate "being imposed for a wide variety of risks regardless of cost." And if the federal government could regulate local tap water quality to this degree, why not have federal regulators take charge of any other facet of local public health and safety—restaurant inspections, for instance, or even traffic signage. U.S. Advisory Commission on Intergovernmental Relations, *The Role of Federal Mandates in Intergovernmental Relations* (Washington, January 1996).

28. President John F. Kennedy, "Inaugural Address, January 20, 1961," *Public Papers of the Presidents of the United States* (GPO, 1962), p. 1. Emphasis added. I credit Richard Reeves for reminding us of how sparse was Kennedy's reference to domestic affairs in his inaugural. Richard Reeves, "There's Always the Option of Giving In," *New York Times,* November 10, 2000, p. 33.

29. President William J. Clinton, "Address before a Joint Session of the Congress on the State of the Union, February 4, 1997," *Public Papers of the Presidents of the United States* (GPO, 1998), pp. 109–17.

30. The Senate enthusiastically adopted the preschooler program by voice vote on June 6, 1986. *Congressional Quarterly Almanac, 1986* (Washington: Congressional Quarterly Inc., 1987), p. 271. By contrast, after a debate, the Senate finally authorized the use of force in the Gulf crisis on January 12, 1991. The vote in the Senate was fifty-two in favor, forty-seven against. *Congressional Quarterly Almanac, 1991* (Washington: Congressional Quarterly Inc., 1992), p. 2-S.

31. Posner, *Unfunded Mandates,* p. 143. The CBO estimated that the near-term cost of the mandate for localities could run to $2.7 billion.

32. Ibid., p. 44.

33. William H. Rehnquist, *The 1998 Year-End Report of the Federal Judiciary,* January 1, 1999.

34. See Juliet Eilperin, "House Votes to Speed Zoning Lawsuits," *Washington Post,* March 17, 2000, p. A12.

35. Corporate interests have long been uncomfortable with outsized product liability awards permitted in some jurisdictions, the disparate regulatory standards and variable rules governing financial services, and local trade barriers. (Some cities, for example, have unilaterally banned the sale of goods and services linked to countries deemed to harbor unfair labor and environmental standards.) See Linda Himelstein, "Going beyond City Limits?" *Business Week,* July 7, 1997, pp. 98–99. For more on this question, see David R. Schmahmann and James S. Finch, "State and Local Sanctions Fail Constitutional Test," *Trade Briefing Paper* (Washington: Cato Institute, August 1998).

36. This hypothesis is more fully developed in Paul E. Peterson, "Introduction: Technology, Race, and Urban Policy," in Paul E. Peterson, ed., *The New Urban Reality* (Brookings 1985), chap. 1.

37. See in general, Jeffrey M. Berry, *The New Liberalism: The Rising Power of Citizen Groups* (Brookings, 1999), especially chapters 5–6.

38. Pietro S. Nivola, "Sweet and Sour Pork: Or Why Regulating Is More Succulent than Spending," paper prepared for delivery at the annual meeting of the American Political Science Association, 1997, Washington, pp. 5–6. See also David W. Brady, Robert D'Onofrio, and Morris P. Fiorina, "The Nationalization of Electoral Forces Revisited," in David W. Brady, John F. Cogan, and Morris P. Fiorina, eds., *Continuity and Change in House Elections* (Stanford University Press and Hoover Institution Press, 2000), p. 146.

39. Pietro S. Nivola, "Last Rites for States Rights? The Rigors of Restoring American Federalism," *Brookings Reform Watch,* no. 1 (June 2000), p. 11. See also Alan Ehrenhalt, "Mandating from Above: The Irresistible Impulse," *Governing,* vol. 8 (September 1995), p. 28.

40. *Washington Post,* December 27, 1998, p. A5.

41. Michael Specter, "Sea-Dumping Ban: Good Politics, but Not Necessarily Good Policy," *New York Times,* March 22, 1993, p. A1.

42. See Dana Milbank, "States Find Federal Powers Grow despite GOP Gains," *Wall Street Journal,* October 3, 1997, p. A12.

43. Derthick, *Keeping the Compound Republic,* chap. 11.

44. Specifically a House bill set aside half of available funds for states that increased prison terms for violent offenders and reserved the other half for states that made convicts serve virtually all of their sentences.

45. Quoted in Edwin Meese III, "The Dangerous Federalization of Crime," *Wall Street Journal,* February 22, 1999, p. A19.

46. Alexis de Tocqueville, *Democracy in America,* J. P. Mayer and Max Learner, eds. (Harper and Row, 1966), p. 248.

47. Quoted in Charles Warren, *A History of the American Bar* (Buffalo: William S. Hein, 1990), p. 217.

48. See Derthick, *Keeping the Compound Republic,* p. 78.

49. The rights revolution has expanded to include, not only persons with alternative sexual orientations but "fetuses, animals, and even vegetation and inanimate nature." William A. Galston, "Between Philosophy and History—The Evolution of Rights in American Thought," in Robert A. Licht, ed., *Old Rights and New* (Washington: American Enterprise Institute Press, 1993), p. 71.

50. Philip K. Howard, *The Death of Common Sense: How Law Is Suffocating America* (Random House, 1994), p. 61.

51. Title VI, perhaps more than any other part of the law, gave force to the federal government's school desegregation effort. See Gary Orfield, *The Reconstruction of Southern Education: The Schools and the 1964 Civil Rights Act* (Wiley, 1969), p. 46.

52. For a thorough account of this expansion, see Thomas F. Burke, "On the Rights Track: The Americans with Disabilities Act," in Pietro S. Nivola, ed., *Comparative Disadvantages? Social Regulations and the Global Economy* (Brookings, 1997), chap. 6.

53. The Honorable Warren E. Burger, "Isn't There a Better Way?" *American Bar Association Journal,* vol. 274 (1982), p. 275.

54. As Melnick observes, "Previous statutes had required citizens wishing to sue administrators to show that they had suffered direct, concrete harm at the hands of an agency. Almost all the regulatory laws passed in the 1970s, though, authorized 'any citizen' to file suit against administrators either for taking unauthorized action or for failing to perform 'nondiscretionary' duties." R. Shep

Melnick, *Regulation and the Courts: The Case of the Clean Air Act* (Brookings, 1983), p. 8.

55. In *Buckhannon Board and Care Home* v. *West Virginia Department of Health and Human Resources*, 203 F 3d 819 (2001), a 5-to-4 majority on the Supreme Court finally curbed fee-shifting opportunities for civil rights and environmental litigants whose cases did not attain an actual courtroom victory or court-ordered settlement.

56. More generally, on private rights of action, see Peter H. Schuck, *Suing Government: Citizen Remedies for Official Wrongs* (Yale University Press, 1983).

57. The definitive treatment of this problem is R. Shep Melnick, *Between the Lines: Interpreting Welfare Rights* (Brookings, 1994). See also Robert A. Katzmann, *Courts and Congress* (Brookings 1997), chap. 3.

58. Archibald Cox, *The Role of the Supreme Court in American Government* (Oxford University Press, 1976), p. 77. For several of the insights here and in the next three paragraphs, see Derthick, *Keeping the Compound Republic*, especially chap. 10.

59. *Cabell* v. *Markham*, 148 F. 2d 737, 739 (2d Cir. 1945).

60. *Monroe* v. *Pape*, 365 U.S. 167 (1961).

61. Paul M. Bator, "Some Thoughts on Applied Federalism," *Harvard Journal of Law and Public Policy*, vol. 6 (1982), pp. 5–58; and "Section 1983 and Federalism," *Harvard Law Review*, vol. 90 (1977), p. 1133.

62. See Derthick, *Keeping the Compound Republic*, p. 142.

63. *Swann* v. *Charlotte-Mecklenburg Board of Education*, 402 U.S. 1, 32 (1971).

64. *Pennsylvania Association of Retarded Citizens* v. *Commonwealth of Pennsylvania*, 334 F. Supp. 1257 (E.D. Pa. 1971).

65. *Mills* v. *Board of Education of D.C.*, 348 F. Supp. 866 (D.D.C. 1972).

66. *Regents of the University of California* v. *Bakke*, 438 U.S. 265 S Ct. (1978).

67. *Firefighters Local Union No. 1794* v. *Stott*, 467 U.S. 561 (1984); and *Wygant* v. *Jackson Board of Education*, 476 U.S. 267 S. Ct. (1986).

68. *Wards Cove Packing Co.* v. *Atonio*, 490 U.S. 642 (1989).

69. *Fullilove* v. *Klutznick*, 448 U.S. 418 S. Ct. (1980).

70. See *Sheet Metal Workers* v. *EEOC*, 478 U.S. 421 (1986); and *Local No. 93 International Association of Firefighters* v. *City of Cleveland*, 478 U.S. 501 (1986); *United States* v. *Paradise*, 480 U.S. S. Ct. 448 (1987); and *Johnson* v. *Transportation Agency, Santa Clara County*, 480 U.S. S. Ct. 149 (1987).

71 . *EEOC* v. *Wyoming*, 460 U.S. 226 (1983).

72. *Griggs* v. *Duke Power Co.*, 401 U.S. 424 (1971). It also might be noted that the Rehnquist court, in the intriguing case of *Reeves* v. *Sanderson Plumbing Prods. Inc.*, 530 U.S. 133 (2000), lowered the bar for proving discriminatory actions on the part of employers. Henceforth, for example, if an employer's

"pretext" for dismissing an employee was not sufficiently convincing, the plaintiff would not need to supply a jury with any additional evidence of possible discriminatory intent.

73. In *City of Richmond* v. *J.A. Croson Co.,* 488 U.S. 469 S.Ct. (1989), the Supreme Court had struck down a minority set-aside program for city construction jobs on grounds that the program had not been strictly tailored to remedy past discrimination. But it was *Adarand Constructors, Inc.* v. *Peña,* 515, U.S. 200, 210, 115 S. Ct. 2097 (1995) that extended this "strict scrutiny" test for such race-based preferences to federally aided activities.

74. *Alexander* v. *Sandoval,* 197 F. 3d 484 (2001). This orientation contrasted with that in 1988 and in 1990, when Congress effectively overturned Supreme Court decisions that were deemed to constrain opportunities for certain types of rights-based litigation.

75. On radioactive wastes and background checks, see *New York* v. *United States,* 488 U.S. 1041 (1992) and *Printz* v. *United States,* 521 U.S. 98 (1997); on sovereign immunity see *Alden* v. *Maine,* 715 A. 2d 172 (1999) and *Board of Trustees of the University of Alabama* v. *Garrett,* 193 F. 3d 1214 (2001); on stretching the commerce clause see *United States* v. *Lopez,* 514 U.S. 549 (1995) and *United States* v. *Morrison,* 169 F. 3d 820 (2000).

76. *National League of Cities* v. *Usery,* 426 U.S. 833 (1976); and *Garcia* v. *San Antonio Metropolitan Transit Authority,* 469 U.S. 528 (1985).

77. *City of Chicago* v. *Morales,* 119 S Ct. 1849 (1999). Here, the U.S. Supreme Court affirmed the Illinois Supreme Court's judgment that the municipal ordinance violated due process on the grounds that it was overly vague. Thus the local ordinance would not have survived, even if no federal review had occurred. It may be noted, however, that three justices dissented. In their view, the Chicago ordinance was in essence an extension of traditional vagrancy laws that dated back to colonial times and that local governments had long been entitled to retain.

78. *Davis* v. *Monroe County School Board of Education,* 120 F. 3d. 1390 (1999) and *Whitman* v. *American Trucking Association,* 531 U.S. 457 (2001).

79. "Judge Blocks a Slag Plant as Violation of Civil Rights," *New York Times,* April 21, 2001, p. A13. For a full and definitive analysis of the environmental justice movement and its implications see Christopher H. Foreman Jr., *The Promise and Peril of Environmental Justice* (Brookings, 1998).

80. *Alexander* v. *Sandoval* (2001). The appellate decision in the Camden case was *New Jersey Department* of *Environmental Protection* v. *South Camden Citizens,* 274 F. 3d 771 (3rd Cir. 2001).

81. Alice M. Rivlin, *Reviving the American Dream: The Economy, the States and the Federal Government* (Brookings 1992), p. 107.

82. R. Douglas Arnold, *The Logic of Congressional Action* (Yale University Press, 1990).

83. Republican congressman William Gooding, quoted in Posner, *Unfunded Mandates*, p. 101.

84. Martin Diamond, "The Ends of Federalism," in William A. Schambra, ed., *As Far as Republican Principles Will Admit: Essays by Martin Diamond* (Washington: American Enterprise Institute Press, 1992), pp. 144–66.

85. Abraham Lincoln, "Address at Poughkeepsie, New York, February 19, 1861," in John G. Nicolay and John Jay, *Abraham Lincoln: Complete Works* (Century Co., 1920), p. 685.


# Chapter 5

1. Accordingly, the public sectors of these countries continue to exceed that of the United States by a wide margin. In 1998 total government expenditures represented 46.2 percent of France's gross domestic product, 43.8 percent of Italy's GDP, 36.9 percent of the United Kingdom's GDP, 32.6 percent of Germany's GDP, but only 19.9 percent of the GDP of the United States. World Bank, *Central Government Finances* (2001), pp. 234–36.

2. Franklin D. Roosevelt, "'Unless There Is Security Here at Home, There Cannot Be Lasting Peace in the World'—Message to the Congress on the State of the Union, January 11, 1944," *Public Papers and Addresses of Franklin D. Roosevelt* (Harper and Bros., 1950), p. 41.

3. Arthur B. Gunlicks, *Local Government in the German Federal System* (Duke University Press, 1986), pp. 104, 112–13.

4. Provisions like this one were retained from a law dating back to 1934. Nicoletta Emiliani, Sergio Lugaresi, and Edgardo Ruggiero, "Italy," in Teresa Ter-Minassian, ed., *Fiscal Federalism in Theory and Practice* (Washington: International Monetary Fund, 1997), p. 257.

5. See John Ardagh, "Local Government in Modern France and Germany," in Maruice R. O'Connell, ed., *Decentralisation of Government* (Dublin: DOCAL, 1994), p. 50. See also Howard Machin, "France," in F. F. Ridley, ed., *Government and Administration in Western Europe* (St. Martin's, 1979), p. 89.

6. Gunlicks, *Local Government*, p. 183.

7. Although the German federal government does not ordinarily aim its environmental mandates directly at municipalities, the latter have been indirectly affected by the government's regulation of the private sector. For example, in the early 1990s, companies were ordered to initiate a massive campaign to collect and recycle packaging material. Soon, industry was gathering so much trash that municipal waste storage facilities were overflowing. Local governments were not adequately indemnified—even as Germany resorted to exporting more trash than

any other country. See James Jackson, "World-Class Litterbugs: German Recycling Mandate Proves Unmanageable," *Time*, October 18, 1993, p. 80.

8. Graham K. Wilson, "Regulatory Reform on the World Stage," in Donald F. Kettl, ed., *Environmental Governance: A Report on the Next Generation of Environmental Policy* (Brookings, 2002). On the prolific output of environmental regulations, see, for instance, David Vogel, "The Making of EC Environmental Policy," in Svein Andersen and Kjell Eliassen, eds., *Making Policy in Europe: The Europeification of National Policy-Making* (London: Sage Publications, 1993), p. 116.

9. See, on this point, Giandomenico Majone, *Regulating Europe* (London: Routledge, 1996); and "The Regulatory State and Its Legitimacy Problems," *Western European Politics,* vol. 22 (1999).

10. The European Union lacks authority to levy taxes. Its budget, though not insubstantial, is dependent on a complex system of contributions from national treasuries. From time to time, there is talk of establishing an EU tax in lieu of this arcane arrangement, but so far the idea has had few adherents. "An EU Tax? The Citizens Will Love It," *Economist*, July 14, 2001, p. 46.

11. This is not to say that the finances of all European municipalities are neatly balanced. The association of German cities reported that local authorities ran an overall deficit of $3.6 billion in 1996. Peter Norman, "German Cities' Deficits Increase," *Financial Times*, January 20, 1998, p. 2.

12. This means, to be sure, that the central governments are overwhelmingly the dominant tax collectors. While the federal government in the United States collected less than two-thirds of all taxes in 1991, the central treasuries of France, Holland, and the United Kingdom accounted for more than 90 percent. Even in federations such as Germany and Australia, approximately three-quarters or more of all revenues were collected by the national governments. See John Norregaard, "Tax Assignment," in Ter-Minassian, *Fiscal Federalism*, p. 56.

13. Most welfare services, including housing, health, education, and social care, are provided by local governments in Sweden. These are "mandatory services," but Swedish municipalities are also in a position to levy the widest possible range of taxes. (Unlike the U.S. government, the national government has not preempted the income tax, for example.) State grants also assist with expenditures on a large scale: more than 60 percent of the cost of local education, for instance, is state supported. Tage Magnusson and Jan-Erik Lane, "Sweden," in Edward C. Page and Michael J. Goldsmith, eds., *Central and Local Government Relations: A Comparative Analysis of West European Unitary States* (London: Sage, 1987), pp. 15, 17, 19–22. Interestingly, however, locally sourced revenues in Sweden and in Denmark greatly exceed revenues from grants. Jørgen R. Lotz, "Local Government in Denmark," in Amadeo Fossati and Giorgio Panella, eds., *Fiscal Federalism in the European Union* (London: Routledge, 1999), p. 139.

14. Jens Blom-Hansen, "Policy-Making in Central-Local Government Relations," *Journal of Public Policy,* vol. 19, no. 3 (1999), pp. 255–59. A somewhat different pattern unfolded, however, when the Swedish and Danish governments contemplated imposing a child-care guarantee on municipalities. In 1995 the Swedish parliament proceeded to make this a legally binding obligation for its municipal governments, but the Danish government did not.

15. Organization for Economic Cooperation and Development, Center for Educational Research and Innovation, *Education at a Glance: OECD Indicators* (Paris, 2000), p. 112.

16. Thus, in 1995 as in 1975 nearly 90 percent of total federal grant dollars were in categorical programs.

17. See Bruce A. Wallin, *From Revenue Sharing to Deficit Sharing* (Georgetown University Press, 1998).

18. See Ehtsham Ahmad, Daniel Hewitt, and Edgardo Ruggiero, "Assigning Expenditure Responsibilities," in Ter-Minassian, *Fiscal Federalism*, pp. 34–39. The leading example is probably the Netherlands, where roughly one-third of total funds going to municipalities from the central government are in the form of an unrestricted grant, and an additional 50 percent are so-called general grants (the equivalent of U.S. block grants). See Robert L. Morlan, "Local Government Reorganization in the Netherlands," in Arthur B. Gunlicks, ed., *Local Government Reform and Reorganization: An International Perspective* (Kennikat Press, 1981), pp. 49–50.

19. On the critically different implications of party-centered versus candidate-centered finance, see Thomas E. Mann, "Political Money and Party Finance," *International Encyclopedia of the Social and Behavioral Sciences,* vol. 3 (Pergamon, 2001).

20. Morris P. Fiorina, *Congress: Keystone of the Washington Establishment* (Yale University Press, 1989).

21. Article 106, section 3, of the Basic Law of the Federal Republic of Germany. See Wolfgang Renzsch, "Financing German Unity: Fiscal Conflict Resolution in a Complex Federation, *Publius,* vol. 28 (Fall 1998). On Canada, see Wallin, *From Revenue Sharing to Deficit Sharing*, p. 148; and Russel Krelove, Janet G. Stotsky, and Charles L. Vehorn, "Canada," in Ter-Minassian, *Fiscal Federalism*, p. 203.

22. Thomas F. Burke, "On the Rights Track," in Pietro S. Nivola, ed., *Comparative Disadvantages? Social Regulations and the Global Economy* (Brookings, 1997), pp. 242–318.

23. See Basil S. Markesinis, "Litigation-Mania in England, Germany and the U.S.A.: Are We So Very Different?" *Cambridge Law Journal,* vol. 49 (July 1990), p. 241; and Annmarie Muth, ed., *Statistical Abstract of the World,* 3d ed. (Gale, 1997), pp. 354, 987, 993.

24. Employment Policy Foundation, "Compensatory and Punitive Damages under Title VII—A Foreign Perspective," Policy Paper (Washington,1992), pp. 3–11.

25. Cited in Employment Policy Foundation, "Compensatory and Punitive Damages," pp. 10–11.

26. See Walter Olson, *The Excuse Factory* (Free Press, 1997), p. 182.

27. "In Germany, a 1980 anti-discrimination law limited financial compensation so strictly that it became known as the stamp law, because the biggest awards available to women barely covered the cost of mailing the necessary documents." The legislation was amended in 1985 and then again in 1994. Compensation may now rise as high as the equivalent of three months' pay. Richard W. Stevenson, "Job Discrimination in Europe: Affirmative Laissez Faire," *New York Times,* November 26, 1995, p. 10.

28. Charles Trueheart, "Questions of Color: Racism in France Persists Despite Egalitarian Creed," *Washington Post,* June 11, 2000, p. A23.

29. Eric A. Besner, "Employment Legislation for Disabled Individuals: What Can France Learn from the Americans with Disabilities Act," *Comparative Labor Law Journal,* vol. 16 (Spring 1995); Carol D. Rasnic, "A Comparative Analysis of Federal States for the Disabled Worker in the Federal Republic of Germany and the United States," *Arizona Journal of International and Comparative Law,* vol. 9 (1992); and Mark C. Weber, "Beyond the Americans with Disabilities Act: A National Employment Policy for People with Disabilities," *Buffalo Law Review,* vol. 46 (Winter 1998), pp. 123–74. The disabilities policies of European countries like Germany and France long predate U.S. policy. In the 1920s, Germany faced the need to reintegrate into society some 900,000 disabled veterans of the First World War.

30. David Vogel, *National Styles of Regulation: Environmental Policy in Great Britain and the United States* (Cornell University Press, 1986), pp. 75–76.

31. Barry G. Rabe, "Federalism and Entrepreneurship: Explaining American and Canadian Innovation in Pollution Prevention and Regulatory Integration," *Policy Studies Journal,* vol. 27, no. 2 (1999), pp. 123–74.

32. See Susan Rose-Ackerman, "Environmental Policy and Federal Structure: A Comparison of the United States and Germany," *Vanderbilt Law Review,* vol. 47 (October 1994), pp. 1587–1622; and Eckard Rehbinder, "The Federal Republic of Germany," in Turner T. Smith and Pascale Kromarek, eds., *Understanding U.S. and European Environmental Law: A Practioner's Guide* (Graham and Trotman, 1989), p. 18.

33. See Carol Cimitile and others, "Balancing Risk and Finance: The Challenge of Implementing Unfunded Environmental Mandates," *Public Administration Review,* vol. 57 (January-February 1997), pp. 63–74.

34. Department of the Environment, Transport and the Regions, *Waste Strategy 2000: England and Wales* (London, August 9, 2000).

35. See R. Shep Melnick, *Between the Lines: Interpreting Welfare Rights* (Brookings, 1994), pp. 10–11.

36. A recent comparative analysis of the policy process in the United States and Canada sought to identify the lead governmental institutions in eight important areas: pensions policies, health care, telecommunications deregulation, tobacco control, nuclear waste siting, military base closings, gun control, and abortion. The authors found that the courts in the United States, were principal players in four of the eight areas and took the lead in at least three of them. In Canada, which also has an active policymaking judiciary, the courts played a part in three but were the principal agent in only one (abortion). Leslie A. Paul and R. Kent Weaver, *The Politics of Pain: Political Institutions and Loss Imposition in the United States and Canada* (Georgetown University Press, forthcoming).

37. See Mary Ann Glendon, Michael Wallace Gordeon, and Christopher Osakwe, *Comparative Legal Traditions,* 2d ed. (West, 1994), pp. 77, 117.

38. F. L. Morton, "Judicial Activism in France," in Kenneth M. Holland, ed., *Judicial Activism in Comparative Perspective* (St. Martin's Press, 1991), pp. 133, 145.

39. *Garcia v. San Antonio Metropolitan Transit Authority,* 469 U.S. 528 (1985); and Donald P. Kommers, "The Federal Constitutional Court in the German Political System," *Comparative Political Studies,* vol. 26 (January 1994), p. 482.

40. On developments in the United Kingdom, see generally Jerold L. Waltman, "Judicial Activism in England," in Holland, *Judicial Activism in Comparative Perspective,* pp. 33–52.

41. Susan Sterett, "Judicial Review in Britain," *Comparative Political Studies,* vol. 26 (January 1994), pp. 431–33.

42. Christoph Fuhr, *The German Education System since 1945* (Bonn: Inter Nationes, 1997), p. 46.

43. Organization for Economic Cooperation and Development, *Inclusive Education at Work: Students with Disabilities in Mainstream Schools* (Paris, 1999), p. 136; and Thomas P. Parrish and others, *State Special Education Finance Systems, 1994–95* (Center for Special Education Finance, June 1997), p. 39. The equivalent of special education enrollments appear to have remained far lower in the school systems of European cities than in those of U. S. cities. In the UK's city of Leeds, as an example, only 4 percent of all pupils in the age group 5–16 years old have a "statement" (classification as eligible for special education instruction). As we have seen, in Baltimore, Washington, New York, and many other American cities, the percentages are several times higher. See S. J. Pijl and A. Dyson, "Funding Special Education: A Three-Country Study of Demand-Related Models," *Comparative Education* (Oxford, 1998).

44. Estimates of expenditures per student at the primary level: Organization for Economic Cooperation and Development, *OECD in Figures: Statistics on the Member Countries, 2000 Edition* (Paris, 2000), p. 66.

45. Marc Landy and Loren Cass, "U.S. Environmental Regulation in a More Competitive World," in Pietro S. Nivola, *Comparative Disadvantages? Social Regulations and the Global Economy* (Brookings, 1997), p. 220.

46. Keith Schneider, "How a Rebellion over Environmental Rules Grew from a Patch of Weeds," *New York Times,* March 24, 1993, p. A16.

47. See John Ferejohn, "Law, Legislation and Positive Political Theory," in Jeffrey Banks and Eric Hanushek, eds., *Modern Political Economy: Old Topics, New Directions* (Cambridge University Press, 1995).

48. Terry Moe and Michael Caldwell, "The Institutional Foundations of Democratic Government: A Comparison of Presidential and Parliamentary Systems," *Journal of Institutional and Theoretical Economics,* vol. 150 (March 1994), pp. 171–95.

49. Arthur B. Gunlicks, "Land Constitutions in Germany," *Publius,* vol. 28 (Fall 1998), pp. 105–26.

50. Mary Ann Glendon, "Rights in Twentieth-Century Constitutions," in Geoffrey R. Stone, Richard A. Epstein, and Cass R. Sunstein, eds., *The Bill of Rights in the Modern State* (University of Chicago Press, 1993), p. 532.

51. Glendon, "Rights in Twentieth-Century Constitutions," pp. 533–34. The recent pursuit of a "Patients' Bill of Rights" in the United States is a vivid, recent illustration of this pattern.

52. Markesinis, "Litigation-Mania in England, Germany and the USA," pp. 243–44.

53. See Harold Wolman and Michael Goldsmith, *Urban Politics and Policy: A Comparative Approach* (Oxford: Blackwell, 1992), pp. 79–84; and Tim Blackman, *Urban Policy in Practice* (London: Routledge, 1995), p. 21.

54. Arthur B. Gunlicks, *Local Government in the German Federal System* (Duke University Press, 1986), pp. 104–06.

55. See John Newhouse, "Europe's Rising Regionalism," *Foreign Affairs,* vol. 72 (January–February 1997), pp. 67–84.

56. Mark Kesselman, "The Tranquil Revolution at Clochemerle: Socialist Decentralization in France," in Philip G. Cerny and Martin A. Schain, eds., *Socialism, the State, and Public Policy in France* (Methuen, 1985), especially pp. 166–74. According to Kesselman, local governments in France subsequently became "effectively autonomous."

57. Yves Meny, "France," in Edward C. Page and Michael J. Goldsmith, eds., *Central and Local Government Relations: A Comparative Analysis of West European Unitary States* (London: Sage, 1987). On the power of French mayors in comparison with English ones, see John Ardagh, "Local Government in Modern France and Germany," in Maurice R. O'Connell, ed., *Decentralisation of Government* (Dublin: DOCAL, 1994), pp. 50–54; and Peter John and Alistair Cole, "When Do Institutions, Policy Sectors, and Cities Matter? Comparing

Networks of Local Policy Makers in Britain and France," *Comparative Political Studies,* vol. 33 (March 2000), p. 255. As John and Cole observe, the mayors of France have "used their power to defend the interests of their cities, particularly over central government decisions to allocate financial resources." Fully 75 percent of all national legislators, and 53 percent of cabinet ministers, in France in the 1980s had held locally elected offices. (The respective figures in Britain were 35 percent and only 14 percent.) Edward C. Page, *Localism and Centralism in Europe: The Political and Legal Bases of Local Self-Government* (Oxford, 1991), p. 59.

58. Maryvonne Bodiguel and Henry Buller, "Environmental Policy and the Regions of France," in John Loughlin and Sonia Mazey, eds., *The End of the French Unitary State? Ten Years of Reorganization in France (1982–1992)* (London: Frank Cass, 1995), pp. 99–100.

59. See, for instance, John T. S. Keeler, "Corporatist Decentralization and Commercial Modernization in France: The Royer Law's Impact on Shopkeepers, Supermarkets and the State," in Cerny and Schain, *Socialism, the State, and Public Policy.*

60. John E. Chubb and Terry M. Moe, *A Lesson in School Reform from Great Britain* (Brookings, 1992), p. 4.

61. See, for instance, R. Daniel Kelemen, "Regulatory Federalism: EU Environmental Regulation in Comparative Perspective," *Journal of Public Policy,* vol. 20, no. 2 (2000), pp. 133–67.

62. Kelemen, "Regulatory Federalism," p. 157. See also Ludwig Krämer, "Public Interest Litigation in Environmental Matters before European Courts," *Journal of Environmental Law,* vol. 8, no. 1 (1996), pp. 1–18.

63. See, for example, Francesco Perugini, "Italy: High Public Debt and Unfinished Reform Agenda," *Liverpool Quarterly Economic Bulletin,* vol. 51 (December 31, 2000).

64. Commune di Milano, *Relazione al Bilancio di Previsione* (Universita Degli Studi Di Cantana, 1999), p. 25. According to officials in Milan, a city now relying for two-thirds of its revenue from own-source collections, there was only one novel obligation that entailed notable unanticipated bills imposed by Rome in the 1990s: the cost of administering a state program of assistance to nonworking mothers.

65. Joseph M. Colomer, "The Spanish 'State of Autonomies': Non-Institutional Federalism," *Western European Politics,* vol. 21 (January 10, 1998), pp. 40–52.

66. See generally, Martin Laffin and Thomas Alys, "The United Kingdom: Federalism in Denial," *Publius,* vol. 29, no. 3 (1999), pp. 89–108.

67. "Demolishing the Dumps," *Economist,* December 9, 2000, pp. 61–62.

68. Robert H. Evans, "Local Government Reform in Italy, 1945–1979," in Arthur B. Gunlicks, ed., *Local Government Reform and Reorganization: An International Perspective* (Kennikat Press, 1981), p. 119.

69. Timothy Beatley, *Green Urbanism: Learning from European Cities* (Island Press, 2000), pp. 153–64; and William Drozdiak, "Automotive Alternative," *Washington Post*, September 20, 1999, p. A9.

70. Quoted in Diel S. Wright, *Understanding Intergovernmental Relations* (Duxbury, 1979), p. 57.

## Chapter 6

1. Michael A. Pagano, *City Fiscal Conditions in 1998* (National League of Cities, June 1998).

2. "Aren't City Centres Great?" *Economist*, August 14, 1999, p. 23. Could, say, Cleveland, which had lost almost 40 percent of its population between 1965 and 1996, now really expect to grow by well over 200 percent from 1998 to 2010?

3. John D. Donahue, *Disunited States* (Basic Books, 1997).

4. For a brilliant analysis of the tobacco war, see Martha A. Derthick, *Up in Smoke: From Legislation to Litigation in Tobacco Politics* (CQ Press, 2002).

5. "The Court and Federalism," *Washington Post*, January 14, 2000, p. A26; and Jack M. Balkin, "The Court Defers to a Racist Era," *New York Times*, May 17, 2000, p. A27.

6. Congressional Budget Office, *CBO's Activities under the Unfunded Mandates Reform Act, 1996–2000* (Congressional Budget Office, May 2001), p. viii.

7. Clyde Wayne Crews Jr., *Ten Thousand Commandments, 2000 Edition* (Washington: Competitive Enterprise Institute, 2000), pp. 27, 31.

8. U.S. General Accounting Office, *Previous Initiatives Have Little Effect on Agency Rulemaking* (June 30, 1999), p. 9.

9. Timothy Conlan, *From New Federalism to Devolution: Twenty-Five Years of Intergovernmental Reform* (Brookings, 1998), pp. 271–72.

10. Conlan, *From New Federalism to Devolution*, p. 271.

11. "Considering the breadth of those rights under present case law," writes one critic of the act, "virtually any mandate can be justified as protecting them." Edward A. Zelinsky, "The Unsolved Problem of the Unfunded Mandate," *Ohio Northern University Law Review*, vol. 23, no. 3 (1997), p. 772.

12. Hearing before the Senate Governmental Affairs Committee, 106 Cong. 1 sess. (Government Printing Office, 1999), p. 10.

13. Andrew Rotherham, "Asking the Wrong Test Questions," *Washington Post*, May 29, 2001, p. A15.

14. See Robert Pear, "States Dismayed by Federal Bills on Patient Rights," *New York Times*, August 13, 2001, pp. A1, A14. Emphasis added.

15. "Patterns of Police Violence," *New York Times,* April 18, 2001, p. A22. Emphasis added.

16. The departures, it should be stressed, were mainly from precedents that liberally discovered "implied" private rights of action. The Rehnquist court mostly held that "state and local governments are exposed to private lawsuits only when Congress has clearly stated, in the language of the statute itself, that it intended such exposure." Michael S. Greve, "Federalism, Yes. Activism, No." *Federalist Outlook,* no. 7 (July 2001), p. 2.

17. Pietro S. Nivola. "Does Federalism Have a Future?" *Public Interest,* no. 142 (Winter 2001), p. 58.

18. Augustus J. Jones Jr., "Federal Court Responses to State and Local Claims of 'Undue Burden' in Complying with the Americans with Disabilities Act," *Publius,* vol. 25 (Summer 1995), pp. 41–54.

19. *United States* v. *Lopez,* 93-1260 514 U.S. 549 (1995).

20. See, on this initiative, Pietro S. Nivola, "Last Rites for States' Rights?" *Brookings Reform Watch,* no. 1 (June 2000).

21. Janet M. Kelly, "Mandate Reimbursement Measures in the States," *American Review of Public Administration,* vol. 24 (December 1994), p. 352.

22. A House bill introduced in 1991, for instance, proposed that Congress extend deadlines for local compliance with its mandates "unless all expenses . . . are fully funded by the United States." HR 2338, 102 Cong. 1 sess. (GPO, 1991).

23. Alan Ehrenhalt, "Mandating from Above: The Irresistible Impulse," *Governing,* vol. 8 (September 1995), pp. 7–8.

24. Kathleen Sylvester, "The Mandate Blues," in Laurence J. O'Toole Jr., ed., *American Intergovernmental Relations: Foundations, Perspectives, and Issues* (CQ Press, 1992), p. 319.

25. For the best general treatment of the political dynamics of "blame," see R. Kent Weaver, "The Politics of Blame Avoidance," *Journal of Public Policy,* vol. 6, no. 4 (1986), pp. 371–98.

26. David Vogel, *National Styles of Regulation: Environmental Policy in Great Britain and the United States* (Cornell University Press, 1986), p. 187.

27. With unification the redistributive transfers to the new Länder amounted to 60 percent of East Germany's gross national product in 1992. Wolfgang Renzsch, "Financing German Unity: Fiscal Conflict Resolution in a Complex Federation," *Publius,* vol. 28, no. 4 (Fall 1998), pp. 127–46.

28. For an interesting analysis of German cooperative federalism, see Michael S. Greve, "Against Cooperative Federalism," *Mississippi Law Journal,* vol. 70 (Winter 2000), pp. 557–624. For another critique, see Clifford Larsen, "States Federal, Financial, Sovereign and Social: A Critical Inquiry into an Alternative to American Financial Federalism," *American Journal of Comparative Law,* vol. 47 (Summer 1999), pp. 41–55. On the more general backlash to "hyper-equalization"

policies in various European countries, see Giancarlo Pola, "A Comparative View of Local Finances in EU Member Countries: Are There Any Lessons to Be Drawn?" in Amadeo Fossati and Giorgio Panella, eds., *Fiscal Federalism in the European Union* (London: Routledge, 1999), p. 49.

29. Edward A. Zalinsky, "Unfunded Mandates, Hidden Taxation, and the Tenth Amendment: On Public Choice, Public Interest, and Public Services," *Vanderbilt Law Review,* vol. 46 (November 1993), p. 1409.

30. See Larson, "States Federal, Financial, Sovereign and Social."

31. See G. Brosio, D. N. Hyman, and W. Santagata, "Revenue Sharing and Local Public Spending: The Italian Experience," *Public Choice,* vol. 35, no. 1 (1980), pp. 3–15; and Ilde Rizzo, "Regional Disparities and Decentralization as Determinants of Public Sector Growth in Italy" (1860–81), in F. Forte and A. Peacock, eds., *Public Expenditures and Government Growth* (Oxford: Blackwell, 1985).

32. Guy Gilbert, "Local Taxation and Intergovernmental Fiscal Relations in France," in Amadeo Fossati and Giorgio Panella, eds., *Fiscal Federalism in the European Union* (London: Routledge, 1999), p. 139.

33. By 2002, with the implementation of a municipal surcharge on the personal income tax, the share of local tax receipts in Italy rose to a level significantly higher than that of the current average among OECD countries. Organization for Economic Cooperation and Development, *OECD Territorial Reviews: Italy* (Paris, 2001), chap. 3, especially p. 154.

34. No fewer than twenty-nine separate federal agencies were eventually involved in writing the regulations for handicapped access under the 1973 Rehabilitation Act. Donald F. Kettl, *The Regulation of American Federalism* (Louisiana State University Press, 1983), p. 11.

35. Congress increasingly appeared to recognize this notion during reauthorizations of various regulatory statutes in the mid-1990s. The Food Quality Protection Act of 1996, for example, finally repealed a zero-tolerance standard for health risks from pesticides (the so-called Delaney clause) and required regulators to subject new proposed standards to benefit-cost analysis. David Hosansky, "Rewrite of Laws on Pesticides on Way to President's Desk," *Congressional Quarterly,* July 27, 1996, p. 2101. For an up-to-date report on the state of play in regulatory reform efforts, see Robert W. Hahn, *Reviving Regulatory Reform* (AEI-Brookings Joint Center for Regulatory Studies, 2000). See also Scott Farrow and Michael Toman, *Using Environmental Benefit-Cost Analysis to Improve Government Performance* (Washington: Resources for the Future, 1998).

36. Council of Economic Advisers, *Economic Report of the President* (GPO, February 1992), pp. 272–73.

37. Reportedly, a motorist who had been ticketed by a police officer for not wearing a seatbelt in a city in Kansas sued it for violating the ADA. James Bovard,

"The Disabilities Act's Parade of Absurdities," *Wall Street Journal,* June 22, 1995, p. A16. A strength test with a 125-pound sandbag for firefighters faced legal challenges in Columbus, Ohio. The suit there was anything but unique, however. Walter Olson, *The Excuse Factory: How Employment Law Is Paralyzing the American Workplace* (Free Press, 1997), pp. 182–83. How such suits became common is a very long story, not entirely easy to follow. Recall, however, that the Civil Rights Act of 1964 explicitly stressed, "It shall *not* be an unlawful employment practice . . . for an employer to give and to act upon the results of any professionally developed ability test provided that such test, its administration or action upon the results is not designed, intended or used to discriminate because of race, color, religion, sex or national origin." PL 88-352. *United States at Large,* vol. 78 (GPO, 1965), p. 257. Emphasis added.

38. Henry Weinstein, "Court Bars Border Stops Based on Ethnicity," *Los Angeles Times,* April 12, 2000, p. 1.

39. The Los Angeles Police Department reported attending to 375 bomb threats between the dates of September 11 and October 10, 2001. Kevin Sack, "Focus on Terror Creates Burden for the Police," *New York Times,* October 28, 2001, p. B4.

40. The best scholarly analysis of police practice, including behavior that has come to be called profiling, remains: James Q. Wilson, *Varieties of Police Behavior: The Management of Law and Order in Eight Communities* (Atheneum, 1972). On page 38 of this classic study, Wilson writes, "Acting in a manner not provided by the law, or acting against some violators but not others, or acting on the basis of a person's attributes—his class, race, appearance, influence, kinship, status, or the like—rather than his behavior is, strictly speaking, unjust. To the patrolman, such a test is unworkable and, in many cases, self-defeating. In preventing crime, the police must make rapid judgements about the probable behavior of a person that often, and necessarily, rest as much on appearance as on past behavior."

41. See David Garrard Lowe, "Urban Lessons from Paris," in Myron Magnet, ed., *The Millennial City: A New Urban Paradigm for 21st-Century America* (Ivan R. Dee, 2000), p. 329.

42. Fox Butterfield, "City Police Work Losing Its Appeal and Its Veterans," *New York Times,* July 30, 2001, p. A1.

43. Quoted in John Leo, "Riot Ideology in the Aftermath," *Washington Times,* July 25, 2001, p. A15.

44. Quoted in William J. Bratton, "A Cloudy Future for Policing," *New York Times,* August 3, 2001, p. A25.

45. See more generally James V. De Long, "The Criminalization of Just About Everything," *American Enterprise,* vol. 5 (March-April, 1994) p. 30.

46. Eleven years after passage of the Americans with Disabilities Act, the Supreme Court was still trying to figure out how serious an impairment has to be

to be considered "substantial" and what constitutes "major life activities." *Toyota Motor Manufacturing, Ky., Inc.* v. *Williams,* 00-1080 224 F. 3d 840 (2001).

47. "A Shot from Justice Scalia," *Washington Post,* May 2, 2000, p. A22.

48. See Robert A. Katzmann, *Courts and Congress* (Brookings, 1997), p. 77.

49. U.S. Advisory Commission on Intergovernmental Relations, *The Role of Federal Mandates in Intergovernmental Relations* (January 1996).

50. The Supreme Court addressed the fee-shifting problem in at least one significant case, *Buckhannon Board and Care Home* v. *West Virginia,* 99-1848 203 F. 3d 819 (2001). Congress has debated the question of legal fees in a variety of programs troubled by legal adversarialism, including the IDEA. Jeffry L. Katz, "Policy on Disabled Is Scrutinized over Discipline Problems, Cost," *Congressional Quarterly Weekly Report,* May 11, 1996, p. 1299.

51. Carol Browner quoted in Rich Henderson, "Green Eyeshades," *American Enterprise,* vol. 6 (January 1995), pp. 83–84.

52. Ellen Nakashima, "Justice Dept. Bows Out of a Civil Rights Case," *Washington Post,* October 2, 2001, p. A23.

53. See Michael S. Greve, "National Power, Post-911," *Federalist Outlook,* no. 9 (November 2001), p. 1.

54. Commission on Intergovernmental Relations, *Civil Defense and Urban Vulnerability* (GPO, June 1955), pp. 1–4.

55. See Edward L. Glaeser and Mathew E. Kahn, "Decentralized Employment and the Transformation of the American City," in William G. Gale and Janet Rothenberg Pack, eds., *Brookings-Wharton Papers on Urban Affairs, 2001* (Brookings, 2001), p. 2.

56. See Joel Kotkin and Fred Siegel, "Terrorism: Attacks Threaten Future of Cities," *Los Angeles Times,* October 14, 2001, p. M6.

57. Kevin Sack, "Focus on Terror Creates Burden for the Police," *New York Times,* October 28, 2001, p. B4.

58. Sack, "Focus on Terror," p. B4; and Michael Janofsky, "Additional Budget Cuts as States and Cities Address Safety Issues," *New York Times,* November 15, 2001, p. B9. See also Kevn Sack, "State Budgets Facing a Fall in Revenues," *New York Times,* November 2, 2001, p. A12.

59. Ed Fouly, *State of the States, 2001* (Richmond, Va.: Pew Center on the States, University of Richmond, 2001), p. 2.

60. Kevin Flynn, "Rebound in City Murder Rate Puzzling New York Officials," *New York Times,* November 5, 1999, p. A1.

61. "United States: A Slow Learning Curve," *Economist,* June 30, 2001, pp. 27–28.

62. Diane Granat, "Virginia V. Maryland," *Washingtonian,* vol. 36 (April 2001), p. 96.

63. A projected deficit of perhaps $245 million seemed in store for Washington in 2002. "Washington May Face a Shortfall Next Year," *New York Times,* October 21, 2001, p. A22.

64. *Davis* v. *Monroe County Board of Education,* 97-843 120 F.3d 1390 (1999); and *Cedar Rapids* v. *Garret F.* 96-1793 106 F. 3d 822 (1999).

65. In the year 2000, barely 53 percent of fourth grade students in central city schools were able to read at or above the basic level. In the suburbs the share was 68 percent. U.S. Department of Education, *The Nation's Report Card: Fourth Grade Reading 2000* (National Center for Education Statistics, 2001), p. 38.

66. Ernest G. Noack, "Comparing U.S. and German Education: Like Apples and Sauerkraut," *Phi Delta Kappan,* vol. 80 (June 1999), p. 773.

67. The United States spends almost 6 percent of its national income on primary and secondary education, more than almost all other industrialized countries. Yet by the twelfth grade, the comparative test scores of U.S. students tend to fall below those in the vast majority of other countries. "America's Education Choice," *Economist,* April 1, 2000, p. 17.

68. On perverse incentives in IDEA funding formulas, see Julie Berry Cullen, "The Impact of Fiscal Incentives on Student Disability Rates," Working Paper (Cambridge, Mass.: National Bureau of Economic Research, June 1999).

69. Joseph S. Nye Jr., "Introduction: The Decline of Confidence in Government," in Joseph S. Nye Jr., Philip D. Zelikow, and David C. King, eds., *Why People Don't Trust Government* (Harvard University Press, 1997), p. 1.

70. The Pew Research Center for the People and the Press, *Deconstructing Distrust: How Americans View Government,* "Confidence and Trust in Government to Handle Problems," (table) Washington, 1997.

71. At the end of 1998, more than three out of every four Americans thought highly of their local government's ability to handle problems. Confidence in the federal government's ability to handle domestic problems was still much lower. David W. Moore, "Public Trust in Federal Government Remains High," *Gallup Organization Poll Analysis,* January 8, 1999. In the wake of the September 11 attacks, the percentage of persons who said they trust the federal government to do what is right either just about always or most of the time rose to 60 percent— the highest point since 1968. Frank Newport, "Trust in Government Increases Sharply in Wake of Terrorist Attacks," *Gallup Organization Poll Analysis,* October 12, 2001.

# Index